THE NURTURING NEIGHBORHOOD

The American Social Experience Series

GENERAL EDITOR: JAMES KIRBY MARTIN

EDITORS: PAULA S. FASS, STEVEN H. MINTZ,
CARL PRINCE, JAMES W. REED & PETER N. STEARNS

THE NURTURING NEIGHBORHOOD

The Brownsville Boys Club and
Jewish Community in Urban America,
1940-1990

GERALD SORIN

NEW YORK UNIVERSITY PRESS
NEW YORK AND LONDON
1990

F
128.9
J5
S67
1990

Library of Congress Cataloging-in-Publication Data
Sorin, Gerald, 1940–
The nurturing neighborhood : the Brownsville Boys Club and Jewish
community in urban America, 1940–1990 / Gerald Sorin.
p.   cm.—(The American social experience series : 15)
Includes bibliographical references.
ISBN 0-8147-7897-6 (alk. paper) :
1. Brownsville Boys Club—History.   2. Jews—New York (N.Y.)—
Social conditions.   3. Brownsville (New York, N.Y.)—Social
conditions.   4. New York (N.Y.)—Social conditions.   I. Title.
II. Series.
F128.9.J5S67   1990
369.42'089'92407471—dc20   89-12167
                                   CIP

New York University Press books are printed on acid-free paper,
and their binding Materials are chosen for strength and durability.

Book design by Ken Venezio

For my brother
David Harold Sorin
1947–1972

Contents

Illustrations

Acknowledgments

There are many people to thank, none more important than the retentive and loquacious Brownsville "boys" themselves. Their names are found throughout and in the appendixes. While several have questioned my reconstruction of a world they knew, and even expressed reservations about some of my interpretations, they have never failed to encourage me. A great many men invited me to their homes, and together with their wives, treated me graciously, and plied me with food and drink. Jacob ("Doc") Baroff, Joseph ("Yussie") Feldman, Martin ("Weasel") Kronenburg, Irving ("Hooker") Levine, Norman ("Webster") Goroff, and Jerome Reiss were especially generous with their time, and supplied important documents and photographs.

I am very appreciative of the cooperation of the Charles Hayden Foundation which allowed me to read and photocopy materials from its files on the Brownsville Boys Club. Elizabeth White, archivist at the Brooklyn Collection of the Brooklyn Public Library, Main Branch, was amiable as well as very helpful. Haig Shekerjian of SUNY, New Paltz, generously contributed his fine photographic talents. The director of the Thomas Jefferson High School Alumni Association, Seymour Janovsky, shared his vast knowledge garnered from several decades of close association with the school. Faye and Sol Cohen, my in-laws, supplied a comfortable Brooklyn nest, and Stuart Pellman graciously provided space in Manhattan.

The manuscript was read closely by immigration historian Richard Varbero of SUNY New Paltz, and benefitted from his criticism.

xiii

Editor James Kirby Martin also made a number of very useful suggestions. Jacki Brownstein, my friend and director of Family and Youth Services for the Mental Health Association for Ulster County, helped shape my thinking about adolescence and led me to the literature on self-help.

My wife, Myra Sorin, shared my enthusiasm for the project, and my sense of affection and respect for the men I met along the way. She also read the entire manuscript, and applied her antijargon blue pencil judiciously. Special thanks are due Deborah Dash Moore, a specialist in the history of second-generation Jews, who drew me to this study in the first place, and then read the manuscript with her usual editorial care and insight.

THE NURTURING NEIGHBORHOOD

Prologue

For the past twenty years and more, former members of the Brownsville Boys Club (1940–55) have been holding reunions in the Catskill
Mountains of New York every fall. Each time, several hundred men
and their wives come together to socialize and to talk about the "old
neighborhood," a depression-impoverished Jewish section of east
Brooklyn, six miles from lower Manhattan. Relatively successful by
many of the measures we use in American society, these men continue
to feel a deep need to share, and share again, the memories of their
childhood and teenage years, and to tell and retell the stories of 1940s
Brownsville: two-hand touch with rolled up newspapers, stickball with
Mrs. Rosen's broomhandle, pick-up basketball games in Nanny Goat
Park, scrap-metal collections to help the "boys" in World War II
Europe, penny candy, Rabbi Miller's stick for discipline, kick-the-can,
stoopball, the phone calls at Leibowitz's drug store, the card games on
milk boxes, and the endless talk about politics and sports and girls.

Second-generation Jews who grew up in working-class immigrant
families near the end of the depression, and "got out," these men
attribute much of their success to Brownsville and to each other. For
together as young boys they developed a sense of identity and a
powerful interdependence in their games, in the parks, and on their
street corners, and they participated in building, on their own, an
extraordinary mutual-aid society and authentic community in microcosm called the Brownsville Boys Club. Amazed still at what they
accomplished many count the experience as "the single most memora-
ble and important 'event' " of their lives.

Four hundred of these "boys," now men, mostly between the ages
of fifty-five and sixty-five, still belong to an active Brownsville Boys
Club Alumni Association. At reunions, breakfasts, and frequent social
gatherings, in large groups and small, the alumni talk among themselves about the club, long and often.[1] They are approaching the
fiftieth anniversary of the BBC in 1990, as well as retirement, disperse-
ment, and thoughts about their own mortality. They want others to
hear their story now. They have persuaded me, a younger former
Brownsville boy, to tell it. It is an intriguing and instructive tale.

Organized in March of 1940, the Brownsville Boys Club grew out
of an informal association of teenage boys who had been closed out of
an afternoon recreation center at Public School 184. One of the few
recreational facilities directly accessible to boys in the heart of the
heavily populated, densely Jewish, Brooklyn neighborhood of Brownsville, P.S. 184 had two small gymnasiums and an even smaller playground. Street-corner clubs and teams of teenagers often used these
limited facilities in athletic competition—when they were not beating
up on each other with fists and sticks and an occasional curtain rod or
baseball bat in defense of "turf." But the New York City Board of
Education in order to increase play space for younger children had
denied the use of the after-school center to boys over fourteen. A
group of the youngsters, under the remarkably spirited leadership of
sixteen-year-old Jacob ("Doc") Baroff, circulated a petition for the
reopening of the center. In a matter of days they had collected over
eight hundred names—mainly from boys who were members of street-
corner clubs and teams.

The Board of Education virtually ignored the petition. Baroff, George
Schmaren, Izzy Lesovoy, Dave Gold, and several others vowed to
continue to act collectively to secure recreation space. They formed a
temporary council, and all the boys' clubs, within an area of approximately one hundred square blocks, were invited to join by sending
representatives. As many as fifty groups, including clubs like the
Chrislotts, the Stonedales and the Newport Indians, names derived
from the boys' streets and street corners, responded, and the informal
association grew, over a period of weeks, from about one hundred to
seven hundred members. With these impressive numbers behind them,
the leaders, now a slightly larger group, including Joe ("Yussie") Feld-

man, Norman ("Webster") Goroff, and Jack ("YD") Deutch (*Y* for Yankel), negotiated with schools and other agencies for space. They were successful in securing a regular meeting place in a story-hour room of the Brownsville Children's Branch Library, and ultimately they succeeded in reopening P.S. 184 for their basketball "tournaments."

At this point, given the fulfillment of its stated objective, the loosely organized confederation of clubs ought to have disbanded. But the process of successful collective action engendered enough neighborhood spirit to form the basis of a more permanent organization. Many of the boys had seen that, in making the larger group effort, a relatively long period of peace had ensued between clubs. They came to see, too, that the youth of Brownsville was underprivileged in terms of recreational opportunities, and they committed themselves to maintaining the confederation and using its strength for their own benefit. They successfully negotiated with other institutions for space for athletic events, equipment, and eventually for tickets to ballgames and shows, and vacations in camps. The Brownsville Boys Club continued to grow, attracting organizations of boys and "independents," and even taking under its auspices several street gangs (i.e., clubs somewhat more aggressive in defending or extending turf, and more often involved in violence and vandalism), thereby further reducing some of the destructive interaction in the neighborhood.

One of the many remarkable things about these Jewish teenagers,[2] who responded vigorously and imaginatively to the crisis of inadequate recreational facilities in Brownsville, is that for six or seven years, and at their own insistence, the boys did it all without adult supervision: without parents, without teachers, and without professionals. Self-government was an important key to the club's appeal. Reformers in cities all over the United States since the late 1880s had attempted to provide play space for street kids. They often had difficulty raising the necessary funds. Even when they were successful in building playgrounds and clubhouses, however, they had the additional problem of "controlling" their wards in those spaces. Teenagers often rejected pre-established adult rules. They did so in 1890 and in 1945; they did so in Chicago, Illinois, and in Worcester, Massachusetts. They did so also in Brownsville; and it is useful to look closely at the Brownsville case to see what empowerment and responsibility meant to boys in at least one troubled neighborhood.

After the Second World War, the club, still operating with no home space other than the small room in the children's library, and still servicing hundreds of boys, with hundreds more clamoring to participate, attracted the attention of various social agencies and civic leaders. The boys active in the leadership of the club, between 1946 and 1953, faced with the need for larger facilities and more services, accepted, with mixed feelings and mixed consequences the help of professional social workers and adult fund-raisers. Abe Stark, a leading Brownsville clothing merchant, philanthropist, community activist, and Democratic politician gave the club much of his time and effort and he inspired a number of generous donors, including the Charles Hayden Foundation, to help procure first a storefront, and then a permanent home for the Brownsville Boys Club. By October 1953, $1,250,000 had been spent to build and open an impressive clubhouse on Linden Boulevard.

Less than a year later, to the disappointment of many, the building had been turned over to New York City, most of its activities to be run by the Department of Parks. This part of the story and the general history of the building will be told in the later chapters of the book. Taken together those chapters can serve as a case study of what may happen when an authentic mutual-aid society is affected by the narrow concerns of traditional electoral politics, or when it becomes part of a large, complex bureaucratic structure. But the building, particularly after it was turned over to the City, was not the Brownsville Boys Club. The boys—"Yussie" and "Weasel", "Yankel" and "Doc", "Sheiky" and "Hooker", "Whitey" and "Red", "Chink" and "Izzy"—and their culture of Jewish Brownsville, were the Brownsville Boys Club.

The club emerged in the context of economic depression, urban blight, social service deficiencies and what at least looked like a rising tide of juvenile delinquency.[3] My goal in this social history is to understand the communal and individual vitality that allowed the achievement of the club, and to explain the relative absence of serious criminality and social pathology among the boys who were part of the process of club formation and development.

An analysis of class and economic experience is necessary and critical here, but there is no escaping cultural factors in the explanation. Ethnic culture, once a "neglected dimension of American history," has become over the last two decades a very useful category of historical analysis. Scholarship prior to the 1950s, particularly the work of Robert Park, Louis Wirth, and a number of other sociologists, confidently assumed that mobility and assimilation were inevitable for ethnic groups in the United States. Within a generation or two the cultures of the immigrants and their children were expected to yield to a "homogenized human brew."[4] Our own experience since the 1950s, and the watershed work of sociologist Milton Gordon, and social historians like Rudolph J. Vecoli and Deborah Dash Moore have made us recognize and reexamine the continuing vitality of ethnicity in modern American society.[5]

By the 1970s many historians were arguing that we must "study the distinctive character of each ethnic group" and neither overemphasize the power of the new environments nor underestimate the "toughness of cultural heritage."[6] Most recently John Bodnar produced what is probably the best synthesis available on the American urban experience of immigrants and their descendants. He has persuasively demonstrated that the "content" of "immigrant mentalities," was as much cultural as it was class-based. The newcomers acted as workers, i.e., as members of a class, but they and their children in the new American context "also remained tied to selected ethnic symbols, . . . institutions," and values. These cultural attachments tended to dilute strictly class concerns.[7]

Jews were very much part of this process of interaction between class and culture, and between the whole self and the American environment. The religious *culture* of the Jewish immigrants as much as their "nonpeasant" *class* experience helps account for the relatively rapid social mobility of their children in this country, and for much of the story of the BBC. Disproportionate numbers of Jewish immigrants did bring with them a more complex economic history and more commercial and industrial experience than that brought by many other groups. But they also brought with them a deeply embedded religious culture, a long-standing commitment to community, and a centuries-old tradition of mutual-aid.

The persistence of this culture in America would be neither total nor linear. Interactions with changing conditions and economic realities in the old countries, but particularly in the new one, produced distinct adjustments which redefined, but did not dissolve the ethnic and religious dimensions of Jewish culture. The adjustments, for many, included reformulated ethical injunctions, remodeled self-help institutions and a progressive politics—in short, an *American* Jewish identity. It was out of this new context, tied to capitalism and urbanization, but simultaneously tied to Jewish tradition, household and community, that the children of Jewish immigrants built the Brownsville Boys Club.

Class experience mattered much. But so did ethnic culture count in shaping attitudes and behavior. It is difficult to determine precisely the relative influence of class and ethnicity on values and achievement; it is also difficult, often, to *separate* class culture from ethnic culture.[8] In any case, in the 1930s and 1940s, non-Jewish white ethnic neighborhoods, relatively similar in socioeconomic status to Brownsville, do not appear to have produced institutions like the BBC. Nor did black Brownsville in the 1960s and 1970s.

The "boys" of the BBC live now in twelve states from Vermont to California, and from Michigan to Texas. But the vast majority reside in the greater New York area, and many are still in Brooklyn (30 percent), though none in Brownsville—at least not physically. Ninety of these men, representing the general geographical distribution of the alumni, have graciously allowed me to interview them, and I have had questionnaires answered and returned by more than 160 others. While looking at their lives in the context of questions about ethnic identity, urban change, and physical and social mobility, I will at points throughout the book allow the men themselves to speak. Their memories are sharp and their feelings run deep. Their perceptions and insights taught me much, including the fact that Thomas Wolfe was wrong on at least two counts: it is not true that "only the dead know Brooklyn"; and in some important ways you *can* "go home again."

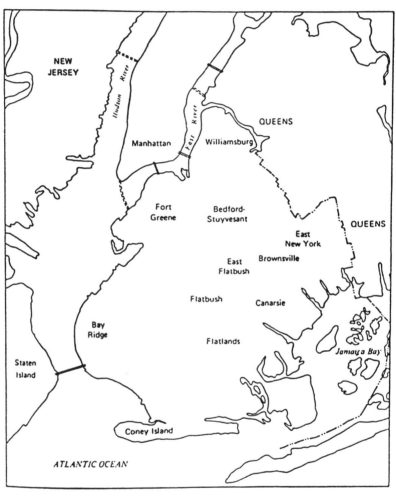

Brooklyn neighborhoods. Brownsville, in the left center portion of the map, is approximately six miles from lower Manhattan. (Adapted by author from Harold X. Connolly, A Ghetto Grows in Brooklyn *[New York: New York University Press, 1977.])*

CHAPTER I

Brooklyn's "Lower East Side": Brownsville Before the Boys Club

"Where ya from?"
"Brooklyn."
"Uhhuh. What section?"
"What section?"
"Yea. 'At's what I said. . . . So what section of Brooklyn d'ya come from?"
"Ahh, whaddya boddring me for? It ain't exactly a section. . . ."
"What section?"
"Well it's kinda near East New York."
"Ahh, stop stallin', willya, what street?"

And as you let the answer trickle slowly forth, you would involuntarily brace yourself—

"Ahah! Dat's in Brownsville, hah hah, Brahnsvil. Noo? howz Peetken Avenue?" [1]

—WILLIAM POSTER,
" 'TWAS A DARK NIGHT IN BROWNSVILLE"

By the time the Boys Club was born near the end of the depression in March 1940, many Jewish residents of Brownsville, a crowded, impoverished neighborhood in east Brooklyn, were preparing to leave or were, at least, dreaming of leaving for "greener pastures." But only sixty years earlier, in the 1880s, Brown's Village was itself surrounded by farms. In 1885 a moderately successful tailor from New York, Jacob Cohen, thinking the fresh country air of Brown's Village would

9

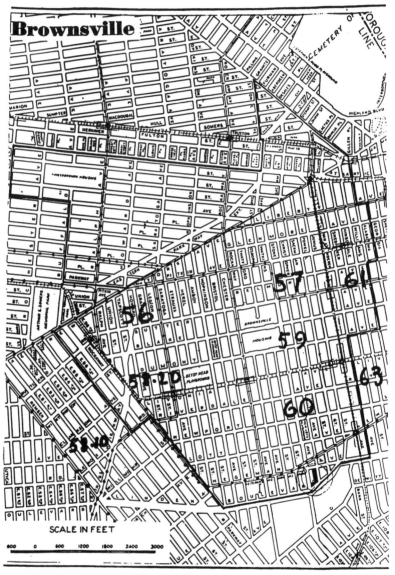

Brownsville streets, with Health Areas marked. (Courtesy of Brownsville Boys Club Alumni Association, adapted by author.)

Shopping was done all along Belmont Avenue in small stores and in the open market. Here, where the avenue met Osborne Street, one could buy fresh produce, kosher meat and chicken, shoes, candy, nuts, cake, a shirt, and perhaps a bottle of rye whiskey or schnapps. (Brooklyn Public Library, Brooklyn Collection.)

be good for his ailing wife, bought a house there. Not long afterward, other Jews from New York's congested Lower East Side followed. Speculators from Manhattan soon bought land from the Brooklyn farmers, subdivided it and began promoting the glories of the new suburb. Some of the land was purchased by New York clothing manufacturers, wholesale garment merchants, and contractors, who, in the hope of producing goods at lower cost, established "outside" shops in Brownsville. The possibility of jobs as well as the promise of less crowded conditions, further stimulated migration and by the end of the nineteenth century, a sizeable town, pronounced *Brahnzvil* or *Brunzvil* by its Yiddish speaking inhabitants, had taken shape.[2]

Another kind of shopping was done on Pitkin Avenue, the "Fifth Avenue of Brooklyn," where an extraordinary number and variety of shops and fine stores, including Abe Stark's men's clothing emporium, served Brownsville's customers. (Brooklyn Public Library, Brooklyn Collection.)

The construction of entrance ramps to the Williamsburg Bridge (1903) and the Manhattan Bridge (1909) dislocated thousands of East Siders and helped transport them and others to several Brooklyn neighborhoods including Brownsville. By 1904, Brownsville had nearly twenty-five thousand people and several small urban settlements. In the next decade population skyrocketed, fed by steady streams from Europe, the Lower East Side and Williamsburg.[3] The expansion of the IRT and BMT subways through to Brownsville continued to push population upward even as World War I and legislation restricting immigration (1921, 1924) reduced the flow from Europe. By 1930 when many of the boys who formed the BBC were approaching school age, Brownsville had nearly a quarter of a million people, more than many American cities, and had become the most densely populated neighborhood in Brooklyn, with considerable tenement congestion, small-scale manufacturing, and a variety of shopping districts.[4] William Poster recalled that

dwellings were of every variety and looked as though they had been dropped chaotically from the sky, while the business establishments gave a curious appearance of systematic arrangement; seven blocks of furniture stores on Rockaway Avenue . . . ; five teeming, pungent blocks of pushcarts, groceries and "appetizing" stores on Belmont Avenue; men's and women's clothing and similar emporia on the ten busy blocks of Pitkin Avenue. A huge six-block

square of junkshops, tinsmithies, stables, garages and miscellaneous small
enterprises surrounded these main arteries. How it all rang and clattered and
hammered and buzzed and smelled! There wasn't a quiet square yard in the
whole district.[5]

Many thought of escaping. Alfred Kazin, who lived at 265a Sutter
Avenue in the heart of Brownsville and spent his 1920s boyhood
exploring the neighborhood on foot, wrote in the late 1940s, after he
had left Brownsville:

> Whenever I went off on my favorite walk to Highland Park in the "American"
> district to the north, on the border of Queens, and climbed the hill to the old
> reservoir from which I could look straight across to the skyscrapers of Manhat-
> tan, I saw New York as a foreign city. . . . They were New York, the
> Gentiles, America: we were Brownsville—*Brunzvil*, as the old folks said—the
> dust of the earth to all Jews with money, and notoriously a place that measured
> all success by our skill in getting away from it.[6]

To be sure, Brownsville by 1940 *was* a place from which many people
wanted to get away. It had already experienced a 4.3 percent drop in
population since 1930 even as the population of Brooklyn *rose* by 5.6
percent. It would experience another 10 percent decline between 1940
and 1950.[7]

Yet those who left and later succeeded in winning a reasonable, if
not disproportionate share of good jobs, durable marriages, psychological coherence, self-esteem, and even fame as in Kazin's case, or as in
the case of basketball star and former Boys Club member, Max Zaslofsky, were likely to feel that growing up in Brownsville had much to do
with their achievement. The Brownsville boys, most now between
fifty-five and sixty-five years old, describe this "district," their combined former corners and streets, as having been a "nurturing neighborhood." Yet *neighborhood*, classically, has been assumed to be "the
product of the village and small town," and not of the "modern city"
with its absence of intimate contact, and alleged lack of group consciousness.[8] Perhaps Brownsville in the 1930s and 1940s, despite its
sizeable population and extraordinary density (140 per residential acre),
was still, as its foremost historian has described it, "an isolated corner,
a provincial world removed from the crosscurrents of the metropolitan
city."[9] Certainly many remember it that way. Kazin said, "We were
of the city, but somehow not in it." Others saw the "provincialism" as
quite positive. Arthur Spetter and Nathan Dassa were among many

BBCers who claimed that their Brownsville days were the highlight of their lives, and who think children living in the anonymity of the suburbs, or within the confines of today's "less sociable" city, are "cheated."[10] Marty Kronenberg, now a junior high school assistant principal and Norman Goroff, a professor of sociology, each characterized Brownsville as a "friendly ghetto" wherein, with the gift of family and *yiddishkayt*, "we nurtured one another" and "developed close relationships and connectedness to a place."[11]

"A kid growing up in the suburbs is lost," Gerry ("Sheiky") Lenowitz complained.

Back in Brownsville when you stepped out of your house there were forty or fifty kids on a corner. There were *always* some friends. You were surrounded by kids. You could round up fifteen at your beck and call for punchball or stickball. Today you see four or five kids walking together you don't know whether they're up to good or evil. I keep thinking of those days—what wonderful days![12]

With perhaps too much nostalgic sentimentality and exaggeration, Brownsville has almost passed into the realm of myth. But Gerald Green, former resident and author of the Brownsville-based novel, *The Last Angry Man*, insists, "It wasn't as Utopian as some recall, nor was it as grim as others remember. Hardly Norman Rockwell country, but a good place to grow up. It offered raw energy, excellent schools, the challenge of the gutter, hope and friendship."[13]

It also offered significant ethnic homogeneity, warmth, and security. As late as 1949 a writer for the *Brooklyn Eagle* described Brownsville as a "close-knit neighborhood," parts of it resembling the Lower East Side of Manhattan. "Here, too, you come upon bearded patriarchs, kosher food stores and Hebrew houses of prayer."[14] Referred to occasionally by the observant as the "Jerusalem of America" Brownsville was indeed densely Jewish. It was the leading area of Jewish concentration in New York City by 1923, and in 1925 the Bureau of Jewish Social Research put Brownsville's Jewish population at 95 percent.[15] By 1930 more than half of all New York's Jews lived in neighborhoods at least 70 percent Jewish, but none (including the Lower East Side of Manhattan) were more Jewish than Brownsville. And in 1940, when the BBC was formed the Jews still made up close to 80 percent of the population there.[16]

The Brownsville boys were not only surrounded by other Jews, but by Jewish religious and social institutions, and by Jewish businesses, all of which helped to define the Jewish character of their environment. In less than two square miles there were eighty-three synagogues, several in "impressive" buildings, but most in storefronts and basements, ten on Stone Avenue alone. There were also dozens of Hebrew and Yiddish schools stretching from Saratoga Avenue east to Sackman Street and from Pitkin Avenue south to Riverdale.[17] Many remember Rabbi Miller who had a storefront school on Powell Street to which they dutifully traipsed for their bar mitzvah lessons at a cost of fifty cents per week. (If you gathered wood for the stove, it was only twenty-five cents!) Miller occasionally used a stick for discipline, and with "extraordinarily good aim," despite his apparent blindness. The stick not withstanding, junior high school principal Isidore ("Red") Karbel recalls, the teacher was "much loved" and respected.[18] The vast majority of boys received at least a rudimentary Jewish education. This was close to inescapable, and sometimes exasperating. As Usher, a character in Arthur Granit's collection of short stories, *I Am from Brownsville*, put it: "I go to Hebrew School there in the basement. It's on Blake Avenue. Plenty synagogues! Plenty rabbis! Plenty Hebrew Schools! That's all they have in Brownsville."[19]

There were exceptions of course. A small number of boys did not go to Hebrew school. Lenny Dryansky was the "only kid on the block not to go to *heder*. I did go to older boys' bar mitzvahs, but I wasn't interested for myself and my father didn't care. My mother cared insofar as it was a *shande* [shame or embarrassment]." Returning home from a bar mitzvah party one afternoon, Lenny told his mother he loved the *kishke* (stuffed derma) served there. "My mother told me I could have all the *kishke* I wanted if I would go to Hebrew school. I agreed." One day, just short of a year of *heder* attendance, Lenny, in Hebrew class, wore a felt beanie he had designed from an old hat. "It was more filigree than hat," Lenny said. "My teacher asked, 'What's that?' A 'hol(e)y hat,' I said for which I received a smack. I told my father I wasn't going back. He said: 'you see what happens when you sell your soul for a mess of *kishke?*' "[20] There was no more Hebrew school for Lenny, and no bar mitzvah, and very little *kishke*.

Of the vast majority of boys who did become bar mitzvah, few continued their Jewish education or frequented synagogues past the age of thirteen. In fact by 1940 only about 9 percent of adult males in Brownsville attended synagogue with any regularity.[21] But on Jewish holidays the public schools were practically empty, stores were closed, and the streets were deserted, except for sidewalks in front of synagogues which were jammed with Jews. "On our streets," said Bernard Berman, a member of the BBC club Condors, and currently a director of Jewish Family Services on Staten Island, "one did not have to be religious to be Jewish,"[22] Larry Kushner, who played BBC basketball as a "130-pounder" and is now a deputy superintendent of the New York City Board of Education, reflected the experience of large numbers of others who "attended synagogue on holidays, sometimes" and "felt a strong commitment to Judaism, but rarely practiced its rituals."[23] A survey of New York City youth published in 1940 found that 72 percent of Jewish males between the ages of sixteen and twenty-four had not spent *any* time in religious services during the year, but nonetheless identified strongly as Jews.[24] Ethnically cohesive neighborhood life, visible Jewish institutions, and the Yiddish language of the street, home, and business, allowed Jews to develop a sense of Jewish identity independent of formal organizational association. Even that handful of Italian boys who made up a very small percentage of the early membership of the BBC could not entirely escape the all-encompassing milieu of *yiddishkayt*. Jimmy Genovese, for example, a member of the Jesters, who served more than a dozen Jewish families as the *shabos goy* (performing services forbidden to Jews on the sabbath), came to be known as Shimmele, and continues to this day to speak Yiddish.[25]

One writer remembers that for him as a youngster and for his friends "Brownsville was a kind of grimy Eretz Yisrael without Arabs. . . . [L]iving in a world all Jewish, where no alien group imposed its standards, he was secure in his own nature."[26] Even at public school, of which there were fifteen in Brownsville, the boys could feel secure in their own "nature." When the bulk of the Brownsville boys were in elementary school, 1930–37, approximately 65 percent of the students were Jewish, as were increasing numbers of teachers. As late as 1940 when many of the boys were in junior high school, more than 50 percent of the students were Jewish. And Thomas Jefferson High School, where the vast majority of the BBCers continued their studies in the 1940s, had a student body which was more than 70 percent Jewish.[27]

The relatively secure ethnic identification of Brownsville boys, however, was hardly matched by their material circumstances. In the early 1920s, when the founding generation of the BBC was being born, the office of the United Jewish Aid Societies testified that "some of the most unfortunate dependent classes" were to be found in Brownsville.[28] And in the same era, relatively upwardly mobile Jews from the Lower East Side and Williamsburg shunned Brownsville, choosing Flatbush, Midwood, and Coney Island instead.[29] By the end of the decade the depression hit Brownsville particularly hard. No neighborhood in Brooklyn, the Bronx, or Queens had higher percentages of families on relief.[30] Widespread unemployment in Brownsville, was exacerbated by the seasonal nature of the garment trade, which employed a disproportionate number of the fathers of the Brownsville boys. "It puzzled me greatly," wrote Alfred Kazin,

when I came to read in books that Jews are a shrewd people particularly given to commerce and banking, for all the Jews I knew had managed to be an exception to the rule. I grew up with the belief that the natural condition of a Jew was to be a propertyless worker like my painter father and my dressmaker mother and my dressmaker uncles and cousins in Brownsville—workers, kin to all the workers of the world, dependent entirely on the work of their hands. All happiness in our house was measured by the length of a job. The greatest imaginable bliss was a "busy season."[31]

Forty-four percent of the boys in this study had parents engaged in some semiskilled aspect of the hard-hit garment trade compared to 30 percent for all New York City Jewish Youth;[32] another 20 percent had fathers who were unskilled, and at least 38 percent of all the families were placed on some form of welfare relief. The librarian at the children's library on Stone Avenue which played so important a role in the history of the BBC reported that "a great many" of the children who registered, listed their fathers as unemployed or named the Works Progress Administration project upon which they were working.[33] And although almost 10 percent of the boys had fathers who would have been categorized as "proprietors" by sociological surveys, this often meant a peddler, as in the case of Abe Zaslofsky's father, or the

Irving Forman outside candy store on Stone and Riverdale Avenues. By the time Irving was twelve his father had been in and out of the candy-store business three times. None of the stores were in Brownsville. (Courtesy of Irving Forman.)

"now and then" owner of a candy store perennially on the margin of folding, as with Irving Forman's father.

The boys, as we will see, eventually took part in the relatively rapid social ascent generally associated with Jews in America, though not without significant struggle. Nathan Glazer explains Jewish success in the United States by the fact that Jews "far more than any other immigrant group" had been engaged in "middle-class occupations. . . ." They pursued callings "associated with a whole complex of habits" including "care and foresight" and "the present postponement of pleasure" in order to obtain long-term satisfactions. Jewish workers, according to Glazer, then, "were not, like the other workers who immigrated with them [i.e.,] sons of workers and peasants, with the traditionally limited horizons of those classes." Their "background meant that the Jewish workers could . . . immediately turn their minds to ways and means of improving themselves that were quite beyond the imagination of their fellow workers."[34]

The adult Jews of Brownsville in the 1930s may have had more industrial and commercial experience in their old countries than other immigrant groups, but the existence among them of a sizeable minority of "unskilled," their significant unemployment, and their general impoverishment makes the description *middle-class* inappropriate. Moreover, the term, as Irving Howe has argued, "does not begin to do justice to the shadings and complexities of Jewish desire." The Jewish immigrants "brought with them not merely habits derived from petty trading but also such additional elements of Jewish experience as messianism," (the promised and expected redemption), *tikn olam* (the repair or improvement of the world) and *takhles* (an orientation to ultimate outcomes). These elements could be adapted to secular persuasions such as progressive politics or militant trade unionism (which also required care, foresight, and the postponement of pleasure), as well as to hopes for personal success.[35]

However the sociologist would slice it, 73 percent of the men, in response to questioning about their boyhoods, classified themselves as having been "poor"—although not entirely aware of it at the time. Jacob ("YD") Deutch, now a social security administrator and professor of economics, "did chew gum *some* days, all day, to stave off hunger," and Milton Kirschner, retired from the field of criminal justice, remembers being allowed "only one cookie per day." These memories were not typical. A large majority reiterated in one variation or another, Ruby Nudelman's point that "we were poor but didn't really know it. What we did have in wealth was family and friends."[36]

Poor housing, a symbol of the material poverty, was—and indeed continues to be—a persistent and pervasive problem in Brownsville. Despite tenement legislation early in the twentieth century, existing buildings originally designed for two families, were remodeled, under the crush of surging populations, into six or eight family dwellings. And by 1933 half the buildings in Brownsville were cramped tenements.[37] From 1920 on through the next three decades, the *Brooklyn Eagle* reported consistently that Brownsville faced an "extremely trying housing situation," or that Brownsville residents were organizing to have slums cleared, or that deterioration was so advanced that public housing was an unquestionable necessity.[38]

Milton Goell, a Brownsville poet, lawyer, and civic leader was indefatigable in his crusade for public housing in the 1930s and 1940s. He described sections and streets, in 1940, just north of the area, from which Jewish youngsters would create the Brownsville Boys Club, as blighted unhealthy slums.[39] Within these streets lived perhaps as many as five thousand of Brownsville's ninety-six hundred blacks (4.3 percent of Brownsville's total population in 1940), and over the next decade that number would increase by 70 percent.[40] Referring to the blacks who lived along Livonia Avenue under the elevated tracks, Jacob ("Doc") Baroff, declared recently with an amazement undiluted by time, "They were even poorer than us!" And perhaps Sid ("Schnitz") Siegel was thinking of these same blacks, when he said "We didn't feel poor. Many seemed poorer than us."[41] But the Brownsville of the Brownsville boys, from Amboy Street, and sometimes as far west as Saratoga Avenue, to Junius Street on the east, and from Livonia Avenue, and sometimes as far north as Belmont Avenue, to Linden Boulevard in the south, overlapped areas with black residents, and was itself (Health Area 60) identified as a "congested tenement district" by a New York City Youth Board Study.[42] Milton Goell, and Rabbi Alter Landesman of the Hebrew Educational Society on Sutter and Hopkinson Avenues (the H E S), and others including Bessie Portnoy, Louis Pink, and Sadie Doroshkin were certainly thinking as much about Jews as about blacks when they insisted that "Brownsville must have public housing."[43]

The civic activists were concerned about what they perceived to be the "unwholesome" effects of impoverished living conditions—poor health, crime, "immoral behavior," and juvenile delinquency.[44] In 1939 the New York City Department of Health reported that infant, neonatal and maternal mortality rates for Brownsville were somewhat higher than for Brooklyn generally, and the morbidity rates for venereal diseases, tuberculosis, and diphtheria were appreciably higher. Similar rates were reported through 1942.[45] Poor health areas and areas with inadequate housing, it was argued, tended to coincide. Reformers drew an even stronger link between bad housing and lack of recreational facilities on the one hand, and crime, gang fights, and juvenile delinquency on the other. Goell pointed out that in 1934 the Commission on Crime and Delinquency, using addresses of offenders and places where crimes were committed, recommended Brownsville as one of five areas in Brooklyn for housing clearance. The commission's "spot maps" indicating arrest areas, crime scenes, and residences of adult offenders and juvenile delinquents, graphically and dramatically depicted Brownsville's problems.[46]

William O'Dwyer, the new district attorney for Brooklyn, agreed with these findings and announced early in 1940 that crime in the Brownsville section had been getting worse for "some time." Twenty murders had been committed in the district in 1939.[47] And O'Dwyer too, made the increasingly classic connection. "Bad housing," the D.A. said, "is certainly a contribution to crime as [are] poor health and improper recreation. There is a new crop in your school room, [which] on graduation day will walk into a life of crime."[48]

When the Brownsville teacher and novelist Arthur Granit wrote, that in Jewish "Brownsville, decaying even in those days, . . . it was nothing unusual to have a body shot up and thrown in some side alleyway,"[49] he surely exaggerated. But by the late 1920s serious crime, mostly the activities of "murder-for-money" gangsters in Brooklyn, and particularly Brownsville, had put the borough and the neighborhood firmly on the national map. New York, over the years, has witnessed the ascendancy of innumerable area gangs whose members were Irish, Jewish, Italian, or whatever ethnic group was fighting to rise up the ladder of economic and social mobility.[50] Jewish and Italian mobsters and gangs, exploited the labor-management conflicts of the 1920s, and took advantage of Prohibition and the large scale of illegal activity it engendered, to expand and unite under the leadership of Charles ("Lucky") Luciano. They became the dominant ethnic element in the world of organized crime by the 1930s.[51] The loose syndicate included such Italian and Jewish gang bosses as Frank Costello (Castiglia), Meyer Lansky, Joey Adonis (Doto), Benjamin ("Bugsy") Siegel, Jacob ("Gurrah") Shapiro, and Louis ("Lepke") Buchalter.

Lepke Buchalter, a native of the lower East Side, and his Brownsville partner, Gurrah Shapiro were regarded as the twenties and thirties "most aggressive, brutal and successful team of gangsters."[52] Lepke (a poor transliteration of Laybke, the diminutive of Layb, Hebrew for Lion) and Gurrah (for his constant and slurred "ged oudda here") specialized in industrial and labor racketeering. But it was their professional, contracted execution of "troublemakers" for the syndicate that captured the national headlines and imagination—and which earned them the title, first used by *New York World-Telegram* reporter Henry Feeny, "Murder, Inc." The gang of Lepke's Brooklyn hit men had its modest headquarters at Midnight Rose's, a Brownsville candy store at the corner of Livonia and Saratoga avenues. The gang roster included Abe ("Kid Twist") Reles, Motl ("Bugsy") Goldstein, Harry ("Happy") Maione, Philip ("Little Farfel") Cohen, and Irving ("Knadles") Nitzberg.[53]

The authorities considered Reles and Goldstein "two of the most important leaders in the city's underworld" in control [of] the rackets of . . . Brownsville." And the police in 1940 credited Brownsville with "spawning more gangsters and criminals than any other section of the city."[54] District Attorney William O'Dwyer also made this attribution. The politically ambitious D.A., perhaps to rival Special Prosecutor Thomas E. Dewey's sweep in Manhattan, determined to purge Brownsville. As part of this process he had his staff reopen previously unsolved homicide cases, and this led to charging Abe ("Kid Twist") Reles and Motl ("Bugsy") Goldstein with murder. Reles, his wife pregnant at the time, turned state's evidence to avoid the electric chair.[55]

Kid Twist had an extraordinary memory for detail and he developed a confession that filled thousands of pages of stenographic notebooks, implicated Lepke in murder (for which he was ultimately executed), and which made the Brownsville-crime connection even more explicit. Reles described activities of his colleagues over a ten-year period. In the process, the public, mainly thorough very wide media coverage, learned that Reles in his late teens, unemployed had spent his "leisure time" in a Brownsville poolroom on Sutter Avenue, where, according to another Brownsville memoirist, you could simply pass the time of day, or you could find "someone to help you break a head, beat up a guy, break a strike, buy junk, set a fire, plan a robbery, or muscle a peddler."[56] It was here that Reles met Bugsy Goldstein and Harry ("Pittsburgh Phil") Straus, who like him had substantial arrest records about which they often bragged.[57] The public also heard once again about Brownsville's vast criminal enterprises including pinball and other extortion rackets, bookmaking, and prostitution, much of which had been controlled by Irving, Meyer, and Willie Shapiro before the Reles gang intervened. The Shapiro brothers in 1930, re-sentful of competition from Reles, killed one of his crew and seriously wounded Reles and Goldstein. Meyer, then Irving, and finally Willie Shapiro were murdered in retaliation. Ultimately the confession accounted for *eighty* previously unsolved murder cases.[58]

The existence of "Murder, Inc." and the exposure of its activities made Brownsville's reputation as a "spawning ground" for crime *appear* to be well-deserved. Most second-generation New York Jews, however, living in neighborhoods of second settlement like Borough Park, Flatbush, Pelham Parkway, and the Grand Concourse, feeling relatively "at home" in America, and knowing that in general Jewish criminality was actually on the *decline*, did not, apparently, become overly discomfited. They "did not see the gang's existence as an indictment of or cause for restructuring the social fabric of New York Jewish life."[59] Brownsville's less upwardly mobile Jews were not quite so dispassionate. One Yiddish paper put it this way: "It is a pity that Brownsville . . . which is known as the 'Jerusalem of New York' . . . should now be known as a nest of dangerous murder gangs. This gives Brownsville a bad name and . . . in turn the Jews a bad name."[60]

Brownsville's Jews did not take adult crime for granted; they were deeply concerned, and they did worry about their "name" and their image.[61] They worried more, however, about their children. While in 1940 juvenile delinquency appeared to be on the decline within Brownsville's Jewish population, Brownsville's general delinquency rate of 83.7 per 100,000 was higher than for most other sections in Brooklyn, and higher than the rate of 63.7 for Brooklyn as a whole.[62] And juvenile delinquency was linked, in the public consciousness, not only to bad housing and inadequate recreational facilities, but to the visibility of adult crime. After all it was not as if there were no examples of " 'the fence,' the racketeer, the dope peddler, and the 'bookie' " who recruited "young prospects to serve . . . illegitimate purposes."[63] Although "Murder, Inc." was ethnically heterogeneous, and although postwar Jewish criminals would be fewer, and much less tied to a Jewish environment, adult crime in the early 1940s was still *part* of the Jewish ethnic milieu of Brownsville.[64]

Brownsville children knew about the adult criminals and even interacted with them to some extent in the neighborhood. The relatively

The Sackonians baseball team, uniforms supplied by "Murder, Inc." Jesse Salit,
bottom right; *Charles Pinchuk,* front and center. Left to right, top row:
Abe ("Boney") Hertzberg, Effie Walitsky, Izzy ("Tim") Becker, Izzy ("Fat")
Hertzberg, Lou ("Turk") Arnyin, Ralph Walitsky; bottom row: *Izzy*
("Whitey") Cohen, Milt Schneider, Allen Novikoff. (Courtesy of BBC Alumni
Association.)

easy contact was facilitated by Brownsville's numerous pool rooms,
often frequented by gangsters. According to at least two studies,
poolrooms were three times as numerous as playgrounds in Brownsville.[65] Although at Label's Pool Hall on Sutter and Rockaway Avenues, "the hoods, after a while . . . got so they wouldn't ask a kid they
knew was all right to do something wrong," the "hoods" obviously did
ask some.[66] One Sunday, two officers of the BBC, Irving Levine,
currently national affairs director for the American Jewish Committee,
and Jack Leavitt, now an attorney in California, were on a "mission"
to a poolroom to recruit members for the BBC. They did find men in
a "comfy Billiard academy" doing nothing more sinister than sitting on
a pooltable watching a religious movie on television. But they were
bowled over by this fact, which flew in the face of everyone's previous
experience.[67]

There was contact on the streets as well as in the pool rooms.

Midnight Rose's candy store, on Saratoga and Livonia Avenues, where "Murder, Inc." conducted meetings over egg creams and pretzels, was one short block from Betsy Head Playground and swimming pool, one of the very few recreational centers for Brownsville youth. Doc Baroff remembers that several of the members of "Murder, Inc.," including Kid Twist Reles played "cops and robbers with the younger kids." Such interaction was more pervasive perhaps than many care to remember. When Jesse Salit's Sackonians, a BBC club and baseball team deriving its name from the corners of Sackman and Livonia avenues where they "hung out" (twelve blocks from Midnight Rose's), were invited to play a team of inmates at Sing-Sing, "Murder, Inc." supplied the uniforms![68] Ben Wernikoff, who insists with some validity that the Brownsville Boys Club prevented him, and his friends, "from seeing 'Murder, Inc.' types as heroes," belonged, prior to the formation of the Club, to a Boy Scout troop that met on Amboy Street and Livonia Avenue, three blocks from Midnight Rose's where his "senior patrol leader became involved with Abie Reles in a kidnapping."[69]

It was not impossible that some Jewish boys saw "'Murder, Inc.' types as heroes." Literary critic Norman Podhoretz, who in his Brownsville youth lived the "life of street corners, pool rooms, crap games [and] poker games . . . was fiercely patriotic about Brownsville, the spawning ground of so many famous athletes and gangsters."[70] The gangsters appeared to have money and power and even status. In working-class Brownsville this was no mean achievement. Criminal activity, as Daniel Bell argued in a classic essay "Crime as an American Way of Life," could be perceived as one more way of achieving social ascent.[71] Moreover as Robert Warshow and Joseph Epstein have contended: "We are hooked on crime, because . . . in our innermost beings most of us *partly* wish to be gangsters ourselves . . . [because] the gangster, at least as popularly conceived, is a man who need suppress nothing.[72] The fundamental attraction of the gangster is that "he is what we want to be and what we are afraid we may become."[73]

The Brownsville Boys Club was fundamentally organized around sports and to some extent, as Ben Wernikoff suggested, it offered an alternative model, or hero, in the athlete. As we shall see in later chapters this helped channel some boys on the threshold of crime into "healthier" activity. There were, however, as we shall also see, even more long-standing, more powerful forces at work than sports. Jewish family, Jewish values, and Jewish community were critical in keeping the Jewish juvenile delinquency and Jewish crime rates disproportionately low. The Jewish constellation made it more likely that Brownsville boys enveloped in it would choose the model of athlete over the model of gangster. In the 1940s, however, even with Jewish crimes on the decline, Brownsville parents continued to worry. The adult criminals were not only visible and their exploits known, sometimes their work was all too apparent. "The *first* time I ever saw a man killed in the street," wrote Sammy Aaronson of his childhood, was "at the corner of Osborne Street and Sutter Avenue in Brownsville, which was maybe the toughest neighborhood in the whole United States."[74] Several boys who grew up together on Christopher Avenue, remember that one Sunday while organizing a punchball game, they realized that a car was parked on what would have been first base. When they went to ask the driver to move, they discovered he was dead—shot in the head. These Brownsville boys, apparently not *too* terribly surprised, and certainly undeterrable, released the brake, pushed the car and played ball![75]

Writers and novelists, later looking back on the Brownsville of the 1930s and 1940s, connected adult crime and juvenile delinquency, and tied these to the poverty and attendant ills of the neighborhood. "Honey" Halpern, the central character of David Dortort's *Burial of the Fruit* lives as a fatherless youngster on Brownsville's meaner streets, and grows up to be a sadistic trigger man for "Murder, Inc."[76] Arthur Granit's *The Time of the Peaches*, with more sensitivity and pathos, shows us, on "one mad Brownsville block" child-geniuses and ordinary boys. But Granit also introduces Bibi who, failing to transcend the personal and social punishments of the depression era, becomes a gangster and is killed.[77] And Irving Shulman's *The Amboy Dukes* draws a startlingly graphic picture of Brownsville gangs that were Jewish.[78] The reefers and guns, the murder and rape by the young, depicted therein, were hardly meant to be representative of pervasive behavior patterns. But the novel, "a combination of the sociologist's research and the writer's art,"[79] proclaimed that Jews, like other groups in modern America, have the problem of juvenile delinquency. Shulman showed in the world of 1942 that for children of Jewish immigrants, the moral mandates, the old world traditions, the "secret treasure of family and Jewish togetherness,"[80] did not *always* take root in the new soil.

Brownsville parents, civic leaders, and police understood what Shulman knew all too well. One set of community responses to the problem included (1) the creation of a Citizen's Committee in 1937 that planned to "cooperate with the Juvenile Aid Bureau of the Police Department in combatting delinquency"; (2) the announcement by the Brooklyn District Attorney William O'Dwyer in 1940 of a drive against youth crime in Brownsville and a vow to cooperate with police in surveying and supervising all hangouts, schools, dance halls, and garages; and (3) the development of new police files with data on hoodlums and potential lawbreakers.[81]

A different response came from the Brownsville Neighborhood Council created in 1938. A confederation of neighborhood organizations, the council aimed "to prevent juvenile delinquency" by a focus on housing, health care and education.[82] Later, a conference on slum clearance meeting at the Labor Lyceum on Sackman Street, among other things a popular forum for socialist and anarchist speakers, insisted that "malnutrition, miserable housing and improper vocational guidance are the three horsemen of the Apocalypse which open wide our jails to young boys who can and should be useful citizens of our communities."[83] Labor leaders, socialists, and other left-oriented political activists—Brownsville's liberal, even radical, political reputation is well documented—recognized the primary significance of class in the delinquency problem, the connection between poverty and social disintegration. Not all of them challenged capitalism directly, but they talked, at least, about the need to improve economic conditions for the poor.[84]

Whether it was the police and prosecutors who emphasized better methods for monitoring youth activity, swifter and stiffer punishment for wrongdoers, and the isolation of gangsters, or it was the neighborhood Socialists, American Labor party members, and other progressive community activists, who emphasized the battle against poverty, inadequate housing, education and health, *all* agreed that "the absence of enough wholesome recreational outlets was a contributing factor . . . of much of the delinquency in the neighborhood."[85] William

O'Dwyer said "improper recreation" is "certainly a contribution to crime;" and the director of the Juvenile Aid Bureau of the Police Department, Byrnes McDonald, said of cellar clubs, poolrooms, dance halls, and junkyards, "It would be useless to close those dives, unless we can offer our youth something better."[86] Similarly representatives of the Brownsville Neighborhood Council, the Brooklyn Council for Social Planning, the Jewish Big Brothers Association, the Jewish People's Fraternal Order, the American Labor party, and other organizations consistently recommended additional recreational facilities, along with other more basic social and economic reforms.[87]

This apparent unanimity notwithstanding, the Board of Education, late in 1939, as an "economy measure," closed night centers in public schools, and ruled that afternoon recreation centers in those schools, in order to accommodate younger children, would no longer be open to boys over fourteen. Dozens of Brownsville boys over fourteen, however, including Doc Baroff, Izzy Lesovoy, George Schmaren, and Norman Goroff, were competing with one another daily on self-organized basketball teams in the two small gyms of Public School 184. The Board of Education decision, in effect, eroded the already minimal recreation space for teenagers. In a densely populated neighborhood "suffering from lack of planning, inadequate community facilities, bad housing [and] more than its share of poverty," but a neighborhood teeming with communal and individual vitality, the Board of Education's fiat propelled a group of extraordinary youngsters toward creating the Brownsville Boys Club.[88]

CHAPTER 2

Founders, Framers, and the Formative Years: The Club Is Born

Our life every day was fought out on the pavement and the gutter, up against the walls of the houses and the glass fronts of the drugstore and the grocery, in and out of the fresh steaming piles of horse manure, the wheels of passing carts and automobiles, along the iron spikes of the stairway to the cellar.[1]

—ALFRED KAZIN,
WALKER IN THE CITY

The Board of Education decision which put boys fourteen years of age and older out on the streets after school was terribly shortsighted, but not *entirely* irrational. There were more children aged five to fourteen in New York City in 1940 than there were in the age group fifteen to nineteen.[2] This was particularly true in Brownsville where more than twenty-six thousand children were in the younger category and just over nineteen thousand in the older.[3] Moreover, East New York and Brownsville, neighborhoods with only 15 percent of the population of Brooklyn in the 1930s, suffered, according to Brooklyn police headquarters, more than 70 percent of automobile accidents involving the younger-aged children.[4]

Perhaps some people could accept the board decision without too much distress by thinking that for the older children, the streets—its

A great deal of time was spent on the streets and stoops, by both children and adults. This is Christopher Avenue near Livonia, c. 1947. (Courtesy of Joseph Feldman.)

stoops and its corners, and even its thoroughfares—presented opportunities for "autonomous forms of recreation, play and community," unrestricted by school.[5] After all, the boys appeared to love the streets, and they fully embraced the life of the street corners. Here, outside of the purview of teachers and parents, the boys developed a powerful sense of identity and peer interdependence. A large part of the day was spent in the streets, going to and from school, running errands, doing odd jobs, arguing, sometimes fighting, and of course playing. Many BBCers reflected the emergence of a relatively independent street culture when they recalled the "amazing camaraderie among those of us who grew up in the streets of Brownsville." Abe ("Lulu") Rubenfeld, said "playing in the streets was our main thing," and Sid Siegel "couldn't wait to finish eating and get out of the house into the street." The streets "were our salvation and sometimes our primary home," Milt Kirschner remembered.[6] And many teams and clubs took their very names from the street corners upon which they hung out.

Punchball and stickball could be played in the streets during the

Punchball was a favored street game and the boys persisted despite innumerable obstacles. (Courtesy of Joseph Feldman.)

day and tag, kick-the-can, and johnny-on-the-pony would substitute as the day darkened. "We came up from a punchball game covered with grime and sweat," wrote William Poster, "gobbled our food and rushed off to one of a hundred feverish nocturnal activities."[7] Sheiky Lenowitz and dozens of others also remember, "We played two-hand touch—most often with a rolled newspaper. We'd fold it in half and tie it. That was our football. My older brother gave me a football— this was a dream fulfilled. A *real* football."[8] Few real footballs or even basketballs, or basketball hoops, were visible in the streets of Browns-ville. But the kids were inventive. Max Zaslofsky, a member of the BBC club Bruins, who went on to play for the Chicago Stags and the New York Knickerbockers, told an interviewer: "We just got those peach baskets and hooked them on to a pole or something like that. And if we were lucky we found a beat-up rubber ball until maybe we could afford fifty-cents to go out and buy one."[9]

Economically squeezed, and politically pressed to provide younger children with play space, the Board of Education could find more than one "justification" for putting the older boys out of school recreation centers. Indeed, many Brownsville boys agreed with the one who said,

Keeping cool on the corner of Powell and Newport streets. (Courtesy of Joseph Feldman.)

"we made our *own* recreation in the streets—stoopball, kick-the-can, and so on—it was wonderful!"[10] One understands the pride of these men looking back on a difficult situation in which as boys they "made do." As "wonderful" as it all was, however, if they had no schoolyards, playgrounds, playing fields, gymnasiums, and recreation centers, there could be no softball or baseball, and there certainly could be little in the way of athletic activity in the evening or in poor weather. Charles Trester, a former vice-president of the BBC, put it simply: "We loved playing street games together when the weather was good, and playing in the schools when the weather was bad. When we weren't alllowed in the schools, we formed the BBC!"[11] While Max Zaslofsky whose "folks were very, very poor people," could be satisfied with a peach basket, when he had no genuine hoop, and a beat-up rubber ball, when he could not afford a decent one, he clearly preferred a "new school" that "had those things in the schoolyard."[12] So did the many hundreds of boys who literally flocked to sign the petition to get them back into the gyms and outdoor playgrounds of Public School 184.

Author on Sutter Avenue near Powell Street (c. 1942), in the sheltering arms of Mom, contemplating the future of Brownsville.

Limited as the school was, with little more than a half-acre of outdoor playspace (most New York City public educational institutions were erected on land scarcely larger than the school building), P.S. 184 was one of the very few recreation facilities directly accessible to Brownsville boys.[13] There was Nanny Goat Park (a little over two acres), but by 1940 it was in great disrepair, and in any case had no indoor facilities.[14] Betsy Head Memorial Park had over seven acres of athletic fields and a sizeable pool. In winter, pool lockers were removed for indoor recreation, but it was nonetheless sorely pressed by crowds of boys. The East New York Young Men's Hebrew Association (YMHA), did open in 1938, but was located in a small remodeled loft over a fish store on Sheffield and New Lots avenues and was in any case not in Brownsville. Nor was there a single public high school in Brownsville. The HES, in the northwest quadrant of Brownsville, had an indoor gym, enlarged and reequipped in 1926. But attendance far exceeded "what would be expected from the building." Only "by use of a carefully planned time schedule," could children be accommodated.[15] Moreover, HES collected dues (as much as $2.50 a year on a sliding age-scale), beyond the budgets of Brownsville boys, and charged additional fees for use of the gym.

Many other more affluent Brooklyn communities had at least some significant provision for indoor recreation and safe outdoor play. There was little in the way of *public* space, but in Flatbush there was a well-equipped Jewish Communal Center, a YMCA, a boys' club (non-Jewish), with a four-story building containing a pool and a gym, and at least two temples (Ahavath Sholem and Beth Emeth) with gymnasiums and clubrooms. The YMHA of Borough Park and the Jewish Community House of Bensonhurst provided similar facilities. Eastern Parkway had the fully-equipped Brooklyn Jewish Center, and on Ocean Avenue, residents of East Midwood could use the Jewish Center with its extensive recreational and social facilities, including gamerooms, social rooms, a roof-garden, a swimming pool and a gym.[16]

Brownsville, like other parts of Brooklyn was "neglected" by the city over "a long period of years during which other parts of Greater New York . . . secured improvements" in parks and playgrounds.[17] But Brownsville, hardly affluent, had more difficulty supplying itself with recreational facilities through private funding. By National Recreation Association standards, Brownsville was cheated in every category. For the size of its population, the neighborhood ought to have had 645 play lots, 162 acres of playground and 8 playing fields (203 acres). Instead, in 1940, it had only 5 play lots, 27 acres of playground, and 1 playing field (8 acres).[18] For years, community centers, parks, and playgrounds had been called for by civic activists, politicians, librarians, social workers, and educators, including Dr. Elias Lieberman, a poet and principal of Thomas Jefferson High School in East New York, and Charles M. O'Neill, the district superintendent of schools for Brownsville.[19] And many, understanding the problem of funding, advocated using available school space at night, putting lights in already constructed playgrounds and expanding and rehabilitating existing facilities like Betsy Head Park. The pleas, during the depression era, however, were generally ignored. Other than some minor repairs made to Nanny Goat Park by a WPA project team in 1939, little was done for Brownsville.

In his 1940 report to the mayor of New York, Parks Commissioner Robert Moses, who was responsible for doubling park acreage in New York City between 1934 and 1939,[20] could state: "In spite of what has been done in the last six years, Brooklyn today is worse off than other boroughs from the point of view of neighborhood recreation. The need for additional playgrounds in [several sections, including] Brownsville . . . is attested by park, police, school, . . . and other authorities."[21]

Whatever park and playground space Brownsville did have, was often taken up by even older boys, those over eighteen or nineteen. "We were caught," concluded George Levine, a member of the BBC club, the Chrisdales, "caught between the 'schools' and the 'parks.' We were too old for the recreation programs in the schools and too young to challenge the 'park boys.' "[22] "Suddenly," said Milt Kirschner, with apparent awe, "a 'Doc' Baroff appeared—another youth—sixteen, not much older than us. He recognized the problems and the potential community response. He helped us get organized."[23] Doc Baroff, who insists that no one person was indispensible in the formation of the BBC, nonetheless appears to have been a central personality supplying energetic and ingenious leadership. Irving Levine, in professional social work now for almost four decades, called Baroff "the most gifted natural social worker I have ever met." And Doc is described by dozens of others as "nurturer," "guide," "mentor," and "companion."[24]

Jacob ("Doc") Baroff played a crucial role in the founding and development of the club from the time of the initial petition drive to get back into P.S. 184 through the 1940s. Several days after the Board of Education's decision went into effect, closing the recreation center to them, Doc and some other Bruins, Baroff's street-corner team that had had its basketball competition interrupted, were out on the street, tossing around a football, one of the rare genuine footballs. Apparently their noise and physical presence rankled a local storekeeper who called the police. "The cops chased us," Baroff said in a radio broadcast in 1945, "and that left us the poolroom on the corner." This sort of thing had occurred in the past, "but no one did anything about it." This time "we got up a petition."[25] Baroff spoke to the captains of approximately ten other street-corner teams and they drew up the petition calling for their readmittance to the afternoon and evening recreation center. The boys clearly aimed at what they believed were important concerns of the adults in the community. "The boys have no other playground or community house," the petition read, "and therefore our only salvation is to resort to other means of recreation . . . without supervision, . . . tending not to encourage the best of citizens."[26] Almost immediately there were eight hundred signatures, and eventually well over one thousand. Doc, Izzy Lesovoy, and Norman Goroff, another member of the Bruins, contacted representatives of the Parent-Teacher's Association of P.S. 184 and convinced them to assist the boys in getting an audience at the Board of Education.

They succeeded. But at the meeting attended by Board of Education representative Mark McCloskey and the head of the Recreation Division, James Brennan, the boys were no more than "politely tolerated." The petition was slipped into a wastebasket. "We were insulted, shocked," Baroff remembered. "We had little. We were angry about being shut out. We were innocent. We believed in democracy and rights. If you ask for something legitimate and sensible it should be done. Also we had a sense of territory and survival. The bureaucracy did not understand us."[27] Democracy, rights, and survival remained critical themes throughout the history of the BBC as it grew from a loosely-organized, single-issue confederation to a well-defined instituion with social vision.

The 1940 petition to be allowed back into the P.S. 184 recreation center, eventually signed by over one thousand boys. (Courtesy of BBC Alumni Association.)

The bureaucracy, the boys noticed, appeared to pay more respectful attention to the members of the PTA, "a bunch of knitting women," than to them. "The secret," Izzy Lesovoy and others concluded, "is organization." An organization of team captains was formed and other

The Brooklyn Public Library, Children's Branch, at Stone and Riverdale avenues, where the Boys Club had its first "headquarters," often witnessed lines of youngsters like these waiting to return and withdraw books. (Brooklyn Public Library, Brooklyn Collection.)

clubs and teams were invited to send representatives. Dues of a penny a month were collected because the boys thought they would need money for letterhead, mailings, carfare, and the phone calls they would be making in an intense coordinated effort to reopen P.S. 184. Pushed outside the system, the boys discovered in their efforts to "get back in," that working together meant empowerment. "We thought we'd last just a couple of weeks," Baroff told a radio audience in 1945, "the time it would take to get back in."[28] But "in our effort to have the school yard reopened to boys over fourteen, we found we could get more privileges by being united and organized."[29]

The very first privilege exacted from the community was an indoor meeting space, for approximately one hundred representatives of the

clubs and teams. A room was secured for Friday night meetings in the Children's Branch Library on Stone and Dumont avenues. This was a familiar place to the boys, many of whom were avid readers. Twelve hundred mostly Jewish youngsters came daily to this Brownsville library—the first free public library for children in the world.[30] Many remember the lines of young people waiting to get in that stretched for a full block. "You needed to show clean hands," one Brownsville boy recalled with obvious fondness, "and you could borrow two books a week—one hard and one easy." For Irving Levine, the library, like the large synagogue Beth Yisrael, was a "spiritual island" in a neighborhood marked by physical deterioration. And for Irving Levenberg "it was a sanctuary."[31] The library was a refuge for many Brownsville children. The writer and Brownsville teacher Arthur Granit described the building which stood

between the market where the pushcarts ended and the abattoir where the sheep were slain. The Tudor-styled brick building would have been more at home in the English Midlands; instead it squatted here, although with great dignity among a vast sea of tenements and an endless array of clotheslines.

BBCers including the Levine twins check out books (c. 1948). (Courtesy of Joseph Feldman.)

Brownsville did not remain silent in its criticism: morning, noon, and night, the clotheslines squeaked against the ivy-studded walls, the beveled windows, the oak paneling, and even into the enormous fireplace where there was enough room for five children to stand with the fire burning and come out unharmed. No matter—the children of Brownsville had a magnificent building where the vaulted vastness of the reading room served as a refuge from the incessant din of the outside—except for the squeaks.[32]

Alfred Kazin, searching for the "beyond"—"to see something new, to get away from each day's narrow battleground between the grocery and the back wall of the drugstore," was another who discovered the spiritual quality of the

Children's Library on Stone Avenue . . . [where] they had an awning over the front door; in the long peaceful reading room there were storybook tiles over the fireplace and covered deep wooden benches on each side of it where I read my way year after year from every story of King Alfred the Great to *Twenty Thousand Leagues Under the Sea*.[33]

"The library was the outside world to us," Baroff said, "and not just the books." He and dozens of others still think with admiration and wonder about the librarians who helped them choose books—"Miss

Beard and Miss Jackson—and about the cooperation they rendered the boys when they needed a place to meet on a regular basis. The librarians also thought highly of the boys. "Their initiative," one remarked, "in contacting social organizations . . . and in trying to get an adequate place for recreation has been amazing."[34]

"Amazing" is the appropriate word. The recreation center at P.S. 184 was reopened to the boys less than a year after it had closed. But the club did not fade away with this achievement. Over the course of that first year the BBCers had learned more about the power of organization and commitment, and they demonstrated an increasing dedication to the survival of their new group of united corner boys. They provided a place and also a process for peaceful interaction between teams, clubs, and individuals. They created a newsletter through which boys could develop and express talents other than athletic. They significantly increased the opportunities for participation in organized play and in athletic competition. They developed relationships with other agencies including the Police Athletic League, the YMHA, the *Herald Tribune* Fresh Air Fund, the Educational Alliance and the Henry Street Settlement, and with schools and local merchants.[35] These relationships provided social nurture, athletic equipment, and a variety of recreations and entertainments including free summer camp, movies and ballgames for thousands of boys. And some of the boys claim the club also made a contribution toward reducing delinquency.

The growth of corner-boy teams and clubs, and even gangs (i.e., clubs somewhat more aggressive in defending or extending turf, and more often involved in violence and vandalism) into a successful self-help and community welfare organization was indeed amazing and probably quite rare. The fact that these second-generation Jewish boys were raised by immigrants who were often active in mutual-aid societies, unions, and progressive social and political organizations (as we shall see in chap. 3) helps explain their emphasis on "rights" and their proclivity for collective peer-group initiative and the organizational mode. Corner boys, in other non-Jewish neighborhoods, faced with some of the same problems as the Brownsville boys, did not respond in quite the same way. Sociologist William H. Whyte's classic study of corner boys in Boston's Italian North End in the late 1930s helps make this point.

Corner boys were playing softball in a small park. Some of the more powerful hitters occasionally drove the ball over the wall bounding the lot and against the building across the street. Several windows had been broken. [In response to complaints] the park commissioner ruled that no boys over sixteen should be allowed to play softball in this lot and the . . . police broke up a hotly contested game one Sunday afternoon.

Sam Franco, the leader of one of the corner gangs, had been organizing a softball league, which was to include sixteen teams. The commissioner's ruling only served to intensify interest in softball, and Sam sought some means of gaining the use of the park. He . . . asked if [the Parks] department could erect a wire netting extension to the wall so that the building would be protected. [This request was ignored]. Sam now consulted Mr. Kendall, head of boys' work at the Cornerville House. . . . Kendall then talked with Sam Venuti a local politician . . . who was not able to accomplish anything.

Meanwhile the corner boys had been holding meetings, and Sam told Mr. Kendall that, unless something was accomplished soon, they would lose interest and the organization would break up. . . . Kendall took some of the team captains to see [an Alderman]. . . . Within a short time the money was appropriated.

Many people were surprised at these results. This was said to be the first time in years that Cornerville had obtained an appropriation for new construction in the park department budget.[36]

The corner boys of Italian Boston did achieve some grass roots organization even if, unlike the Brownsville boys, they were helped by an adult social worker. And they were effective. In the North End boys did get to play softball. They did not, however, seek additional benefits and they failed to sustain their organization. The Italian boys, apparently, did not gain a sense of empowerment from their "victory." They continued, according to Whyte, to remain cynical about politicians and were generally "fatalistic,"—pessimistic about their ability to make a difference. Their daily activities continued to proceed along very "narrowly circumscribed channels."[37]

More than two decades after Whyte's *Street Corner Society*, Herbert Gans wrote his widely-cited *Urban Villagers*, a participant-observer study of Boston's West End. Gans confirmed many of Whyte's observations about circumscription and fatalism among Italian-Americans. The primary relationship for Gans' Italian-American West Enders was the "peer-group society," made up of people of the same sex, age, and life-cycle status. The peer-group society "dominated the life of the West Ender from birth to death," reinforcing parochialism, circumscription, and nonparticipation. Although most male adolescents married and developed stable family relationships, great numbers continued to spend a significant part of their nonwork hours with male companions, many entirely "unable to get off the corner."[38]

This was hardly the case with the Jewish corner boys. The "founders," of the BBC, particularly Baroff and George Schmaren, Joe ("Yussie") Feldman, Jack Deutch, Izzy Lesovoy, Dave Gold, and Norman Goroff, had begun by making the corner rounds to collect the one-cent monthly dues, to touch base, and to encourage attendance at the Club's weekly library meetings. They and others democratically elected to a council by club representatives (seven to fourteen members equalled one vote; fifteen or more equalled two votes) appropriated monies from the dues collected. They used these to pay expenses incurred in contacting various social agencies. Although the representatives and the members, jealous of their rights and attuned to democratic procedures, wanted full reports and accountability from Baroff, now president, and Lesovoy, now treasurer, they were generally pleased with the results of the council's efforts. This was particularly true in regard to the leaders' success in "booking" basketball games for the BBC teams with teams from the Flatbush Boys Club, the Madison Square Boys Club and other organizations that actually had home courts.[39] "This was great stuff," Joe Feldman said. "We had duffle bags, we traveled." By arranging for this kind of athletic activity, said another member, "the club gave us a feeling we were somebody, and bigger than ourselves." And new boys were attracted and joined. "It gave me the opportunity," said Sol Altman, "to play real basketball, a game I dearly loved."[40]

Arranging games in a variety of sports for the street-corner teams in the BBC confederation and eventually also for the "official" or All-Star BBC teams, remained a centrally important function of the organization. And as early as 1941 George Schmaren filled the elected post of athletic director. In that first year the club also claimed Nanny Goat Park as its turf, liberating it from the older "Park Boy" monopoly. Club members persuaded others in the community to help at the park,

Jack Baroff, George Schmaren, and Izzy Lesovoy (from left to right), *key figures in the founding of the Brownsville Boys Club in 1940. (Courtesy of Jacob Baroff.)*

and together they cleared play spaces of debris and made some necessary repairs. The boys also lobbied to have the park lighted at night,
and after a time, they won. The park supervisors, impressed with the
discipline and maturity of the club's leaders, allowed them to regulate
the use of the park and its equipment. A BBC boy, even an older "park
boy" could turn in a membership card and get a basketball. With a
ball, a boy could get a game, or mount the expected challenge for a
court. "We took over Nanny Goat Park," Doc Baroff explained. "The
supervisors gave us control of the basketballs and we gave them order."[41]

Sometimes the boys got old equipment donated by other organizations. George Schmaren and others remember that through Joe Mc-
Govern, a retired motorcycle cop, who held a job with the Police
Athletic League, they got baseball bats. McGovern also helped the
boys get free tickets for the circus, and "knothole" tickets entitling
youngsters to free seats at Ebbets Field, the home of the much loved
Brooklyn Dodgers baseball team. "We could get twenty-five tickets for
the 'knot hole' entry to Ebbets Field from the Police Athletic League,"
Baroff recalled, but

there was so much demand from our nearly one thousand members that we
had to develop lists and take turns. When I told Joe McGovern this, he asked
how many tickets we would need for any single game to meet demand. I had
'chutzpa' [nerve], and asked for two hundred. He said OK. The kids didn't
think it possible, but we piled on the subway to see the Dodgers. When I saw
McGovern he had only twenty-five tickets, and he saw I actually had two
hundred kids. I said 'Joe, come through for me or I'm dead—two hundred
kids just paid full carfare to get here.' He got us in by passing the same
twenty-five tickets back and forth eight times![42]

The reputation of the club, and the esteem of the leaders rose
dramatically. "Things like this never happened before in our neighborhood," Baroff said. "When we took boys to the ballgame it was the
first time ever for almost all of them. To their parents a big outing was
the zoo."[43] In addition to ballgames, there were free outings to museums and concerts and movies. Robert Solow told a radio interviewer
in 1945 that "going to museums and concerts gave me ambition to
really make something of myself. I began to read and study as much
as possible."[44] Boys were inspired, but more often simply entertained.
Norm Goroff took fifteen boys to the movies at the Stone Theater

every weekend, and there were tickets for the rodeo and the circus, often supplied by Joe McGovern.[45] The relationship with Joe Mc-Govern solidified. As George Schmaren put it, frankly, "McGovern needed 'statistics' and we needed entertainment and an occasional 'bailout.' "

The BBC, young and without resources, in needy Brownsville, was "doing good," but basic social conditions were generally unchanged and continued to produce "delinquent" behavior in the area. Mc-Govern, the former cop, having learned by 1941 to trust Baroff, would sometimes succeed in convincing the police to turn "offending" boys over to Doc. Except for a small number of auto thefts, the offenses were mostly relatively minor—shoplifting, vandalism, sneaking onto the subway, gang fighting. Doc Baroff that "gifted, natural social worker," would take the boy in trouble to an older relative, preferably to a brother, and only rarely to parents. "I got him off once," Doc would say, "and I can't get him off again." The idea was to use the family for discipline and monitoring, and to use the knowledge that exposure would be a *shande*, or shame.

The club, insisting on the same "democracy" from its own struc-tures that it demanded from the larger community, also had a "penal code" accompanied by all the accoutrements of due process. A member or representative could be disciplined for breaking club rules. If for example, a street-corner club delegate failed to show for a BBC meet-ing, his team could be deprived of a game.[46] The same discipline was rigorously applied to clubs engaged in street fighting. Baroff and others believe the games were so important to the boys that over time a reduction of gang conflict was achieved.[47] "Before we had the club," William Goldberg admitted in 1945, "my friends and I roamed the streets. We gambled, stole and cheated; and many did much worse. BBC gave us baseball, basketball and swimming teams—travel to games . . . and they sent us to camp!"[48]

A significant number of men remember going to camp as boys through the BBC. Seymour Brief, who went into social welfare work himself, and several others said, "It was the only time I *ever* went to camp." And nearly all the men mentioned how much time and energy the BBC leaders put into the camp program that developed in the second year of the club's existence. The older boys, led by Doc Baroff, secured places for younger boys in camps run by the more established, more affluent Boys Clubs, including Flatbush and Madison Square. The BBC also made placements for the "Fresh Air Fund" run by the New York *Herald Tribune*. "We recruited for camps," Baroff still says proudly, "before we ran our own. They liked using us. We provided manpower, time, and reliability. And we could even deliver types. For example the Fresh Air Fund would ask things like—'Get us a twelve-year-old white boy,' or 'a ten-year-old black girl.' "[49] Sometimes in order to get a boy to a Boys' Club camp for two weeks, the BBC workers had to convince parents that it would be all right. "We would give carfare if necessary and we told them you don't need a suitcase—a paper bag will do. We picked the kids who needed it the most—the poorest, and those who had lost parents. And we ran the whole thing—the interviews, the contacts, the arrangements." No one, Norman Goroff said, "could not take advantage of the opportunities we created, for lack of money."[50]

One of the best camps—and "the quality of the camp was judged by the amount of weight the kids gained," said Baroff—was Cold Springs Camp run by the Educational Alliance. The alliance—a curious mixture of settlement house, night school, and gymnasium—had been set up by German Jews in the late nineteenth century to help their East European brethren "acculturate." The goal of "uplift" was often pursued with blatant condescension, but the immigrants nonetheless derived tangible benefits. Despite some resentment at being "treated like inferiors," many of them knew they were being helped at the time, and remember the experience now as generally positive. Eddie Cantor, the child of immigrants, first attended the Cold Springs Camp when he was eleven. "Cold Springs was a strange place," Cantor recalled. "There wasn't a horsecar or a deli store in it." There were instead "endless playgrounds." What "a strange magic world with fruit on trees instead of [on] pushcarts." Cold one night at the camp, Cantor, a self-described, "typical New York street boy," took two blankets from other boys' beds. He was caught by the camp director who said softly: "I know you feel chilly at night and like to keep warm, but when you steal two blankets from the other cots, that means that two other little boys lie all night without blankets and feel very cold. Now is that right?" Eddie Cantor, embarrassed at the time, wrote of the experience: "I had never been reprimanded quite so gently. . . . Instead of a scowl, I got a smile; instead of a blow, a pat on the cheek. Yes, life was totally different in this marvelous boys' heaven. . . . The next night I stole only one blanket."[51] The "reform" dimension of this camp and others was real enough, but the boys who attended them were not only resistant to the subtle manipulations of reformers, they were also appreciative of the camps.

Clearpool Camp run by the Madison Square Boys' Club served mainly Irish and Italian boys. The BBC, with Baroff as counselor, brought Jews—and in 1942, two blacks. Herb Grosswirth recalled, sadly,

It was at Camp Clearpool that I ran into anti-Semitism for the first time. We were called "Baroff's Bagel Boys." We took the two black kids into our bunk because no one else wanted them. They were called the "Burnt Bagels." However, we showed the gentiles what the Brownsville Bagel Boys could do: we finished first or second in every event they had.

"I made all the kids play," Baroff said, "and we won games—Jews!— We amazed them all. And going to camp through us became even more popular."[52]

Norman Goroff contended that the camp program was not only "popular with all the boys in the neighborhood," it accomplished remarkable results even with [the] 'problem boys' recommended by local public schools."[53] George Levine's sharpest memory is "helping younger boys keep out of trouble," and Abe ("Lulu") Rubenfeld characterized the BBC with its camps and other activities of social concern as "an organization to contribute to younger kids coming up behind us. This was the whole point."[54] Although it was not "the whole point" at the very outset—sports played that role initially—"helping out," for these Jewish boys familiar with mutual-aid organizations and progressive politics, quickly became central to the meaning of the BBC. "We got games all right," Robert Solow said in 1945, "but after we were in the club a while we found other things. . . . We learned about loyalty to our friends and our obligations to society."[55] Joe Feldman, long-time and current president of the BBC Alumni Association agreed, "The need for helping was part of us, and became part of the organization."[56]

Who were the boys who created such an organization? Who for

example was Jacob ("Doc") Baroff, the sixteen-year-old, who in Milton Kirschner's words "suddenly appeared" and offered "such good advice and help to troubled children and children in trouble, and who trained and developed others to work with him and after him?" The child of Jewish immigrants from Minsk and Vilna, Baroff grew up surrounded by relatives, "all of whom lived in the neighborhood." His mother worked as a seamstress upon her arrival in the United States in 1911, but stopped when she married Baroff's father who was employed on the excavation that helped expand the New York City subway system, and then peddled secondhand clothes. "We were pretty poor," Baroff recalled.

I remember my mother saying to me when I was eleven years old, "You were *so* sick, I *almost* took you to the doctor." I slept on a foldaway bed in the kitchen, and at night I used the table there for my homework, after the others went to sleep. For my bar mitzvah I was told I could have one present only. Of course I chose a basketball. With a basketball you could get a game in the yard. And games were what we wanted, though we had little equipment and almost no place to play. But we made do. We all loved basketball. We could play all day every day. We even shovelled snow to make space when necessary. Touch football with cereal boxes was also popular.

Poor in property, "we were rich in tradition," Baroff said.

On one side of my family was a long line of rabbis and yeshiva *buchers*. My own parents were relatively observant. And of course we kept kosher. In our neighborhood you couldn't *find* any food but kosher. My father was in Minsker Young Friends [a *landsmanshaft* or mutual-aid society of people mainly from the same town in the old country] and went to *shul* [synagogue]. But he had to work some Saturdays and shul attendance was sporadic. Once he was offered an *aliyah* [honor of being called up to the Torah to read] which he turned down, feeling "tainted" from working on *shabos* [the Sabbath].

Although it was not always possible for them to be strictly observant, Baroff's parents taught him "the *shtetl* tradition of showing respect," told him stories of the old country and read the Bible with him, "pointing out the moral and ethical lessons." Doc Baroff (*Doc* for his love of *Doc Savage* magazine stories) said his understanding of Jewish tradition and the respect for his parents in the community, gained him entree and trust. In the process, for example, of convincing poorer parents to allow their children to go to camp, via the BBC, "we tried not to make it feel like mere charity, but part of the larger

tradition of *tsedaka* [justice and righteousness as well as charity]."
Baroff's parents taught him ethical lessons not only from "the Book,"
but by their behavior. They were always ready with their time, their
spiritual support and their money (little as there was) for people in
distress. And the *visible* examples were apparently only the tip of a
moral iceberg. In illustration Doc told the following story:

When my father died two men I did not know came up to me at the funeral
and told me that my pop had loaned them money when they first arrived in
the U.S. from Minsk. He had done this quietly, he never told me or anyone.
These immigrants did fairly well and paid my father back eventually, but they
had not seen him for many years. They had come to the funeral to pay
respects, to thank him again, and to make sure I knew this story about my
father.

Years later Baroff himself was thanked for aid rendered. When Doc
was honored by the BBC Alumni at their annual reunion in 1984, a
man came up to thank him. Baroff did not recognize him, but his
memory was soon refreshed. He was one of the car thieves whom
Baroff had bailed out in 1942. "When I heard you were going to be in
this area," the man said, "I had to come so that my wife could meet
you, and so that I could thank you for saving me. I'm now a very
successful businessman and I have three beautiful cars." Doc was
moved but could still quip—"Did you buy them?"

Doc Baroff "saved" a number of youngsters, mostly by tapping into
the old world tradition of family and community. Occasionally it was
necessary to threaten clubs and individuals with loss of privileges—
games, trips, camp—or worse, with loss of membership. But using
the family, particularly the older brothers, significantly reduced the
need for the harsher discipline. When Baroff was ten, "kicking a
garbage can and making a mess," he was interrupted by an elderly
neighbor who said in Yiddish, "Aren't you Baroff's boy? I knew your
grandfather in Europe. He would be upset." In his work a short time
later with younger boys, Doc remembered that invocation of family,
community, continuity, and ethnic solidarity. It often worked. "The
police trusted me, because with the boys they gave me there was
almost no recurrence." Baroff's values and behavior were influenced
by the "secret treasure of family and Jewish togetherness," as well as
by the Jewish concept of *qmiles-khesed* (applied religion). "My social
work," he said, "was 'practical religion.' "[57]

NEW YORK UNIVERSITY
SCHOOL OF EDUCATION
WASHINGTON SQUARE, NEW YORK

March 7, 1942

Mr. Jacob Baroff
427 Osborne Street
Brooklyn, New York

Dear Mr. Baroff:

In my course on Juvenile Delinquency and Crime Prevention, which meets on Monday evening from 6.15 to 8.00, we have been discussing the various methods of delinquency prevention. During the past two weeks the work of the Boy Scouts and the Y.M.C.A. has been presented.

I would appreciate it very much if you and the members of your club who spoke in my other course could visit this class on Monday evening, March 16th, and present a complete picture of your club and its activities. You would have from 7 until 8 o'clock for this presentation. That would enable the various members to present different phases of your work and to have some time for class discussion and questions.

I hope this plan appeals to you because, of course, it means wider publicity for the fine work you are doing. I am looking forward to being with you on Friday, March 20th.

Very sincerely yours,

FREDERIC M. THRASHER
Professor of Education

FMT:MM

P.S. Please tell Mr. Gold that I received the instructions as to how to get to your club and thank him very much.

Professor Thrasher invites Baroff and others for a return visit to "lecture" at New York University, 1942. (Courtesy of BBC Alumni Association.)

Others also thought Baroff's approach to "delinquency" worked, or at least was interesting enough to expose to students. And Baroff was invited by professors to speak in sociology classes at Brooklyn College, New York University, Fordham, and Columbia. Frederick Thrasher, the author of *The Gang: A Study of 1,313 Gangs in Chicago*, "one of the most quoted books in American sociology," and professor of educational sociology at NYU was concerned with "the informal processes of education, such as the street, the poolroom and the 'candy store hangout.' " He had also, between 1927 and 1936, directed a study "to determine the effects of a large New York City Boys' Club on juvenile delinquency."[58] Thrasher had Baroff, Feldman, Schmaren, and others tell the Brownsville story in his classrooms during 1941 and 1942. After the boys made their first set of presentations at NYU, Thrasher sent a thank-you note and enclosed a dollar bill to cover the cost of their round-trip subway fares. the boys at their weekly meeting voted to donate the dollar to the Red Cross.[59]

In late 1942, Baroff, now eighteen, was called upon to serve in World War II. He and many of the early leaders, and hundreds of older BBCers were separated from the Boys Club for several years. Younger boys, as we shall see in chapter 4, successfully filled the vacuum until 1945. About to begin a furlough in 1945, Baroff, before his arrival stateside, wrote the following in a letter to his family:

Today we heard the war here is over. I know you must all be happy. I myself am happy but I have also some sad feelings. I never wanted to tell you [all of] what I have seen and been through.

When I left N.Y. on my ship I went into action so fast that I didn't know what was happening. I fought through France then had it pretty fair [for] a little while in Luxembourg. Then when I went to Germany I really saw hell and I was glad to be alive from one minute to another. I was buried alive for a few minutes. I was hit by shrapnel but (you won't believe it) my bible stopped it. I have prayed oftener and harder than I ever did in my life. Some of my best friends died in front of me, some in my arms. I took care of wounded. I killed Germans myself. Right now it is easy and I [am] very restless. I hope I can settle down again.

I read today that I probably will be home for a 21-day furlough and then to the Pacific.

So when I get home . . . I want you to have plenty of soda and *hoch fleish* [chopped meat]. If I get temperamental and shout every once in a while, forget it. . . .

I met the Russians here and they are big heavy-set soldiers. And lots of their equipment comes from the United States. The Germans are afraid of them and deserve to be so—I saw one of their concentration camps.

I have seen a lot and [done] a lot in the last 9 months. And I hope it will be over in the Pacific before I get there, but if not I will do my best to end it as soon as possible.

I hope someday this will be [just] a memory and I can laugh about it. But now it's too fresh. God was with me and I thank him for everything. So you see why I feel a little sad but happy today.
Forgive me if this letter sounds a little foolish.[60]

Doc's identity as a Jew was intensified by his participation in the war and by the Holocaust, some of whose consequences he witnessed directly. When he was home for good he rededicated himself to BBC work. "I worked even harder. I survived the war. I owed." In his later professional social work, after earning an M.S.W. at the University of Pennsylvania School of Social Work, Baroff had an opportunity to speak with Vietnam veterans, who like himself had "gone through hell" but survived. Doc told the vets, invoking the Jewish concept of *tikn olam* (the repair or improvement of the world), "You have a mission to do good on earth."[61]

Other boys among the BBC founders and framers also felt a sense of mission. Like his close friend, Baroff, Norman Goroff, was the son of Jewish immigrants. He too claimed, "We felt we could make a difference. We weren't alienated." Goroff's mother was the janitor in their Brownsville tenement in exchange for rent. His father lost his grocery store and worked during the depression on various WPA projects until he died in 1940. "We were very poor," Goroff made clear. "I was the sole supporter, doing 'war work' after school. I almost dropped out of high school when I was sixteen, but the dean convinced me not to."[62] The dean must have been possessed of patience and foresight, because Norman's senior class yearbook at Thomas Jefferson High School implied that he was something of a troublemaker. "He knows a million ways to give a teacher grey hair," Goroff's fellow students wrote about him in 1943.[63]

But Norman Goroff went on to be a teacher and social worker himself. Now professor of sociology in the School of Social Work at the University of Connecticut in Hartford, Goroff says he was very much influenced by *yiddishkayt* (Jewish ways and values) and the politics of his active social democrat father, a devout reader of the socialist *Jewish Daily Forward*. Norman attended the socialist Workmen's Circle school for several years and says, "A socialist orientation permeated the entire community." Indeed, as late as 1924 Brownsville gave a majority of its votes to the Socialist presidential candidate, and Brownsville Jews, like other New York City Jews, showed more than twice the readiness of the city as a whole to support Socialist candi-dates for all offices right through 1940.[64] They also elected Peter V. Cacchione, the first Communist ever, to the city council in 1941 and sent him back again in 1943 and 1945.[65]

Goroff remembers that, at the height of the depression, and before the BBC, he and others, who eventually helped create the club, would come to the aid of people evicted from their apartments. "Some of us would kick ash cans and create a general ruckus; this would divert the marshall and others of us would help the families put the furniture back up. It was a war of attrition."[66] Alfred Kazin also remembered "those terrible first winters of the depression, when we stood around each newly evicted family to give them comfort and the Young Com-munists raged up and down the street calling for volunteers to put the furniture back and crying aloud with their fists lifted to the sky."[67] Raised on Jewish ethical injunctions, Goroff reflected the concept of *tikn olam,* when he said: "We wanted to make a better world. My original commitment to social justice," he continued, "was intensified by my struggles over the dispossessed." Surely Norman Goroff's sympathies were reinforced, too, when he, in 1940, was himself dis-possessed. He lost his father; and at the same time he was being thrown out of P.S. 184 by the New York City Board of Education because he was "too old."

Looking back at Brownsville, Goroff reflected that this was a section capable of producing "authentic community," community that could soften the shocks of dispossession. The BBC, he wrote recently, was such a community, where boys and young men had "the need and the capacity to love . . . to be creative . . . to grow and develop." Norman ("Webster") Goroff (*Webster* because he used big words) believes the BBC presented "opportunities to develop the fullest human potential; to be creative in an interdependent world, to be responsible to others, to share, care, understand, to find meaning in one's existence by making a commitment to help create a humane world."[68] Like nearly a dozen other boys Goroff says he became a social worker because of his long and active experience with the club.

It is worth noting here that by the 1940s social work had already undergone more than a decade of significant transformation. At the beginning of the depression there were very few social workers in the

United States, and the majority of them were young upper-class and upper-middle-class men and women, who worked for institutions supported by private philanthropy. In the early 1930s an important rank and file movement developed among social workers, which emphasized the links between social work on the one hand and social action and social change on the other. In the later 1930s the movement added a strong interest in organizing social workers along trade-union lines. All of this was occurring at the same time that college-trained Jews looking for new careers based on educational credentials, were moving into social work in increasing numbers. The long hours and relatively low wages of social work make it clear that Jews did not choose this profession simply to "make a living." Culturally predisposed by the "socialist orientation" of their parents' generation and by the *yiddishkayt* that surrounded them, disproportionate numbers of second-generation Jews were attracted to the *new* social work for its recently established focus on social action and social change.[69]

With an M.S.W. earned in 1952 from Case Western University, Norman Goroff began his career with the Educational Alliance, to whose camp he had helped send younger boys earlier. He has been in social work and social work teaching ever since. Recently Goroff was thanked officially by the State of Maine for helping to establish the only publicly sponsored graduate school for social work education in the New England region. The State Legislature cited his "outstanding work and years of dedicated service in providing . . . much needed graduate social work training and significantly improved delivery of social and health services to the region."[70] Connecting his BBC past with his social work present, Goroff wrote in a recent letter to Joe Feldman: "Sometimes we attempt to repeat history, particularly if it is good history."[71]

Joe ("Yussie") Feldman also thought the BBC was "good history," as was growing up in Brownsville, despite the hardships. His immigrant father died when Yussie was four years old, and the family lived "on welfare" and a small income from boarders. But "we loved it as kids—we enjoyed ourselves," he said, "even though we had no material things." Feldman's family was "traditional," but not intensely religious. "Our parents and people we grew up with," Joe explained "all held views sympathetic to socialism." He went to Hebrew school,

Joseph Feldman (upper right) *working as day camp counselor at an outing with boys at Alley Pond Park Queens. (Courtesy of Joseph Feldman.)*

though, as he said, he would rather have played ball "all day." He did put enough time in to become bar mitzvah, and Joe generally felt "surrounded by *yiddishkayt*," wherever he went and whatever he did in Brownsville.

Yussie, fatherless, and another of those prohibited from using the public school afternoon recreation center, was drawn to the slightly older Baroff. Although Feldman reflected, "I never considered myself a leader," he was early an active participant in the founding of the BBC. Joe helped write the original constitution and was the first district attorney of the club. He also nurtured the younger boys, taking them on trips and later acting as a counselor for the BBC at its day camp in Alley Pond Park. Joe Feldman was one of the lecturers in Professor Frederick Thrasher's sociology classes and the confidence he gained there convinced him he should go on to college. After a three-year stint in the armed services, Joe finished a degree at Brooklyn College, and earned a master's degree at NYU in 1952, while working for the BBC. Joe continued to commit himself to youngsters in a long career as a public school teacher of social studies.[72]

Jack ("YD") Deutch, whose intelligence gave the early organizers "credibility," according to Feldman, also became a teacher—a professor of economics at Townsend State College in Baltimore. He started out, like virtually all the boys, as the son of poor Jewish immigrants, and lived in the same building on Powell Street as several future BBCers including Joe Feldman and George Schmaren. His father, originally from Poland, was a scrap dealer in America. In the old country, Jack said,

My father had been a yeshiva *bucher*, but here he rebelled. My mother, however, continued to be observant. And despite my father's rebellion, he gave *me* a Jewish upbringing. He taught me Hebrew and Jewish history and civilization. What he imparted to me were values. And he trained me for bar mitzvah—though in the end he did not come to the synagogue to see it.

Jack Deutch's father was also a member of the International Workers Order (IWO), the Communist's version of the Workmen's Circle (WC). His affiliation, however, Jack explained "was more fraternal than political." Fraternal or political, his father's friends were mainly "left-wingers," like the parents of Dave Kitzes another BBCer. Jack early on, then, was embraced in progressive political values as well as Jewish ethics and tradition.

In 1938, at the age of thirteen, YD read about housing codes in his ninth grade civics class. He promptly wrote an essay about the violations in his building and won a Community Civics Prize. On the basis of this essay a building inspector visited and forced the landlord to rectify the violations Jack had identified, and "a number of others." Landlords remained a target for Deutch. In 1941, his family still residing in the same building, paid their $31 rent, by the new landlord's apparently idiosyncratic demand, in cash at 9:00 A.M. the first Sunday of every month. Jack's parents had offered to mail the landlord a money order, saving him the three flights of stairs, and them the Sunday morning disturbance. The landlord refused. Jack, over a period of months, and unbeknownst to his parents, saved his meagre allowance and whatever he earned in odd jobs after school. And one Sunday morning he greeted the landlord by dumping $31 dollars in small change out of a bag onto the kitchen table.[73]

The New York City Board of Education may have played the role of landlord, for Jack, when it "evicted" him and his friends from P.S. 184. In any case, socially conscious YD was attracted to the early circle of BBC founders by "the promise of politics," as he put it, "and the power and respect inherent in organization." He finished high school in 1942. Recognizing Jack's talent, his classmates quipped "Riley's economic theories will become absurd, after this young man is heard."[74] He went on to be heard as an excellent, outspoken student through City College (interrupted by service in World War II) and through Johns Hopkins University where he earned three master's degrees. He continued to be active in the Boys Club after the war, eventually becoming, along with Feldman, Goroff, Baroff, and others, a hardworking representative of the alumni on the postwar BBC adult board of directors.

George Schmaren and Isidore Lesovoy, a retired New York City fireman, also served on the board of directors after returning from service in World War II. As Izzy put it,

When we returned we found that the club was being run by fellows we had recruited—guys four or five years younger than us, like Irving Levine and Marty Kronenberg. We were amazed that the thing hadn't fallen apart, and we thought: "We must have done a good job with these boys." This was incentive for us to continue.

Izzy Lesovoy, captain of the Bruins, competing in P.S. 184 at the time of the close-out, was the energetic treasurer of the club for many years. He was also the Brownsville boy who fished the original petition to the Board of Education out of the wastebasket where it had been tossed. Izzy was another of the originators of the club who lost his immigrant father early, and like Goroff, in that critical year 1940. The elder Lesovoy, a glazier in the old country and the new, had been sick for five years before he died and the family was on welfare. Izzy's mother who had come to the United States in 1923, went to work in a garment factory after her husband died. And Izzy worked Sunday mornings in a dry-goods store on Belmont Avenue. Although "we had very little," Izzy said with no bitterness, "we had a normal life." His mother was an "observant woman" and Izzy carried some of this over into the BBC where he said "we didn't play or schedule events on Jewish holidays."[75]

The boys did not see their club as a Jewish organization, but they certainly saw themselves as Jews. It is clear in their memories, and it is clear in what they said and wrote in the 1940s. Their ethnic identity was made even stronger by Hitler's "war against the Jews." A 1948 survey of BBC members concluded that although Jewish boys continued, disproportionately, to be concerned about universal social justice, they also held pronounced "nationalist" views.[76] War veterans reflected this intensified commitment to ethnic identity even more powerfully than the younger boys. Izzy Lesovoy was no exception. After his service in the navy from 1943 to 1945, he considered himself "something of a zionist." Once demobilized, Lesovoy, like many other veterans rededicated himself to BBC work.

George ("Shtime") Schmaren, too, was an extremely hard worker for the BBC, handling the day-to-day activities and problems. He was also responsible for special programs. George, a quiet boy dubbed Shtime (voice) somewhat facetiously by his buddies, described his contribution as "inside work" compared to Baroff's equally effective but more dramatic "outside work" of public relations. Schmaren, now a restaurateur in North Carolina, was the son of a "mostly unemployed" tailor who came to the United States in 1907. His mother arrived seven years later from Russia and is remembered—she too died in 1940—as observant. George's older twin brothers "Berl" and "Yankl" described their father as a "shul mensch," who spoke only Yiddish and who made certain they had a Jewish education and became bar mitvah. By the time it was Shtime's turn, his mother was ailing and his father was suffering a failure of will, so George "escaped" bar mitzvah. After their mother died the Schmaren boys, along with their father, moved in with an aunt and uncle. George now had only a peripheral relationship with his father, whom he saw Sundays for dinner, but a strong and abiding relationship with his older brothers.

Though George and some of the other boys sought help from older members of the community in getting back into P.S. 184, he "did not trust most adults." Too "many of them," he said, particularly those from outside the community, "did not trust *us* or any boys from Brownsville." Their attitude George said, was: " 'Everyone in that neighborhood is a juvenile delinquent.' "[77] One is reminded of Samuel Abelman, the doctor in Gerald Green's *The Last Angry Man*, who explodes at a policeman he thinks is too soft on delinquents: "The trouble is . . . that *everybody* is a criminal. Am I right or wrong? Being a hoodlum is now the *rule*, not the exception."[78]

The BBC proved Dr. Abelman wrong and changed the minds of many non-fictional characters as well. "We created real community. And Doc got kids out of jail and out of trouble. Imagine." said George Schamren with obvious delight, "kids being paroled to kids." Schmaren also changed his mind about adults, at least about some—such as the settlement-house workers who "considered the job the BBC boys did the most effective in the city"; and Joe McGovern of PAL, who "paid attention to us because he knew we had nobody"; and NYU professor Frederick Thrasher, who "befriended us and supported us." Although they accepted the help of these adults and others, "the boys," Schmaren insisted, "did not accept their control. We continued to run the show."

We were not "politicians, nor professional social workers," George Schmaren pointed out: "We were just street people—we knew everything about all the families and the neighborhood. We cared and we helped. We had a desire and a *need* to do this. I don't know why. I didn't know then and I don't know now."[79]

Whether, like Schmaren, they were not particularly conscious of the reasons for their actions, or whether like Baroff and Goroff, they were acutely self-aware, these boys appear to have been acting out of a host of complex motives developed in the "nurturing neighborhood" of Brownsville. They were surrounded by kin, and supported by ethnic solidarity and communal norms. Most were saturated in Jewish ethics and tradition including *tsedaka* and *tikn olam* and their political environment was "permeated with a socialist orientation." All of this was experienced by the boys at an age when, according to the foremost student of adolescence and politics, "serious politics begins," when intelligence, struggling with the "ideal and the practical" is "brought to bear on the problem of the social order."[80]

No doubt Doc Baroff's energy and persuasiveness brought a unique dimension to the equation, and no doubt several of the founders were attracted to him because of their condition of fatherlessness. But all of them, whether through *yiddishkayt* or progressive communal consciousness, or some combination of both, had earlier internalized the norms of social interdependence. As Yussie Feldman said, "the need for helping others was part of us;" and when the "recreation crisis" struck and Baroff "appeared," the boys were ready, not only to "defend their turf," and not only to help themselves; they were ready also, by dint of their personal and sociocultural histories, to grow into a community, or as one of them put it, into a "real neighborhood, not just street corners."

CHAPTER 3

Corner Kids and Cultural Cornerstones: The Brownsville Boys in Context

The amazing thing . . . was not that Brownsville produced some criminals,
freaks and barbarians, but that so many did manage . . . to obey the laws,
attend school, and go on to become proper or even distinguished citizens.[1]
— WILLIAM POSTER,
" 'TWAS A DARK NIGHT IN BROWNSVILLE"

The boys who made the Brownsville Boys Club were raised in a
Jewish immigrant culture, within which family and community were
central. The parents of the boys, in the vast majority of cases, emigrated from the old country *with* family, or came *to* family already in
New York City, or they did both. Although there was uprooting and
dislocation, families were fairly quickly reconstructed in America.
Dozens of the men repeated stories they had heard as boys about
relatives brought here by other relatives. It was hardly ever easy.
George Berch, vice president of the Brownsville Boys Club in 1946,
and now a supervisor for the New York City Board of Education
Work-Study Program, recalled that his father, having lost his parents
in the old country as a youth, had to be brought here by an uncle.
Seymour Smolin's uncle helped bring to the United States, one at a
time, six of his brothers including Seymour's father—who was already
married and who left temporarily a pregnant wife. A seventh brother

died in Russia, just before it was his turn to leave, and the "extra" visa and *shifscarte* [paid passage] was given to Seymour's mother. This was why Smolin's older brother was born in a freight train "somewhere in Romania." Leonard Gerber, the only first-generation Brownsville boy in this study, arrived here from Poland in 1936 at the age of eleven. His father had been here since 1929 and despite the depression, managed to bring over, one at a time, his wife and three of his children, including Leonard. One daughter, the last child scheduled to emigrate, was caught in the Nazi onslaught in 1939 and killed.[2]

Overcoming innumerable hardships, Jewish families resettled and reconstituted themselves, and in Brownsville they remained "extended" families, at least for a time. Most of the boys remember being surrounded by relatives in the neighborhood, a significant minority by relatives in their buildings, or even in their apartments. Sid Siegel, Morris Levine, William Brief, Isidore ("Red") Karbel, and several others had grandparents who lived with them. Siegel's grandmother taught him about *tsedake* (charity and social justice), and Levine's "wise and sensitive" grandfather served as a "spiritual model" for the young Morris. Brief's grandfather, with whom William had a "close relationship," conducted *shabos* services in their basement; and Red Karbel insists that his "close-knit family," with Orthodox grandparents living in the same building, accounts at least in part for "the ability to transcend the social pathologies that surrounded us."[3]

Jewish identity and values were transmitted within the context of the family. We saw in chapter 1 that almost all of the boys received some type of formal Jewish education. Most were also trained for bar mitzvah, and though a good deal of the text they studied was probably incomprehensible to many of them, the months of intense preparation, and the "performance" in front of relatives, friends and neighbors gathered in a synagogue was a rite of passage; it was ascension into Jewish adulthood and a demonstration of attachment to family, folk, or neighborhood tradition—as well as to the larger Judaic tradition. The boys would respond with sympathy to Alfred Kazin's description of his confirmation.

Whether I agreed with its beliefs or not, I *belonged;* whether I assented to its rights over me or not, I *belonged;* whatever I thought of them, no matter how far I might drift from that place, I *belonged.* This was understood in the very nature of things; I was a Jew. It did not matter how little I knew or understood of the faith, or that I was always reading alien books; I belonged, I had been expected, I was now to take my place in the great tradition.[4]

Although the parents of the boys could be described as Orthodox in only 20 percent of the cases, 54 percent of the boys had mothers and fathers who lived intensely Jewish lives. This included at least some shul attendance during the year, *kashrut*, Friday night rituals, and modified *shabos* observance. And 44 percent had at least one parent who was moderately observant, that is, at least High Holy Days *shul* attendance, *kashrut*, and Passover seders. Only 2 percent of the boys had parents whose attachment to Judaism appeared to them to be minimal. Nearly all, then, were raised by adults explicitly committed to an identifiable form of Jewish religious culture.

Literary critic Norman Podhoretz, who grew up in the northwest corner of Brownsville before "making it," gives us a description of his moderately observant father that would sound familiar to most of the Brownsville boys:

He was sympathetic to Socialism, but not a socialist: he was a Zionist, but not a passionate one; Yiddish remained his first language, but he was not a Yiddishist. He was, in short, a Jewish survivalist, unclassifiable and eclectic, tolerant of any modality of Jewish existence so long as it remained identifiably and self-consciously Jewish, and outraged by any species of Jewish assimilationism, whether overt or concealed.[5]

Although fathers were most often too "busy trying to make a living" to develop what would be described today as a "relationship" with their sons, they were nonetheless a visible and felt presence in these households. Fifteen percent of the boys, before they were sixteen years old, experienced the death of a father, but in only 3 percent of the families was there divorce or separation. And the fathers, in the vast majority of the cases, stayed around even during the depression, despite unemployment. Novelist Arthur Granit's observations about Jewish Brownsville help reinforce this point:

Situated so that one could see the spires of Manhattan on a clear day, and close enough so that one could get there by subway, the district served as a supply center for the garment industry of New York. With the depression, Brownsville was assailed on all sides. The men began to lose their jobs and appear wheeling baby carriages. Soon they began to shop for their wives and argue with the peddlers. And as times grew worse, the long, fascinating noses of our Jews got closer to the ground and began to sniff through the very walls to see what was transpiring on the other side.[6]

[W]hen they went to the corner grocery to borrow on the bills so that they could have carfare to go looking for jobs, this was the bottom. And as if that were not enough, this particular winter was extra cold, so that, without money, we sat around without heat. This was below the bottom. And when the pipes began to freeze and burst, this was further down. Really, there was no end to how far down things went. Even the bottom had a bottom.[7]

It is instructive to compare these observations with writer Gilbert Sorrentino's impression of mainly Italian South Brooklyn, during the depression:

One of the things most remarkable to me was the scarcity of fathers actually living with their families. Most of the children on my block lived with mothers, grandparents, or uncles and aunts. . . . It was a simple time, but it was not that glorious age that phony nostalgia has made it out to be; there was no enormous warmth about it all.[8]

Blacks also experienced a relative "scarcity of fathers." In 1925, 84 percent of black children lived with their mothers and fathers. During the 1930s, however, blacks suffered unemployment, subemployment, and wage decline at twice the rates of whites. They were also disproportionately the victims of a welfare policy which fractured households. Not surprisingly, therefore, the rate of black family breakup as measured by male absence also increased.[9] There were hard times for all; but fathers for only some.

The fathers—and mothers—of the Jewish boys had been raised in Eastern Europe on the concept of *takhles*—an orientation to ultimate outcomes, rather than immediate benefits. There could be "neither meaning nor satisfaction in simply living one's life"; one had to achieve.[10] Traditionally, this meant success in mastering a body of Jewish knowledge and living one's life according to that knowledge. This would bring one not only coherence and satisfaction but *yikhes* (status, based on family lineage or achieved by learning). But when the *shtetl* world dominated by religion began to erode, the search for *takhles* was transferred, at least in part, to the secular world. And many of the parents brought with them to this country high aspirations—if not for themselves, then for their children. "Our parents' job was to feed us," Jacob

Baroff said, "and our responsibility was not to disgrace them, and to accomplish something."[11]

For Jewish immigrants school became an important arena within which hopes could be fulfilled, and wherein children, who had internalized the drive to achieve, could prove themselves. One East Side mother wrote to the *Bintel Brief* section of the Yiddish-language *Daily Forward:*

I am a widow . . . [with] five children . . . I have a store and barely get along. . . . I . . . employ a salesman. If I were to withdraw my [15-year-old] son from high school, I could dispense with the salesman, but my motherly love and duty . . . do not permit me. . . . So what shall I do when the struggle for existence is so acute? . . . I cannot definitely decide to take him out of school, for he has inclinations to study and goes to school dancing. I lay great hopes in my child.[12]

These hopes were no less intense in Brownsville. Samuel Tenenbaum, a writer and former Brownsville student, remembered that:

School to Brownsville represented a glorious future that would rescue it from want, deprivation and ugliness. It did not matter how poor . . . these ex-East siders themselves may have been—when it came to education nothing was too good, no sacrifice was too great for them to make. . . . We were all measured in educational potential. Next to an allegation of illegitimacy, nothing more damaging could be said than: "He has a stuffed head."[13]

Herb Grosswirth, occasionally in trouble as a youngster, now an educator himself, was told by his parents: "Stay in school. It is the only way you will ever leave Brownsville." George Berch said the "great disgrace was to be left back,"[14] and Alfred Kazin put it most directly: "Anything less than absolute perfection in school always suggested to my mind that I might fall out of the daily race, be kept back in the working class forever, or—dared I think of it?—fall into the criminal class itself."[15]

Ninety-two percent of boys who were members of the BBC in the 1940s completed high school. And most of them did it in four years. This compares with the fact that in 1940 less than half of all those who entered high school in New York City stayed to earn a diploma. Forty-two percent from white-collar homes "completed . . . high school . . . and only 20 percent of the sons and daughters of manual workers had done so. Only about one in ten Negro youths had finished high

school." Drop-out rates for New York City, including Brooklyn, increased dramatically through 1944 because of "the impact of the war
effort with its greatly increased industrial opportunities and concomi-
tant shortage of man-power."[16] The Jewish Brownsville boys, however, stayed in school.

In school they not only received diplomas, but the boys were also
often reinforced in their ethnic identities. By 1934, 70 percent of the
student body of all local high schools in New York City was Jewish.
A somewhat higher percentage obtained at relatively new Thomas
Jefferson High School in East New York where most of the boys were
educated, and which was one of two high schools in New York City
authorized to teach Hebrew classes. In addition, the percentage of
Jewish teachers was high and increasing.[17]

Comparative figures for college attendance are even more startling
than the high school figures. William Poster's impression of educational mobility in the 1920s was that: "Out of the hundred or so boys
I knew best in Brownsville, I don't think more than ten got to college,
despite fairly good opportunities. And many sons of fairly affluent
parents never got past grade school, the lure of punchball, movies, and
'workin' proving stronger than parental authority or desire."[18] The
Brownsville boys of the 1930s and forties, however, often went to
college. Fifty-six percent of the BBCers entered college, and 48 percent
finished—though rarely in four years. This is a rate higher than the
general Brownsville rate and four times higher than for all New York
City youths of student age.[19]

Not only parents were responsible for this achievement. Several
who were not on "college track" were encouraged to continue their
education by older Brownsville boys, including Doc Baroff and Norman Goroff. The G.I. Bill was also critical. "Given our economic
circumstances," Baroff said, "we might not have dreamed of going on
in school otherwise." Even for those who did continue, military service, or the need to earn money, often interrupted education. The long
ride to a college degree was hardly ever smooth. The case of Morris
Levine, now a New York City schoolteacher is not atypical. Morris's
father was injured and could not work from the time Morris was nine.
After working part-time jobs until he was sixteen, Morris quit school
in 1944 to take the full-time job his uncle secured for him in a book-

binding establishment. His mother had also gone to work sewing coats for the Army. Earning twenty-six dollars a week, and an active union member, Morris Levine went to Thomas Jefferson in the evening and gained a high school diploma. In 1948, he started Brooklyn College as a part-time student while working for the Post Office, spent two years in the army after being drafted, and completed his college education, while working, after his discharge.[20] Levine and dozens of others were indefatigable in the pursuit of education, and were part of a pattern respected in the neighborhood, of combining work and school.

This emphasis on education in Jewish culture was special, but not entirely exceptional. Fortified with relative stability and "better" jobs providing greater economic security, Jews, as well as Scandinavian farm-holders, and Greek and Japanese entrepreneurs, could afford to keep their children in school and out of the work force longer.[21] But as several works on Jewish mobility demonstrate, this is "something they wanted to do anyway." The high hopes of the Jews were partly fashioned by class, "by a nonpeasant experience in Europe" as well as "by a *cultural* ideal that respected academic learning."[22]

These attitudes should be compared with the attitudes of those groups for whom education was generally a matter of indifference or even hostility. The most studied people, and those who present the sharpest contrast are the *contadini* (roughly peasants and/or farm laborers) from the *mezzogiorno* in southern Italy. There was nothing irrational about the active disparagement of education found among them. The *contadini* lived in the old country in a state of significant material deprivation. They resided in towns with castelike social structures rather than in homogeneous peasant villages, and their condition was made even more painful by the close proximity of more fortunate neighbors.

Education in these circumstances was correctly perceived as having no relevance to upward mobility. Moreover parents believed that schools would deprive them of their children's incomes, and would likely teach values at variance with those of the home. (This dimension of resistance to acculturation is not dissimilar to Jewish reaction to state schools in Galicia and Russia in the early nineteenth century, and particularly to the "Crown Schools" under Tsar Nicholas I in the 1840s and 1850s; but Jewish parents did not withhold their children—

primarily boys—from education. They enrolled them in their own communal *hederim* and in *yeshivot*).[23]

When the first compulsory school attendance law was passed in Italy in 1877, it met with great resistance including rioting and the burning of schoolhouses. This noncompliance and discouragement of children by the family was, in the main, a practical response to the social and economic realities of that time.[24] These attitudes and behaviors, however, would persist, at least to some extent, among Italian-American immigrants, and for more than one generation of their offspring. A leading educator and student of Italian-American teenagers, Leonard Covello, demonstrated that parents resisted compulsory schooling for their children in the United States as well as in the old country. One father said: "Someone decides not to allow the drinking of wine, so he makes a law without asking the people. Same with going to school. How can you respect such a law?"[25]

Indifference to education among first-generation Italian-Americans was at least partly reinforced by their high repatriation rate. Between 1892 and 1896, forty-three Italians returned to Italy for every hundred who emigrated to the United States. For the period 1907–11 the number increased to seventy-three repatriates for every one hundred Italian immigrants. In the same era only 7 percent of Jews from the Russian Empire returned to their countries of origin. Moreover, several studies, particularly those of Miriam Cohen and Richard Varbero suggest that the educational choices made by the transplanted *contadini* were rational in the light of the occupational opportunities their children confronted, and that there *was* a gradual shift in attitude and attendance with the inception and extension of vocationally-oriented programs in the schools.[26]

The pursuit of education, however, remained a relatively low priority among Italians. Children by the 1920s were more often allowed to finish elementary school, but not without considerable grumbling. "The schools made of our children persons of leisure—little gentlemen," complained one mother. "They lost the dignity of good children to think first of their parents, to help them whether they need it *or not.*" This parent's statement at least implies that the choice was as much between education and family as between education and work. Children who could not obtain jobs also stayed away from school, or withdrew at the earliest legal age.[27]

Even in the mid-1950s, at least in Boston's Italian West and North Ends, education continued to be suspect, "with student disinterest and parent approved truancy a major problem." Children who did well in school were called "sissies." They could not excel and expect either encouragement from their parents or continued acceptance by their peer group.[28] Jonathan Rieder was able to report that, as late as the 1970s, Italians in Canarsie were saying: "The Jews in Canarsie push their kids to excel in school. They really pressure their children. They won't see past 'My kid will be a doctor.' That's happening a little more now with the Italians, but we mainly say we want our kids to have a good job and to provide for the family."[29]

The repression of aspiration among Italian-Americans, so uncharacteristic of the Jews, can also be detected among the Irish. Andrew Greeley in *The Most Distressful Nation* contends that there is an Irish-American terror of "standing out." The slightest

risk-taking beyond the limits of approved career and personal behavior is unthinkable. Art, music, literature, poetry, theatre, to some extent even academia, politics of any variety other than the traditional, are all too risky to be considered. The two most devastating things that can be said to the young . . . Irishman who attempts to move beyond these rigid norms are "Who do you think you are?" and "What will people say?"[30]

Novelist Mary Gordon, supporting Greeley's conclusions wrote recently that:

The second of these two questions, "What will people say?" is used by nearly all but the most courageous parents from every ethnic group. But the first question ["Who do you think you are?"] is a rarer one. The implied . . . right answer for the American Irish . . . is "I'm not much." . . . [I]t isn't mere immigrant inferiority. "I'm not much" doesn't mean, "I'm not much but the WASPs are a lot." It means that the human condition isn't much, and anyone who thinks it is is merely a fool. And the proper response to the fool is ridicule.[31]

The fatalism and the disparagement of outstanding achievement among Italian and Irish Americans appears to have outlasted the historical factors that gave them birth. The extraordinary persistence of these attitudes suggests that we are looking at something that transcends economic and political experience and is at least partly ethnocultural.

In any case Jewish parents raised in the old countries and saturated in the religiocultural concepts of *takhles* or long-term achievement, and *yikhes* or status, not only expected success from their boys at school, they also expected not to be disgraced by their behavior in the streets. "As we left the house," Milton Kirschner said, "parents constantly reminded us of two things, 'Don't get into trouble, and don't tear your trousers.' " And "anybody else's mother," Baroff added, "could discipline you. They'd even make you *eat* if they thought you were too skinny."[32]

Leo Yedin, a retired New York City policeman, who for a time played the role of liaison between the Hasidic Community of Williamsburg and police headquarters, recalled how his parents handled him when he got into trouble:

> There were three or four of us; we were shooting seagulls with a BB gun in Canarsie. Two "giant" men who said they were detectives picked us up, put us in the car and drove us home. They brought me to my mother, where they introduced themselves as police officers. She didn't even wait to hear what I had done. She immediately pulled out the wooden ladle and beat the living daylight out of me, right in front of the cops. And then she says to me, "Wait, your father will come and you're going to get it." And I did, this time with a strap.

That night and from time to time thereafter, Yedin's parents reminded the fourteen-year-old that just across the street lived a butcher whose son had been executed for murder![33]

When Seymour Schlosberg, a basketball player for the Brownsville Boys Club Square Deals, and now an electrical engineer, proudly told his father that he did not have to give him carfare anymore because he had learned how to sneak onto the subway, Seymour was beaten soundly. It is no wonder that when these Brownsville boys did get in trouble—and there were a small percentage of window breakers, school cut-ups, fighters, gamblers, and shoplifters—they tried desperately to hide it from their parents. Ruby Nudelman, with three other boys

> took a beating one day in coney Island from Italian kids. And we got stitched up at Coney Island Hospital. We didn't dare tell our mothers and fathers. And we wore "pupke" hats to cover our wounds. We told them it was "for the club." To take out the stitches we went to Beth-El Hospital which was closer than Coney Island. They refused to take them out; we tried the local doctor who wanted 50 cents each, an extraordinary sum for us. We thought of the corner druggist, but he was a "yenta," and our mothers would surely find out. So, we walked all the way back to Coney Island Hospital from Brownsville [seven miles] to get the stitches out.[34]

Households often witnessed beatings, quarrels, screams, theatrical sobs, and bitter accusations, "but that did not mean even that someone disliked you."[35] Parents "were simply honest and beat us if we were bad," said Ben Wernikoff. "They were less ambivalent than some of us are now about values and goals." There was anger, but rarely hopelessness. "The dirty stuff was there if you wanted," Abe Rubenfeld remembered, "but the majority of us turned out pretty good." Reflecting the power of both immigrant home and American street corner in the lives of young Brownsville Jewish boys, Lulu continued: "We were lucky we came from quality people. They had values. We also influenced each other."[36]

Seymour Schlosberg agreed that the boys had positive impact on one another and that part of it was "luck—being in the right place at the right time. Y.D. [Jacob Deutch] influenced me; he lived in my building." Joe Feldman and the three Schmaren brothers also lived in that building on Powell Street. Jack Schmaren's remarks support the memories of dozens of others who recall the influential combination of street and home in their upbringing. "We brought *ourselves* up as far as 'Americanizing' was concerned." Jack Schmaren said, "but our *families* taught us the basics—values—how to be good people."[37]

Family and household "were the predominant form in which *all* immigrants . . . ordered their lives. Members of nearly all groups received indoctrination in the need to remain loyal to the familial and household unit," and to its values.[38] Despite this fundamental similarity among immigrants, however, there were important differences in economic position, religion, and cultural background that accounted for variations in family strategies and behavior.

Many scholars have demonstrated that "[t]he Jewish migration was much more a movement of families than that of other European nationalities and groups."[39] Yet Jewish devotion to family went hand-in-hand with loyalty to the larger society and the Jews brought with them to the United States, a history of commitment to wide-ranging communal networks. For the *contadini*, *la famiglia* was the primary social unit, and *paese* (country) or *villagio* carried little more than physical connotation. Apparently in southern Italy there is no synonym for the English word "community," or for the Yiddish *kehillah*—"the community where each is responsible for all and all are responsible for each."[40] The "consequences of these differences," Thomas Kessner

persuasively maintains, left Italians *relatively* unorganized and uninte-
grated, but "produced a Jewish community in New York," and elsewhere in urban America, with perceived ethnic, and to an important
extent, universalist obligations.[41]

Brownsville Jewish boys learned about these obligations and the
value of community outside of their families and buildings, as well as
in them. They lived, after all, in a neighborhood culture pervaded by
association and institution, formal and informal. As we saw in chapter
1, there were *shuln* and Jewish schools all around them. The *shul* very
often played the role of mutual aid society. While organized primarily
for religious purposes and always constituting itself as a congregation,
the shul often subordinated these functions to ethnic needs. These
khevrot (societies) reinforced social bonds and collected dues in order to
underwrite loans, help the stick, offer cash relief, and pay for funeral
and burial expenses.[42] The more secular Jewish immigrants served
themselves in these ways in their *landsmanshaftn* and fraternal lodges.
Forty-six percent of the Brownsville boys were aware at the time that
their parents belonged to *landsmanshaftn*, and understood the mutual-
aid character of these associations. Jack Oventhal even remembers
going to meetings occasionally and seeing there, in addition to the
herring and the whiskey, lots of other boys.[43]

There were, as well, other charitable and mutual-aid institutions
visible every few blocks, including the Brooklyn Hebrew Home and
Hospital for the Aged on Howard Avenue, the Hebrew Ladies' Day
Nursery, the Ladies' Free Loan Society, and the Hebrew Educational
Society, all on Hopkinson Avenue; the Pride of Judea Children's
Home on Dumont Avenue, the Hebrew Free Loan Society on Pitkin
Avenue, and the Brooklyn District office of the Jewish Board of
Guardians and the New York Free Loan Society on Stone Avenue.
And six other organizations were doing Zionist work of one form or
another in the neighborhood.[44]

Another community organization, the Brownsville Neighborhood
Council, was mainly formed by Jews in 1938, two years before the
birth of the Brownsville Boys Club. Its objectives were to stimulate
active and effective citizen participation in public affairs, to secure
neighborhood improvements, and to cooperate with public and private
agencies to promote the welfare of the Brownsville community. The

boys were well aware of the council, which in its general concern over inadequate recreation, had voiced some protest over the closing of public school recreation facilities in 1940.[45] The council was known and respected too because it occasionally coordinated "pressure rallies," some of which were ultimately effective. Council members, for example, helped secure public housing, child care centers, and a new health center for Brownsville.[46]

Well before the formation of the Brownsville Neighborhood Council there were, in the immediate vicinity of the boys, Workmen's Circle and Industrial Worker's Order Clubs, (Socialist and Communist mutual-aid societies respectively), local "headquarters" of unions, and on Sackman Street the Labor Lyceum, which was often an arena for political mobilization and a forum for radical speakers. Later (1942–43) the Congress of Industrial Organizations (CIO) set up its own community councils in Brownsville.[47] These associations were not only visible; 45 percent of the boys reported that their parents belonged to the Workmen's Circle, the Industrial Workers' Order, or unions. Many were quite active, including Seymour Schlosberg's father, a socialist who was "very outspoken" and "once pulled down a Nazi flag at a rally in New York City," and Harold Radish's mother, a factory worker and militant left-unionist.[48]

Of course the majority of Jews were not radicals, and the "regular" political parties had local offices in the neighborhood, too. Democratic politics was for all practical purposes the rule. Many remember Sam Curtis, a Democratic city councilman elected from Brownsville who, when they had been boys, held "grievance nights" on Mondays in a storefront on Powell and Riverdale. Ben Werbel, president of Yeshivah *Torah M'Zion*, and his wife were Democratic co-leaders of the Brownsville-East New York Assembly District, as well as the parents of three sons who became members of the Brownsville Boys Club in the early 1940s.[49] In the late 1940s, progressives who had participated in the unions, the American Labor party, the Liberal party, and Brownsville tenants' groups founded the Fifth Assembly District Independent Democrats.[50] "My father would take me up on Pitkin Avenue on Sunday morning," a furrier's son recalled. "By 10:00 A.M. the sidewalks were jammed with people having political discussions. A liberal Democrat was about as [far] right as you got."[51] Several boys' parents, who did not read or speak English well, had to be instructed on how to vote. "Vote Democratic, vote the 'Star,' we told them. The joke was, if you voted Republican in the booth a bell would ring and you would disappear."[52]

Radical or liberal, politics in the immigrant Jewish community was seen as a vehicle for remaking society, for the "repair or improvement of the world." And this view of politics was passed on to the children. Dozens of the second-generation Jewish boys from Brownsville participated in election campaigns for Democrat Abe Stark and American Labor party candidate Sammy Kaplan. Several including Leonard Scholnick, Jack Oventhal, Dudley Gaffin, and Morris Levine ran for office themselves. For Italian immigrants, on the other hand, politics was generally suspect. In the old country it was "assumed that whatever group is in power," or for that matter sought power, "is self-serving and corrupt."[53] Most of Herbert Gans's second-generation Italian-American urban villagers in Boston's West End in the 1950s continued to be convinced that elected officials were corrupt and they continued to avoid "political participation [or] any . . . other forms of civic activity."[54] In the 1970s, Italians in Canarsie told Jonathan Rieder: "The only thing we think about is our home and family. . . . But we don't vote. It's incredible. We complain, but we just don't vote." Rieder concluded that second- and even third-generation Italians continued to reflect, though somewhat less intensely, fatalism and "the values of particularism represented by loyalty to family, reliance on personal networks and private settlements of disputes." Jews in the same neighborhood, however, though beginning to waver, were still marked by the "mode of universalism and faith in the democratic state."[55]

We should not overstate these differences. Italians in America, like all immigrant groups, did create institutions outside of family and personal networks. Formal institutions including mutual-aid societies and even unions functioned as "educational" devices enabling the Italian immigrants to feel secure about the compatibility of their ancestral heritage and the principles of their adopted country.[56] And informal institutions such as the religious *festa* also promoted a sense of ethnicity that could satisfy the need for an intermediate social affiliation to a group larger than the family. The Italians creatively synthesized parts of their past and parts of their present. They reinforced or reformulated institutions, values, and behavior patterns to give coherence, meaning, and a measure of autonomy to the immigrant condition. They passed this new social cohesion on to their children, who continued to use it as a method of countering the fragmentation of contemporary life. But *la famiglia* remained central. Very few institutions could compete with it—neither political parties, nor labor unions, neither self-help organizations nor the church. Although the great majority of Italians were Roman Catholic, formal religion did not provide a cultural anchor in the new world. The American Catholic church, controlled in the main by the Irish, failed to play a major role in uniting Italian immigrants, or in integrating them and their children into the wider society.[57] One respondent reflected the views of many when he quipped: "Fatalism is our religion. The church just supplies the pageantry of life."[58] Familism and fatalism—partly reshaped to the American environment—combined to promote a coherent and viable lifestyle for Italian-Americans, but one that maintained some distance from the wider community, and one that was different from the lifestyle of the Jews.[59]

The Jewish boys of 1940s Brownsville were raised in an environment—at home, in the streets, and even at school—that was Jewish, and increasingly American Jewish. Their parents had made a relatively successful transplantation of important parts of the rich and long-evolving East European Jewish culture in which *they* had earlier been steeped. Like Italian parents, Jewish mothers and fathers "adjusted" but did not discard their ethnocultural traditions. That meant, as we have seen, that the Brownsville boys would be strongly influenced by the values of family *and* community, by the concept of *takhles, tsedaka*, and *tikn olam*. It meant that they would be surrounded by institutions of mutual-aid and would see examples of the viability of communal self-help. It also meant that their political environment, with its widespread allegiance to the Democratic party, would be given shape and tone by a vital minority of left-oriented street speakers and activists.

Jewish culture, manifest in the community and its institutions and values, together with progressive politics, in the broad sense of that term, created the context within which the Brownsville boys were made, and within which they in turn made the Brownsville Boys Club.

In addition, the combination of Jewish culture, formal and informal mutual-aid, and a progressive political and social orientation helps account for the disproportionately low rate of juvenile delinquency and for the relatively high rate, given the materially impoverished base, of educational, occupational, and economic mobility.

Among the boys who formed, or who later joined and were active in the Brownsville Boys Club, there were many who attributed their "success"—in escaping the "dirty stuff" and in "bettering" their material situations—to the interdependence they developed in the streets and to the values of their parental generation. Sometimes this was simply implied, but in most cases, as with Norman Goroff, Jack Schmaren and Doc Baroff, and with Lulu Rubenfeld and Ben Werni-koff, it was conscious and explicit. Many also believed that in addition to Jewish culture and the values and models provided by parents and community, and slightly older boys, another factor—sports—helps accounts for their ability to transcend the negative social conditions and inadequacies of Brownsville. "Athletics deflected gang wars," claimed Max Stavitsky, who had done some numbers-running in his youth. "We were surrounded by crime but 99 percent of us turned out good." Irving Forman, who eventually served as an athletic director for the Brownsville Boys Club, remembered that "we did some foolish things, but never of a serious nature. We were busy playing ball." And Don Rosen, a member of the Comets, and now retired from the bakery business, "knew hundreds of kids. I only knew two kids who had problems. We had things to occupy us, good solid relationships. Most of all, sports kept us busy."[60]

It may come as a surprise to some who continue to hold stereotyped views, that there was a strong Jewish interest in sports and a significant amount of participation as well. Moreover, interest and participation did not begin with the 1940s boys of Brownsville. As early as 1903 Jewish interest in sports elicited a long essay by Abe Cahan, editor of the Yiddish language *Daily Forward* which read in part:

> A father has written us a letter about baseball and wants our advice. He sees baseball as a foolish and wild game. But, his boy is eager to play. This father expresses the view of the majority of the immigrant parents:

> "Here in beautiful America, big people play baseball. They run around after a piece of suede and fight with each other like small boys. I believe a boy should grow to be a man not a wild American runner."

We say let the boys play baseball and become excellent at the game. Why not? It should not interfere with their studies and they should not become dragged down to bad company. In a healthy body lives a healthy mind. In a quick body a quick wisdom. Mainly, let us not raise the children to grow up foreigners in their own birthplace.[61]

Jewish boys on the Lower East Side became addicted to the American game of baseball, as players and fans. In the streets, of course, baseball was narrowed to stickball, played with broomsticks and rubber balls. But some would go to parks (there were very few diamonds on the Lower East Side!) and play with genuine equipment.

"I couldn't tell my father I played ball," one East Sider admitted, "so my mother would sneak out my baseball gear and put it in the candy store downstairs. . . . Later, when I played semipro baseball I'd bring home five dollars and give it to my mother."[62]

Jews became fans as well as players. In 1915 Jewish baseball player Benny Kauff, an extraordinary hitter and base-stealer (aptly dubbed the "Ty Cobb of the Feds") playing for a Brooklyn club in the new Federal League, drew many Jewish spectators to the ballpark. John McGraw, the manager of the New York Giants, was so impressed by Benny Kauff's drawing power he virtually kidnapped the ballplayer.[63] Jewish fans could also follow the fine pitching performances of Barney (the "Yiddish curver") Pelty who played with the St. Louis Browns from 1903 to 1912 and of Eddie Reulback, the only man ever to pitch shut-outs in both ends of a doubleheader, who played with the Chicago Cubs from 1905 to 1913.[64]

In Brooklyn, Manhattan, and the Bronx, in the early decades of the twentieth century, baseball was extraordinarily popular. Many Jewish boys and young men were doing whatever they could to get to the New York ballparks, including hitching rides on the back of trucks delivering ice to the Polo Grounds, where the New York Giants played baseball.

That Jews were significantly interested in sports was also indicated by the fact that in 1908 the Yiddish press was carrying results of boxing matches. They were moved to do this by the success of Jewish boxers like Joe ("Pride of the Ghetto") Bernstein, and Abe ("the little Hebrew") Attell.[65] A poor boy from a large San Francisco family, Attell learned to fight at an early age. "We were Jews living in an Irish neighborhood," he recalled. "You can guess the rest. I used to fight

The Slappy Aces, a club and team from Powell Street, between Newport Street and Riverdale Avenue. Named for Arthur ("Slappy") Slapion (second from left, top row), a key figure in the group, the club poses outside of Nanny Goat Park. (Courtesy of BBC Alumni Association through Martin Greenberg.)

three, four, five, ten times a day."[66] Abe Attell, the world featherweight champion from 1901 to 1912, was considered to be one of the best fighters of all time by many, including Nat Fleisher, an East Side Jewish boy born in 1897 and one of the major pioneers of modern boxing.[67] Interest in this sport was reinforced with the career of Benny Leonard, who held the world lightweight title from 1917 to 1924. The son of Orthodox Jews, Benjamin Leiner (his real name) was one of the most famous Jewish-American personalities of his time.[68]

There was also an increasing number of Jewish professional and college basketball players who in turn helped increase the number of Jewish amateur players and the number of Jewish basketball fans. Harry Fisher was a well-known "All-American" at Columbia College in the early 1900s. And five-foot, four-inch Barney Sedran, called "the best little man" ever to play basketball, eventually (1920) ended up on the same team with Max Friedman, who started in 1908 with the University Settlement House on the Lower East Side and turned pro in 1910.[69]

Touch football with a rare genuine pigskin on a Brownsville corner. (Courtesy of Joseph Feldman.)

By the time the Brownsville boys were old enough to develop an interest in sports in the mid to late 1930s and right through the 1940s, there were enough Jews *in* games, and *watching* games to reinforce the boys' natural enthusiasm for play, to stimulate more participation by them in organized sports and even to engender dreams of pro careers. Barney Ross was the world welterweight boxing champion from 1934 to 1938 (There were seventeen Jewish boxing champions in the 1920s and 1930s!). Between 1939 and 1947, Brooklyn-born Sidney Luckman led the Chicago Bears football team to five Western Conference titles and four National Football League championships. In 1943 he threw seven touchdown passes at the Polo Grounds in New York and five in the National Football League title game. He was voted the league's "Most Valuable Player" that year.[70]

In the same era, Henry ("Hank") Greenberg, like Barney Ross, the son of Orthodox Jews, nearly broke Babe Ruth's record for hitting home runs. He played superbly for the Detroit Tigers baseball club from 1933 to 1941 and from 1945 to 1947. In 1934 Greenberg refused to play on Yom Kippur, despite the fact that the Tigers were caught

Brownsville boys (c. 1946) in general admission seats at Ebbets Field about to watch the Brooklyn Dodgers play baseball. (Courtesy of Joseph Feldman.)

up in an exceedingly tight race for the American League Championship (They lost the game but won the pennant).[71]

It was possible for Brooklyn Jewish boys to dream of playing pro ball and several BBCers actually had tryouts with major league baseball teams: Fred Feit with the Dodgers, Jesse Salit with the Giants, and Julie Isaacson and Sam Geller with the Yankees. Another Brooklyn boy, Sid Gordon, was "a typical Jewish kid . . . whose ambition was to become a major league baseball player."[72] In 1941 he joined the New York Giants, who by this time had four Jewish players on the team, including Harry Danning, an outstanding catcher and hitter for the Giants since 1937. Sid Gordon, who had played at Betsy Head Memorial Park in Brownsville as a youngster, loved playing in Brooklyn's Ebbets Field against the Dodgers, and always did well there. When asked about his consistently good performance at Ebbets Field, Gordon said, "If thirty thousand fans were in the park, I knew twenty-five thousand of them." He became so popular, that in 1948 his hometown admirers gave this "opposing" ball player a "day" at Ebbets Field.[73]

Some of Gordon's fans were undoubtedly "Brownsville boys" who entered the park with knothole passes secured by the Brownsville Boys Club. Brownsville, like all of Brooklyn, loved the Dodgers. The team was part of every neighborhood's culture and gave the whole borough status. "Maybe Brooklyn was a minor borough compared to Manhattan," Joe Flaherty recalled, "but Brooklyn had the Dodgers . . . with the Dodgers you could swagger." The games, the players, the team's "chances," were major topics of conversation on Brownsville street corners throughout the 1930s and 1940s. People waited up for the late edition of the *Daily News* to catch the box scores and stories.[74] It was a love affair, and a loyal one. For as Doc Baroff put it, "Anybody could be a Yankee fan. To be a Dodger fan you had to go through thick *and* thin."[75] After all, when the Brownsville Boys Club was formed in 1940, the Dodgers hadn't won a championship for twenty years. And as Pete Hamill remembered it:

All through the 30s they were the clowns of the league, an outfielder named Babe Herman had been hit on the head with a fly ball; three Dodger runners once ended up on third base at the same time; a player named Casey Stengel once came to bat, tipped his hat, and a bird flew out. But in 1941 they won the pennant and Brooklyn welcomed them home like champions. All the schools were closed. There was a motorcade from the Brooklyn Borough Hall right up Flatbush Avenue to Ebbets Field, and in the huge crowds people were laughing and cheering and crying, lost in that kind of innocent euphoria that comes when underdogs win out against all odds. . . . They lost the World Series to the hated Yankees. . . . But nobody gave up on them. "Wait 'till Next Year" became the perennial battle cry, and for the next fifteen years they were one of the finest baseball clubs in the country.[76]

Jews nourished a powerful connection to baseball. This could manifest itself in many contexts as Brownsville–born-and-raised Norman Podhoretz's meeting with Eliot Cohen, the editor of *Commentary* magazine makes clear. "In that first hour I spent with [Cohen]," Podhoretz wrote, "he jumped from literary criticism to politics to Jewish scholarship, from Jewish scholarship to the movies, from the movies to sports, and indeed spent a good deal of time trying to find out how much I knew about baseball. I did as it happened (a Brownsville legacy), know rather a lot, if not as much as he." After a complex conversation about Casey Stengel and American life, Cohen abruptly handed Podhoretz a book, *The Natural* by Bernard Malamud. "Well," he said, "you seem to know something about novels, you know something about symbolism, you know something about Jews, and you know something about baseball. Here's a symbolic novel by a Jewish writer about a baseball player. I guess you're qualified to review it."[77]

If baseball was important, basketball was supreme. Nat Holman, an outstanding Jewish basketball player with the original Celtics (1921–29), became even more famous as the extraordinarily successful coach of City College of New York basketball teams from 1920 to 1953, teams on which many Brownsville-born boys played. Moe Goldman, for example, captained a team in 1934 to a record of fourteen wins and one loss.[78] Holman also coached Brownsville Boys Club member Seymour Schlosberg. Seymour, an engineering career in mind, had played basketball for Brooklyn Technical High School through 1944. In 1945 he played at City College where Holman "liked my playing enough," Schlosberg said, "to get me a one month's extension from the draft, so I could finish the season." During his Brownsville Boys Club days Seymour was friendly with Sidney Tanenbaum, an East New York boy, "who was close to many BBCers." Tanenbaum starred at Thomas Jefferson High School and played often for the BBC All-Star basketball teams. He went on to captain the New York University team in 1947 and was according to the sports editor of the *New York Sun* "the finest all around basketball player to don violet livery." Tanenbaum terminated a short pro career with the New York Knickerbockers and the Baltimore Bullets, because he was a family man "who didn't like the road."[79]

"One of the ablest" high school and college basketball stars, Harry Boykoff, played for Thomas Jefferson High School while dozens of BBCers were students there, including Joe Feldman, Ruby Nudelman, Jesse Salit, Jack and Bernie Schmaren, Jack Deutch, Leo Yedin, and Irving Forman.[80] A brilliant player with St. John's University, Boykoff was selected for the annual college All-Star game in Chicago, in 1943 and 1946.[81]

Some of those same BBCers who watched Boykoff play, and an additional number including Harold Radish, Walter Werbel, Norman Goroff, and Ben Wernikoff, had the pleasure of seeing one of their own Brownsville Boys Club members play at Jefferson as well. Max Zaslofsky, an early and active Brownsville Boys Club member, played for Jefferson coach Mac Hodesblatt from 1941 to 1944. His classmates thought "Zaslofsky was sensational, averaging over fifteen points per game, and showing wonderful team play,"[82] Zaslofsky had loved plaything street ball, but his

> big desire as a youngster, forgetting the monetary end of it, was to be one of the best basketball players that ever lived.
>
> I was always attracted to the game. The first time I had a basketball in my hand I was six years old, and when I was eight or nine I wanted to be a professional player. This is what I always dreamed of and wanted. As a result I spent countless hours in the schoolyards and the playgrounds playing ball— eight, ten, twelve, fourteen hours a day meant nothing. I would rather be playing than eating.
>
> My folks were very, very poor people, but we were very happy. There was an awful lot of love in the family. I have two bothers and there was enough to eat but no luxuries. We never had a nickel or dime in our pockets. So at a very early age I said that sports were very wonderful things; you could make some good contacts and they were a good stepping stone to something else. And because of the fact that we had no money, I always felt if the time ever came when we, or I, ever did have money, I would appreciate it and know what to do with it.[83]

After two years of playing basketball at St. John's University (1945– 46), Max married the Brownsville girl he had been dating since she was thirteen, and he began playing in the National Basketball Association. He was with the Chicago Stags for four years, played for the New York Knickerbockers from 1951 to 1953, moved around the league for a few years, and retired in 1956. He led the NBA with a 21 point average in the 1947–48 season, and ended his career with a 14.8 points per game average, and a total of 7,990 points, the third highest scorer in the NBA history to that time.[84]

The excellent notices he got in the media meant little to him, Zaslofsky said,

> I would rather hear praise from my teammates. When my own peers could say that Max Zaslofsky for the year so-and-so was the best athlete in the entire city of New York—coming from them it meant everything in the world. . . . [M]y ego would be built up. . . . I don't see how you can perform without having an ego.
>
> Two of my most glorious moments in basketball were in 1952 when they had a night for me at Madison Square Garden. I was the first New York player ever to have an evening in his honor. And the other, to top it off, was

they had my name on the marquee. This was my dream, that my name would appear on the marquee of the old Garden. Zaslofsky night. I was on cloud nine. My mother and father and my wife came out to center court. It was a dream fulfilled and that's it.[85]

Ethnic and neighborhood pride and ambition, reinforced by Brownsville "success" stories, promoted an already established love of the game and increased participation. Irwin Sandler said, "I played basketball all day long. . . . My parents didn't mind so much, except when I . . . missed lunch, and sometimes dinner." Irving ("Hooker" [for his hook shot]) Levine said, "We were all preoccupied with the game." And Doc Baroff remembered clearly that "we all loved basketball and would often play all day, every day, after school."[86]

No doubt some of the boys, because they played basketball all day, had less time to be vandals, thieves, gang fighters, and drug users. Irwin ("Whitey") Gladstein, who, as a child, broke his elementary schoolteacher's nose, said "sports took away all my bad energy." And Nathan Dassa and his friends "never got involved" in the "dope scene" because "we had no money and we were *always* playing ball." Several others, including Max Zaslofsky, thought participation in sports was valuable in reducing gang wars in Brownsville.[87] And early on in the history of the Brownsville Boys Club it appeared to some of the leaders that nothing could be more true. Before their Brownsville neighborhood had well-organized athletic competition, it had been marked, they said, by fights between street gangs since at least as early as the 1920s. Brownsville memoirist William Poster wrote of those twenties:

When two Brownsville kids who were strangers had some contact, the first question was, "What's your block?" and the answer established identity. A gang might not inhabit a full block but only a specific sector of it. . . .

Between the Pitkin Avenue gang and the Italian clan in the middle of [my] block, relations were slight, consisting of brief, jittery moments of sociability, and bursts of warfare in which, despite a considerable inferiority of numbers, the Italians maintained equality. We were physically stronger, I think, and won our share of individual fights, but their group fighting tactics were much more advanced than ours: they stuck together like a unit of the Mafia, swooped down on us suddenly while we were dispersed in twos and threes, feinted frighteningly at our testicles, batted us over the head with stockings full of ashes, and sometimes even succeeded in taking our pants down. By the time we could get organized to counter-attack, they would have disappeared into their lairs. Once we went to a lumber-yard and armed ourselves with thin

Basketball at Nanny Goat Park (c.1945). (Courtesy of Joseph Feldman.)

Basketball at Nanny Goat Park (c. 1945). (Courtesy of BBC Alumni Association.)

twelve-foot lances with which we kept them off the streets for days, but they soon procured lead pipes of equal length and wreaked havoc among us. There were also occasional flurries of ash, garbage, tin-can, stone, and bottle throwing.[88]

And Doc Baroff said of the middle 1930s: "Petty differences express themselves in gang fights. Like, it used to be in Brownsville, if a boy walked by another block outside his own, he was pushed or yelled at by [that] block's gang. Then he would go back and get his gang and there'd be a fight."

Baroff's gang, "the Bruins, were organized," he said in 1947, "for self-protection, against other gangs." By putting these gangs into a confederation, through which they could compete with each other peacefully on fields and courts, and by giving them a common bond, Baroff believed the Brownsville Boys Club reduced gang fights. In addition there was the "penal code," wherein gang fighters would lose club privileges.[89]

The belief grew that sports helped some boys avoid "going bad." Boys had formed the Brownsville Boys Club in order to keep on playing ball, and in the process thought they saw in sports the power

Seymour Smolin in his BBC tee shirt about to shoot a foul shot. (Courtesy of Seymour Smolin.)

to control gang fights and juvenile delinquency. It is probable that several boys were helped in this way by the Brownsville Boys Club. The Police Athletic League, Doc Baroff said, in 1945,

> used to send boys to us who got into trouble in our vicinity. When they first came to our meetings they expected to show off and let us see how tough they were. However, when they looked around, they saw some of the toughest fellows in our neighborhood and some of the best ball players, who were quiet and interested in what was going on. Instead of treating them as a special group, we gave them the right to vote and the same privileges as any other. . . . If they liked basketball some of our best players would act as coach. If they wanted to go to camp, we tried to arrange that. After a while, the spirit of the club got into these fellows and for five years we haven't had any trouble with our members.[90]

Still, boys could not be *forced* to become members of the Brownsville Boys Club; they could not be *forced* to play; they had to *choose* between sports and other forms of "excitement." The impressionistic evidence suggests that while the Brownsville Boys Club did indeed have a number of dramatic successes with individual boys and may even have contributed to a reduction of gang fighting within its immediate vicinity, the Brownsville delinquency problem persisted and within some populations even grew worse between 1941 and 1946. Almost exactly one year to the day after the founding of the Brownsville Boys Club, the Slum Clearance Council for Brownsville held a conference on the increasing problem of street gangs and youth crime —crime that went beyond vandalism and disorderly conduct, crime that included "robbery, murder and rape."[91] Even the *Brooklyn Eagle*, a paper that perceived its role as "stressing Brooklyn's positive qualities," found it necessary to run a special series on juvenile delinquency, from September 29, 1943 to September 24, 1944. Though the series, as the paper's foremost historian put it, was a "frightfully inadequate treatment of crime and gangs," it made a number of troubling references to Brownsville.[92]

In 1944, the Brooklyn Council for Social Planning launched a pilot program directed toward the problem of "delinquency and other antisocial manifestations." In deciding upon a demonstration area, it considered the following factors essential: (1) that the area be religiously and racially diversified; (2) that it have *serious* (though not extreme) *delinquency problems;* and (3) that it already be served by programs for youth, yet *clearly in need of further help.*[93] The council selected a one-square-mile site that included approximately 130 square blocks of the heart of Brownsville, at least 30 square blocks of which were in Brownsville Boys Club territory, between Livonia and Sutter avenues, and Rockaway Avenue and Junius Street. Some Brownsville civic leaders were critical of the council's choice. The Brownsville Chamber of Commerce charged that "it would bring adverse publicity to the neighborhood." But the only real "defense" mounted by critics of the council was that "Brownsville is no worse and no better than any other community."[94] Abe Stark, a leading Pitkin Avenue Merchant and philanthropist, said, "Brownsville is not a setting for 'Green Pastures,' —but neither is it a place out of Dante's *Inferno.* All it asks is fair treatment in the apportioning of blame for sundry evils."[95]

The Brownsville Boys Club, as extraordinary as it was, would be no match for those "sundry evils" as they developed over the course of the next decade. The Brownsville Boys Club *had* made a difference, and would continue to do so, but it could not perform miracles. Recreation could, in the main, "save" boys who were ready to be saved because they had had other socioeconomic and cultural supports. Boys victimized by poverty and its attendant ills, and who for whatever social or personal reasons, were outside that cultural constellation of family, community, long-standing ethical tradition of mutual-aid, and hopefulness, were less likely candidates for "rehabilitation."

The gangs portrayed in Irving Shulman's novel, *The Amboy Dukes,* such as the Herzl Street Boys, the Pitkin Giants, the Sutter Kings, and the Dukes of Amboy Street themselves, were based on the Jewish gangs in Brownsville that were outside that Jewish communal constel-lation, and who were, to use one of the Amboy Dukes' favorite words, irredeemably "hard."[96]

The Dukes were different. Dudley Gaffin, now a lawyer and an active reform Democrat, remembered that before he became a member of the Brownsville Boys Club, his Boy Scout troop was located in a basement on Amboy Street. "It was a few blocks south of where the gang which was the model for the 'Amboy Dukes' hung out. I knew some of them. In 1943, Big Al Chotiner and I were at a party in their cellar. A gun was pulled. We left."[97] Up from poverty, with an infusion of war work for their parents, but not far enough up to escape their "dirty, stinking block" of tenements, the Amboy Dukes lived in a world of Ramses, reefers and guns, and they "fought for the sheer joy of bloodying and mauling."[98]

The Dukes and the boys in the other "unredeemable" gangs were only nominally Jewish; they had almost no Jewish background, no time or respect for their families, and no familiarity with books, Jewish or otherwise. Their sense of Jewish identity was peripheral, and there were no Jewish traditions or precepts that influenced their lives. With minimal Jewish education, formal or informal, and even less culture, these boys had nothing to draw on to counteract the mean effects of poverty. There is only one youth in the novel, Frank Goldfarb, with the capacity to come to the threshold of understanding moral choices; but with no deeply internalized ethical values and no reinforcement from his immediate environment, his vision is never clear and he is unable to act upon those choices.

Stan Alberg, the novel's social worker at the Jewish Community Center, tried to channel the energies of some of the Dukes, including Frank, by offering basketballs instead of bullets. He thought he was

doing a worthwhile job. Every juvenile he was able to interest in the gymnasium was someone who made his day a success. It was a tough job to go out and drag the boys off the street corners and make them want to meet in the Center gymnasium instead of the poolroom, make them want to meet in the center clubrooms instead of the corner candy store, and make them want to go out and recruit their friends to join the athletic teams instead of the gangs.[99]

Frank *is* disturbed by Alberg. Maybe he *should* get rid of his gun. But he tells the social worker: "You guys make me sick. That's why we never come around here. You're always trying to make us reform. What the hell have I got to reform for? I haven't done anything wrong."[100] Goldfarb who did do some thoughtlessly irresponsible, dangerous, and harmful things, occasionally comes close to remorse; but the feeling is fleeting, overwhelmed by the fear of getting caught.

By the 1940s Brownsville already included populations of such children—a relatively small, Jewish minority, that history and social conditions had pushed outside of a strongly supportive cultural constellation. In the same era, Brownsville would begin to fill with an increasing population of other children whose families and culture had been victims of unprecedented historic disruption, even brutalization. There was a relatively rapid influx of black migrants into Brownsville from the rural South even before the end of World War II, as well as some in-migration of blacks from other New York neighborhoods including Harlem, Fort Greene, and Bedford-Stuyvesant. Between 1940 and 1950 the black population of Brownsville doubled.[101]

School registration figures showed a steady increase in the proportion of black children after 1940, and as one report on Brownsville put it: "Negro children suffer special deprivation. They . . . are . . . even more deprived than the White population from the standpoints of economic welfare, acceptable housing, good health; and with many mothers working away from the home, no . . . nursery schools, and with so little . . . play space for them, the needs of this group are obviously acute."[102] And by 1945 black children in several sections, including thirty square blocks in the northern end of Brownsville Boys Club territory, constituted 30 to 80 percent of the students in public schools.[103]

Simultaneously the absolute number, as well as the relative proportion of Jews in the community were steadily declining. Population mobility contributed to instability of neighborhood life and to increased frustrations. "We didn't have the wealth to give us mobility, and we were stuck," Jack Newfield remembered,

and I saw friends, whose fathers were doing well, . . . and one by one they began to move out of the neighborhood, some to Sheepshead Bay and Flatbush, more to Queens, some to Long Island, some to Jersey. They had upward mobility. But we were stuck there. And with the blacks moving in there came a great fear. There was blockbusting. There was panic selling. There were real estate speculators, the piranhas and vultures who circle any changing or transitional neighborhood.[104]

Community instability and social and personal frustration, according to one careful report, led to "substantial racial tensions among children in school and in the playgrounds," as well as to "considerable delinquent behavior including such serious offenses as burglary, robbery, stabbing and arson."[105]

The Brownsville Boys Club, as we shall see in the chapters to follow did what it could in the face of this situation. But recreation would not be enough. The Brooklyn Council for Social Planning predicted that more adequate play space would only deflect such minor offenses as "ballplaying [and] riding bicycles [in prohibited areas], breaking windows, trespassing and throwing stones." And it recognized that

the family problems and neighborhood conditions which help produce delinquency are complex and there are no easy solutions. The Committee is aware that what happens in the City . . . State . . . nation and the world will have [an] important effect on family and neighborhood life here. . . . This interdependence must not be forgotten.

We know that healthy family life depends in large part on progress in raising economic standards and improving living conditions, especially housing, for *wholesome neighborhood environment and basic economic security provide the underpinning of happy family life.* Furthermore, there must be continued effort to overcome tensions which arise from cultural and religious differences and to develop the understanding and ways of cooperation which make for sound community morale.[106]

The Brownsville Boys Club also reflected, in its rhetoric and behavior, some understanding that in addition to increased recreational facilities and other social services, changes in more basic social and material conditions were necessary. In March 1946 at the Sixth Anniversary Meeting of the founding of the BBC held at the Stone Avenue Library, it was announced, "We must try to obtain certain improvements for Brownsville. Although a settlement house is our immediate goal, we will campaign for health centers, housing projects, high schools and other facilities."[107] In 1947 Norman Goroff wrote that the goal of the club is "not to keep the boys off the streets, but to make the streets attractive and safe."[108] Pointing also to the fact that a small but increasing percentage of BBCers were black, Goroff, now an alumnus and volunteer worker for the club, said that all the boys, black and white, were striving "for better understanding through working and playing together: and above all knowing each other."[109]

The Brownsville Boys Club was a stunning achievement. A group of young boys created an organization which enabled them and others to do what they loved to do most—play ball. The club made possible large-scale participation of boys in recreation. It tapped into an already deeply-rooted sports culture, provided athlete-heroes as types for emulation, and channeled energies into "healthy competition." It tapped even more into the Jewish community culture of *tsedaka* and mutual-aid, and progressive politics. The BBC quickly developed into an extraordinary self-help institution providing nurture for many young Brownsville boys in need and acting as a powerfully successful negotiator in gaining benefits and resources from other established agencies. The club also provided social models and guidance. Most important perhaps it created a sense of authentic community and of belonging. As Ben Wernikoff put it: "At the outset our object was to get back into the playground. But, then belonging to the BBC was as natural for us as that our families were members of shuls and 'societies.' "[110]

Almost all the boys, when they talk about the BBC experience, convey a sense of deep satisfaction and fulfillment resulting from what was virtually total involvement and interdependence. Several studies have found that men and women as old as seventy and as young as thirteen, from a wide range of cultures, East and West, describe the times when they are at their peak of fulfillment in very similar terms. They talk about a nearly complete immersion in whatever they are doing,

a deep concentration on the activity at hand, which leads to a forgetting of everyday problems; a clarity of goals and feedback; a loss of self-consciousness and . . . a sense of transcendence, as if the self had shed its puny shell and become part of a much larger entity, a more dynamic force. And they all say that this experience . . . called the "flow" experience because so many respondents likened it to a merging with a stream of energy—is made possible by the balancing of personal skills with environmental challenges.[111]

Creating and maintaining the BBC together was a "flow" experience for the Brownsville boys. These boys, products of Jewish home life and environment, helped themselves and were able to help others. "I really believe that the BBC made me a better person," said Nathan Dassa, and many others remembered that "the older BBC boys picked us up when we needed them," or that the "BBC strengthened our self-esteem as Brownsville boys."[112]

The Brownsville Boys Club, which had impressed other social agencies with its energy and commitment, was to become in the postwar era an "established" agency itself. But it would continue to provide, perhaps even more effectively, all the older valuable services as well as some new ones. Postwar club leaders included war veterans —former BBCers, who felt enough attachment to their Jewish neighborhood to return to it at least for a time. They were apparently not yet as ready as many other Jews were to "move up and out." The veterans and other leaders stayed in Brownsville, and tried, beginning in the mid-1940s, to contribute, in their own small ways, to the alleviation of the enormous social problems brought during the war, and in its wake.

CHAPTER 4

Soldiers, Storefronts, and Social Change: The Club Carries On

It is Better to Build Boys
Than to Mend Men.
—BROWNSVILLE BOYS' CLUB SLOGAN

The war brought a number of problems to Brownsville and to the Brownsville Boys Club. Virtually all of the "older" boys who had been most responsible for the founding and framing of the BBC were, along with nearly five hundred other club members, serving in one branch or another of the armed forces.[1] Doc Baroff, Yussie Feldman, Y.D. Deutch and George Schmaren were in the army, and Izzy Lesovoy was in the navy. Only Norman Goroff, of the "originals," because of a heart problem, stayed on the home front. But the club carried on.

Goroff, with the help of the fifteen- and sixteen-year-olds, including Irving Levine, Jack Leavitt, Seymour Brief, Bernard Berman, and Marty Kronenberg, kept the club alive and active. There was a temporary decrease in membership (approximately 60 percent), but the newsletter came out with relative consistency, games were booked and there were still trips to movies, and outings to museums and circuses. One BBC serviceman stationed in Texas, received a copy of the newsletter, and was delighted. He wrote to thank the editors and to encour-

On Pitkin Avenue, members of the U.S. armed forces demonstrate weaponry for the "education" of the public, including a number of BBCers. (Courtesy of BBC Alumni Association.)

age them: "I am glad to hear that you are still going places and getting in gratis. I got a big kick out of it when I went to the Rodeo with you boys at Madison Square Garden. I enjoyed myself because I saw happy kids all around me." He went on to say, "We have God to thank for this country where we can still laugh and do as we please. . . . I think it would be a good idea if you boys went out and hustled up things to help our country."[2]

Brownsville generally did its part for the war effort. Civilian defense volunteer organizations were very active writing letters to soldiers, running canteens for servicemen home on furlough, cooperating with the Red Cross and selling war bonds. Fifteen million dollars in war bonds were sold in Brownsville. *Landsmanshaftn* in Brownsville also raised large sums for Russian war relief.[3]

The boys in the Brownsville Boys Club were no exception to the general Brownsville trend of war aid and enthusiastic support for the

A war bond rally on Powell Street sponsored by Ben Werbel, Democratic party leader, and father of three BBCers. Other Brownsville Boys Club members participating included Ruby Nudelman, Sheiky Lenowitz, and Joe Feldman. (Courtesy of BBC Alumni Association.)

soldiers, many of whom were their own club mates. Boys going on BBC-sponsored trips, for example, were required to "buy at least a ten-cent war stamp." The boys also participated extensively in local "scrap drives."[4]

Aid continued even after the war. Having heard the stories and seen photographs of children who had spent time in concentration camps,

Bernard ("Red") Geller, Dudley Gaffin, and Gerald ("Sheiky") Lenowitz in Gaffin's father's bar and grill, on Rockaway and New Lots avenues, sending Ruby Nudelman off to war. (Courtesy of BBC Alumni Association.)

the boys decided to adopt a war orphan. Saving pennies, nickels, and dimes in a month-long no-bubble gum and no-candy campaign, the BBC boys accumulated $365. The money was given to Salmon Rzepko, selected, the boys said, because "we kinda liked his picture," and what they had read about him in the newsletters.[5]

Brownsville Boys Club newsletters were sent to servicemen throughout the war, and were an important part of the boys' general support and aid. Certainly they were no small thing to the soldiers who received them: "I just got [the] newspaper you mailed me," wrote Private Joe Skope in a letter reprinted in the BBC newsletter:

It was great and I want to thank you boys for helping to build up my morale. I guess the other fellows that you mailed the paper to feel the same way as I do. It was great to read about the things back in the old neighborhood and know that you boys are helping us here.

I'm some where in New Guinea and when a fellow gets news from the old gang you can see the sparkle in his eyes and he knows that some of the boys still think of him and it makes him fight all the harder so he can get back to his prewar friends.

Thanks again for the paper and I hope when the next one comes out you will remember to mail one to me.

I'll be seeing you after final victory.[6]

Hy Rabinowitz wrote:

It was certainly swell to hear from the "mob" again. Only a serviceman knows how it feels when his friend writes to him. In my opinion a letter, or a paper as you sent, is the best present one in the service could ask for. . . . Reading it brought back memories—memories of us fellows playing ball, arguing, and laughing together. Yep, those were the "good old days". . . .

I must stress again keep sending those papers to us continuously . . . and thanks again.[7]

Private First Class Sid ("Schnitz") Siegel also expressed his gratitude not only for the newsletter but for the Brownsville Boys' Club generally:

Congratulati[ons] . . . on your Third Anniversary, and thank[s] . . . for the B.B.C. paper which you sent. . . . The fellows in my barrack really enjoyed reading [it] especially the Honor Roll of the fellows in the service and their nicknames. I guess I am very lucky to be one of the first members of the club and see it grow from a small disorganized group to a large and powerful organization. You may laugh when I use the adjectives large and powerful but it really is powerful as it got me things which I never dreamed of. . . . I do not think that any of us would have thought of playing in the different settlement houses all over New York City. . . . Let us hope that on the Fourth Anniversary of our club the war will be over and that we all once again will be seated in the library or perhaps in a new settlement house, and listen to Doc's pleasant jokes and his inspiring speeches.[8]

Doc's speeches and general leadership apparently had been very inspiring. Boys he recruited and "trained" in 1941 and 1942, including Levine, Kronenberg, Lenny Dryansky, Irving Sikora, and Sam Schneider, all of whom held executive office in the war years, continued to do the work of the Brownsville Boys Club. As early as December 12, 1941, five days after Pearl Harbor, Baroff said that some of the older officers of the club were likely to be called into the armed services. His main objective, Doc said, was to "train members not to depend on him alone."[9] He succeeded. The younger leaders were informally tutored earlier by Doc; he took several of them with him on his "public relations rounds" as well as to his social agency negotiations and his police station dealings, and they helped keep the club from disintegrating. Several, including Berman, Brief, Levine, and Dryansky, later went into social work buoyed by this "preprofessional" experience. With Doc and many of the other older leaders gone, the younger boys maintained the valued schedule of athletic competitions; the Sackonian baseball team won the Kiwanis League City Championship at Ebbets Field in 1942, and the Brownsville Boys Club basketball team came in second five years running in the Boys Athletic League competition, finally winning in 1947.[10] The new boys also continued to chaperone outings, publish the newsletter, and send youngsters to camp. These boys, constituting a second generation of leaders, dubbed the "best and the brightest" by returning veteran Joe Feldman, also continued to recruit members for the club. They went "out to pool rooms, candy stores and street corners in their efforts to recruit" BBCers, and to remove boys from "the dangers [inherent] in these menacing environments." Learning, as the first generation of leaders had learned, that "waiting for the boys to seek out the club [was] . . . unsatisfactory," they determined to "bring the club to the boys."[11]

Bringing the club to the boys also brought an intensified sense of purpose and meaning to the new leaders. Several of them as we have seen became social workers and even more entered teaching as a result of their BBC work. Marty Kronenberg chose education as a vocation "because of the joy derived from working as a mentor and guide to boys in the club." Now an assistant principal in the New York City Public School system, Marty was only eleven when the club was formed, and he described himself as a "hanger on," in 1940 "but a leader among the young."

His mother, a "Yiddishe Mama," according to Marty, arrived in the United States from Russian Poland in 1910 at the age of eleven. Marty's father left the Russian Empire in 1900 just after he became bar mitzvah, and not long after his arrival here he brought his two younger brothers to the United States. "The *shul*," Marty says, "was my father's life." The elder Kronenberg was the unofficial cantor and rabbi for a congregation of thirty to fifty friends, most of them from the same general area in the old country. They prayed and socialized in a basement *shul*, and were constituted as a *landsmanshaft khevra*, providing numerous mutual-aid services.

"I loved my father," Marty said warmly,

though he wasn't what you would call a powerful presence or a real role-model for me, an American kid. He did send me to Talmud Torah till I was sixteen, and he even made me go to *shul* regularly until I was fifteen. Of course, when I went to college I moved towards the "left," and gave that up. But I miss it now.

My father's real power lies in the fact that he was not a hypocrite. He never cheated; he never lied. And a good part of that's in me. The closest thing to a "lie" that my father told was when he turned a blind eye to my Saturday afternoon movies. He would come home from shul on *shabos*, have lunch and take a nap. And I would say, "Ma-a-ah?" And she knew I was asking for movie money. I'm pretty sure my father knew, but he never confronted me.

Marty Kronenberg's "second mother and father," he said, was the Brownsville Boys Club. The charismatic Doc Baroff filled out that part of "the role-model my father couldn't provide. Doc was a guide and nurturer, like my father, but also a companion—*and* a ballplayer!" The neighborhood, the street corners, the teams and the Brownsville Boys Club generally, Marty said, "gave me something really important —it extended the boundaries of my home." [12]

Receiving and then giving back or passing on was a rich dynamic that lay at the heart of the Brownsville Boys Club, and it is embodied in Marty Kronenberg's life and career. Kronenberg having had the boundaries of his home extended by the BBC went on to extend the boundaries of others boys' homes. Larry Kushner, for example, now a deputy superintendent for the New York Board of Education, was coached by Marty in basketball, and remembers him as "very supportive, very intellectual and an influence on us all." [13] One of the wartime presidents of the club, with the nickname "Weasel" (having to do with the way he moved on the basketball court), Marty, in addition to coaching and playing basketball, wrote a column for the newsletter ("Krony's Korner"). Though thoroughly dedicated to his studies at City College of New York from 1946 to 1950, Marty stayed very much involved with the club. With a law degree as well as a master's degree in educational administration, Kronenberg said in 1975 that his "years of work with the Boys Club have meant more to [him] than any other single experience." And he continues to believe in the Brownsville Boys Club slogan that "it is better to build boys than mend men."[14]

For some time even during the war, several of the leaders at home and abroad began to think that "building boys" could be more effectively accomplished in a real clubhouse instead of through a combination of their small "headquarters" in the library and the "extended facilities" belonging to others. Beginning as early as May 1940 a number of adult speakers were invited to the library to address the possibilities of a settlement house in Brownsville.[15] By the mid-1940s the boys realized that if they were to obtain financial assistance in this goal, "they would need the advice and aid of an older and more experienced group." The leaders contacted Milton Goell of the Brownsville Neighborhood Council; Edward J. Lukas, the Executive Director of the Society for the Prevention of Crime; Judge Daniel Gutman; and other community notables. These men became an "advisory board," one of whose functions was to help procure the strongly desired clubhouse.[16] Serviceman Sid Siegel's 1943 letter mentioned the possibility of a "settlement house," and Baroff on furlough in 1945 told a radio audience that "when our members come home from the war their greatest delight would be to have a building—either in the making or waiting for us."[17]

There was no building waiting or in the making. But the Brooklyn Council for Social Planning had received in late 1945, perhaps as a result of the radio broadcast, an anonymous donation of twelve hundred dollars earmarked for the Brownsville Boys Club.[18] This gave some of the boys the feeling that enough money could be raised for a clubhouse. And at the Sixth Anniversary Meeting of the Club, held at the Stone Avenue Library on March 22, 1946, it was announced that a "primary goal of the club was a settlement" house.

Abe Stark, a prosperous men's clothier and president of the Pitkin Avenue Merchants' Association, though not on the original advisory board, had since 1946 been interested in a clubhouse for the Brownsville boys. He persuaded several others that it was possible, incorporated the club, and set up a new board of directors consisting of local businessmen, bankers, and lawyers. In 1947 they raised enough money to open a storefront on Christopher and Riverdale avenues, and to bolster the club's activities financially.

Jacob ("Doc") Baroff on furlough in 1945, outside of Nanny Goat Park, speaking (what else?) with Norman Goroff (left) Zeke Levy (right), and others about the war and the future of the BBC. (Courtesy of Jacob Baroff.)

The boys, however, still trying to abide by their earlier proscription, "No Adult Control," continued to "run the show." They continued their "extended facilities" operation from their larger storefront headquarters and took care of the day-to-day management of all the club's affairs. Moreover, three alumni members of the Brownsville Boys Club (after becoming twenty-one years old, one could no longer be a member of the Brownsville Boys Club proper) were elected by the younger boys' representative council to sit on the board of directors, and council members themselves could attend board meetings as observers.[19]

In 1947, the "twenty-one-year rule" meant that neither Baroff nor Schmaren, nor indeed any of the founders' generation could be officers of the club. However, Doc Baroff, now twenty-three, was hired by the Board, with the voted approval of the boys, as a professional group worker at $110 per month (all he was allowed under the G.I. Bill while going to school). George Schmaren, Norman Goroff, and Isidore Lesovoy sat on the board of directors and they, along with others includ-

The rear yard of the Christopher Avenue storefront (c. 1947), with makeshift basketball hoop in the upper righthand corner. (Courtesy of Joseph Feldman.)

ing Joe Feldman and Jack Deutch, became part of a volunteer staff for the boys.[20]

The overriding goal in the late 1940s was to raise funds for a building. But at this point, at least, the building was still a means to the end of magnifying and extending the services the Boys Club had always provided. The Christopher Avenue storefront had a number of back rooms—remodeled and refurbished by the boys themselves—and the boys were able to secure contributions of ping-pong tables, enough photographic apparatus to set up a darkroom laboratory, radios, a library of hundreds of books donated by the boys and their families, and a significant amount of athletic equipment. Basketballs, bats, and punchballs were loaned by the Brownsville Boys Club to members of all ages for use in parks, playgrounds, and streets. The inside activities, even a "quiet corner" where a boy could get help with his homework, were also popular.[21]

"We closed from 5:00 P.M. to 6:00 for dinner," said Baroff, "and on our return there were always twenty to thirty guys waiting outside to get in."[22] Individual clubs were allotted space for their meetings to

*Outside club "headquarters" at 417 Christopher Avenue. Increasing member-
ship, and the boys' sense that they could do more with it, intensified the desire
for a building with space, and a "real gym." (Courtesy of BBC Alumni
Association.)*

enable them to come out of the "cold park" and off street corners. The
boys also successfully negotiated with P.S. 184 for meeting rooms in
the school's newly reopened evening center.[23]

The boys, in the late 1940s, were assisted by paid workers including
Baroff, Harold Radish, Irving Forman, Jack Oventhal, and Isidore

("Red") Karbel as well as volunteer staff. All were former BBCers, and virtually all, like Baroff and Lesovoy, were toughened war veterans. Forman had been in the navy's submarine service, Karbel in the air force, and Radish had even been a prisoner of war for several months in Europe. Survivors, these Brownsville-raised boys, rededicated themselves to Brownsville Boys Club work. And they transcended, by their internalized resources, the troubled experience of significant numbers of other veterans. Writer Gilbert Sorrentino described some of these "other veterans," on their return to South Brooklyn, "home from the slaughter ready to take their places:"

> But how strange that so many of them had become drunkards, brawlers, bums content to stand on the corner with the boys who had been just too young to get into it. They fought, they ogled high school girls, drank wine, shot crap, played the horses.
> The last half of the decade was one of drift and disillusionment. The Depression and the war had made the young adults of the neighborhood restless, strangely malcontent. Alcoholism flourished, and most young men seemed to live their entire lives in saloons.[24]

Journalist Bradford Chambers wrote in 1946 that servicemen returning to all parts of New York were aggravating the problem of gang wars by supplying weapons brought back from the international conflict:

> Jobless veterans themselves are slipping back into the gang environment. New York's courts are filling with veterans held on criminal charges, and I have talked with many veterans who are hanging out again on the same old street-corner with their former pals. They're not happy about the employment situation, and they are not at all pleased at the wartime invasion of Negroes, Puerto Ricans and Jews into their neighborhood[s].[25]

The scene was different for the Jewish war veterans of Brownsville, at least for those who helped at the Boys Club. Although these returning servicemen were with their "former pals" and even on street corners, they do not appear to have been "disillusioned." The veterans not only returned to school, they, along with other staff aided the boys with activities at the storefront, and helped them sustain their program of securing vacations for boys in camps, and free admission to a variety of entertainments. They rendered service, too, of course, in helping with organized athletic competition. Thousands of boys participated

Marty Kronenberg, vice-president of the Brownsville Boys Club in 1949, displays prizes BBC received for winning the Boys Athletic League basketball championship (1947–48), the district championship for softball (1946), and the Division B championship for foul shooting (1946–47). (Courtesy of Martin Kronenberg.)

in intramural and citywide competitions, in baseball, softball, basketball, volleyball, track, and boxing, with equipment donated by the American Baseball Foundation, the B'nai B'rith (boxing gloves!) and other organizations.[26] The Brownsville Boys Club teams entered citywide tournaments, and in 1949 Marty Kronenberg appeared in the *New York Herald Tribune* proudly displaying prizes and trophies awarded the teams between 1946 and 1949.[27] The veterans, the older staff, and the younger boys like Irving Levine who became athletic director in 1947, continued to maintain that sports were "therapeutic" and rehabilitative. And they would continue to try to bring the "recreational solution" to Brownsville's problems.

Brownsville's troubles, however, increased and intensified. Club leaders and workers recognizing the disadvantages caused by class differences and racial discrimination, began to move away from sports as the *primary* route to social health. They began over time to focus more steadily on "all aspects of the boys' lives," including the socioeconomic conditions in which they lived. The postwar years produced in Brownsville, as in many American urban areas, not only an increase of youth crime and in the number of gang wars, but an escalation of brutality.[28] New York's answer to juvenile delinquency and the gang problem was to assign extra policemen in Brownsville and elsewhere "to halt [the] hoodlums' reign."[29] Boise S. Dent, a black minister who would soon sit on the Brownsville Boys Club board, requested in 1947 that the cops assigned to Brownsville be mostly blacks. For although "both whites and Negroes were the victims," Dent said, the petty thievery and vandalism was mostly perpetrated by black youth and the street fighting was mainly between black gangs like the Nits and the Socialistic Gents.[30]

In addition to calling for more police, civic leaders, along with the Brownsville Boys Club, continued to push the "recreational solution." Shocked that the city had recently eliminated gymnasiums and indoor play spaces from proposed new elementary school buildings, and had closed the Glenmore Avenue public library, "one of the few youth resources in Brownsville,"[31] men like Milton Goell increased their lobbying for local facilities. Pointing to the "homelessness" of the Brownsville Boys Club, which he described as a "potential power for tremendous good," Goell said, "Recreational facilities have been so meagre in [Brownsville], the surprising thing is not that there is juvenile delinquency in the area, but that it is not tenfold."[32]

Abe Stark, chairman of the Brownsville Boys Club Board in 1947, also recognized the organization's "potential power." Referring to a "new bad young gang," in Brownsville, Stark said: "Our boys went after them but couldn't interest them in any games or activities until they asked the gang leader to join a baseball team. That did it. All the gang began playing ball. Now they are getting into other club activities and they're behaving themselves." Staunchly invoking the "recreational solution," Stark went on: "I'd like to see every city in the country take these boys for an example when they're wondering how to combat juvenile delinquency."[33] And by May of 1948, even New York City decided to push a "War on Juvenile Delinquency" with an outdoor "play program in strategic areas." It marked Brownsville for special attention.[34]

Brownsville was becoming increasingly a "borderline" or transitional district of diverse racial and religious groupings. Instability, tension, and frustration pervaded many sections of Brownsville and particularly those with relatively sizeable black populations.[35] Here (e.g., Health Areas 57 and 59), boys tended disproportionately to get "into trouble," whether they were black or white, and whether the perceived "palliative" of recreation was or was not available.

Fifteen-year-old Stanley Fox, for example, a basketball and softball player, living on Sutter Avenue in the heart of the most troubled district was the fatal victim of a shooting in February of 1949. The Fox boy (apparently white and Jewish, but never so identified) was, along with several others, readying a variety of weapons for a gang fight, when a gun accidentally fired and killed him. Stanley was a member of the Black Hats, which was initiated as a social club and sports team in June of 1948 (not part of the BBC). The club was "officially recognized" by P.S. 156 at which the "rather loosely organized" group met. A dispute between the Black Hats and the Bristol Street Boys, another social and athletic club, arising from a softball game played in the schoolyard of P.S. 156, apparently led to plans for revenge. A third group, the Musketeers, involved themselves in the confrontation as allies of the Black Hats. Because of the accidental shooting the "showdown fight" never took place, but eight boys were arrested at eight different locations in Brownsville and a virtual arsenal was rounded up: ten hand guns, eight rifles, a machete, five daggers, fourteen knives, and three hundred rounds of ammunition.

The principal of P.S.156 said the Black Hats had created "no disorder or trouble at the school," and the slain boy's father (an air force staff sergeant) said the Black Hats were not a gang, but a club which held meetings and games at school, and mostly "watched television at home." The Foxes were among thirteen hundred families living in the Brownsville Housing Project, into which they had moved when it first opened in April 1948. Sergeant Fox said they found almost immediately that it was a "bad neighborhood."[36] Ironically, the housing project was, in good part, the product of long-term lobbying by reformers, like Milton Goell, who aimed at reducing delinquency and was labeled by them "Brownsville's greatest improvement."[37]

The Fox case showered "negative publicity" on Brownsville, and prompted many to rise to its defense. Abe Stark, in response described the neighborhood as "a nice place, with a fine community spirit and with thousands of fine upstanding boys and girls." At the same time he continued to insist, despite the failure of sports to "save" the Black Hats and the Bristol Street Boys, that the way to fight "boy gangsterism" was for the city to finance new recreational facilities.[38] Doc Baroff's "talks" in the immediate aftermath of the accidental shooting, though more sophisticated than Stark's, followed a similar pattern. "Recent accounts in the newspapers have been exaggerated," the Brownsville Boys Club director said, but the club's approach to the delinquency that does exist in Brownsville, is not to break up a gang; it is to bring it into the central group, and redirect its energies "along less brutal lines," like athletic competition.[39]

Recreation continued to be the proposed "solution," too, of eighteen-year-old Jack Leavitt, president of the Brownsville Boys Club from 1947 to 1949. Talking to television, radio, and newspaper reporters after the Fox affair in 1949, Leavitt said, the Brownsville Boys Club is a federation of clubs

which might be gangs if they had not all been supervised and led into the excitement and adventure of athletic competition and taught the rules of self-government.

[Recently] there was a gang of about thirty boys around here who were really bad. They would stop kids in the street and beat them up and take their money. And they were giving the storekeepers along here a bad time. I guess they carried knives and guns. We tried to bring them into the club, because once we got them into the club we knew they would change, but they thought we were a bunch of sissies. Then we learned that their leader loved to play basketball. We asked him to play on our all-star team. He came, and he came again, and the others came to watch him. Pretty soon they were all in the club. They're fine fellows and we're all proud of them.[40]

But Baroff and Leavitt, despite their rhetoric for the media, knew as did many of the other boys that "athletic competition," even supervised athletic competition, and "self-government" were not cure-alls. They knew that these things, alone, while valuable, were no substitute for changed social conditions. They knew that the "recreational solution" they celebrated and which was being touted by the Brownsville Parent Teacher Associations, the Brownsville School Council, City Youth Board Head Nathaniel Kaplan, the police, and the district attorney's office, was not really enough.[41] The Brownsville boys, particularly Jacob Deutch, Norman Goroff, and Lenny Dryansky—socialist sons of socialist fathers—knew, for example, that "better paying jobs were also essential." And all knew too that decent shelter was critical. Having been exposed to more than a decade of highly visible public lobbying for state and federal funds to improve housing in Brownsville, Baroff and Leavitt and many of the other boys were well aware of the housing issue and were supportive of reform.[42]

Speakers at the Brownsville Boys Club meetings throughout the early 1940s focused on the need for a postwar reconstruction of the neighborhood.[43] In 1945, when the Brownsville Neighborhood Council was at the forefront of the fight for public housing, Doc Baroff invited Council Representative Flora M. Davidson to a meeting at the Stone Avenue Library. Over one hundred boys came to hear and be heard.[44] Less than a year later, in March 1946, the boys publicly dedicated themselves to campaigning for housing projects, health centers and high schools to improve the social conditions of Brownsville.[45] Throughout the following year Norman Goroff ran a column in the Brownsville Boys Club newsletter called "Pamphlets in Review" in which he dealt with a variety of social justice issues including inadequate shelter and race discrimination. And in 1948 Brownsville Boys Club executives, including President Jack Leavitt, held a number of meetings with the Brownsville Neighborhood Council about "interracial understanding," and about public housing.[46]

During this period 1947 and through 1948, Werner J. Cahnman, a professor of sociology at Brooklyn College, set out to study the leisure-

Norman Goroff conducting a meeting of the BBC at the Brownsville Children's Library (c. 1943). (Courtesy of Norman Goroff.)

time activities and attitudes of "minority youth" in Brownsville. He focused on the "cultural consciousness" of Jewish youth but he also interviewed many blacks. Cahnman was less interested at the initial stage of his research in intergroup relations, as in group "structure." The professor and the students in his introductory sociology course did street-corner interviewing and engaged in discussions with leadership groups, especially of the Brownsville Boys Club. On the basis of these exchanges they designed a questionnaire to which the youngsters responded. Among the many interesting "findings" were the following: Blacks recognized discrimination as a major problem, but at the same time pointed to a number of "group disabilities": drinking, fighting, physical violence, lack of community spirit, and lack of political organization. Jewish youth, like blacks, recognized the oppressiveness of racial prejudice and discrimination; but the Jews, disproportionately, demonstrated an orientation toward political action and social justice.[47]

Cahnman dubbed the Jewish youth of the Brownsville Boys Club, "social actionists" when he completed his study in 1949. The BBC leaders had demonstrated, from at least as early as 1945, some concern

about negative social conditions. Many of them had also agreed by
1947 that "sports, however important they may be, are not when one
comes down to it, the sole and main factor in our lives."[48] Many
Friday evening meetings were spent discussing and debating other
things than sports. Often there were presentations by educators, community leaders and activists, and occasionally there were documentary
films.[49] The boys did continue to see athletics as a very positive force,
not only in terms of the joy of play, competition and accomplishment,
and not only as a way of diverting "negative energy," but also as a
vehicle for "getting to know one another," and "having a common
bond." These last two acquired particular importance in the face of
Brownsville's growing black population.

In Alfred Kazin's 1920s Brownsville,

Negroes were the *shvartse*, the blacks. We just did not think about them. They
were people three and four blocks away you passed coming home from the
subway. I never heard a word about them until the depression, when some of
the younger ones began to do private painting jobs below the union wage
scales, and when still another block of the earliest wooden shacks on Livonia
Avenue near the subway's power station filled up with Negroes. Then some
strange, embarrassed resentment would come out in the talk around the supper
table. They were moving nearer and nearer. They were invading our neighborhood.[50]

Undoubtedly some of the 1940s Brownsville boys were also resent-
ful of what could have been perceived as an even larger "invasion" in
their era. And one small group of boys at least, led by "Shimmy,"
chased and beat blacks whenever they saw them on their block.[51] The
main thrust, however, was "integration." As early as March 1943 "the
Negro question was brought up" at BBC meetings, and one speaker,
at least, representing the Society for the Prevention of Crime, asked
the boys to continue "to promote interracial relations." In September
1943 Norman Goroff followed up by encouraging club members to
attend a Negro Freedom Rally at the Premiere Palace.[52] In 1947 the
Reverend Boise S. Dent, a black man, joined the Brownsville Board of
Directors, and a black program director, Vincent Tibbs, was hired to
work out of the Christopher Avenue storefront.[53] In April 1948, in
conference with the Brownsville Neighborhood Council, Brownsville
Boys Club representatives agreed that "the speed with which the

Brownsville Houses were being inhabited . . . posed the need for a welcome by the community. . . . [T]his would take the form of an Easter-Purim festival to underwrite the intercultural and interfaith implications of the housing project which was nearly 45 percent Negro." Later in the year the Brownsville Boys Club contributed refreshments for a Halloween Youth Dance at the housing project.[54]

A small number of boys, particularly Irving ("Hooker") Levine, took an intense interest in racial integration. The child of Jewish immigrants, who were "the poorest of our relatives," Levine had joined the club in 1941 when he was eleven years old. The very next year he was president of the club's Junior Division (seven-to-thirteen-year-olds). Irving then went on to become president of the Brownsville Boys Club during the war years. In 1946, at the Stone Avenue library, Irving, who "identified strongly with the Brownsville Neighborhood Council and its policies" of progressive social action and vigorous pursuit of interracial cooperation, initiated a free-wheeling discussion about active recruitment of blacks for teams and clubs.[55] Only when the storefront opened on Christopher Avenue in 1947, however, were there any appreciable number of blacks visible at the club.

There were at least three black BBC teams by 1947: the Cobras (who gathered at P.S.184 and prayed before each meeting), the Saints, and the Nobles. And at least two other clubs, the Rams and the Spartans, included blacks.[56] In addition, several of the Cobras were on the Brownsville Boys Club All-Star Softball Team. Irving Levine recalls that there were blacks on the Brownsville Boys Club track and boxing teams as well. The general pattern then, with a few exceptions, was that clubs and teams organized themselves by race, but that intramural competition and Brownsville Boys Club "varsity" teams were forces for integration, as were the general meetings to which all clubs sent representatives. "Proof," read the Brownsville Boys Club newsletter that "the boys of Brownsville can work and play together in perfect harmony."[57]

Irving Levine "identified with black kids," he said, on a number of levels. "We thought of them as strong physical types, and some of us even believed, in the immediate aftermath of the Holocaust, that if we were black, we would have killed the Nazis instead of them killing us." Earlier, in junior high school Irving had won a civics medal for an

An integrated softball team (c. 1949). Izzy Lesovoy and George Schmaren were the coaches. (Courtesy of BBC Alumni Association.)

essay he wrote on black-Jewish relations. He had been stimulated by American Jewish Committee and American Jewish Congress materials on the subject and "proud and delighted," when he discovered how much the Jews were tied into the movement for civil rights. Hooker got to know blacks more directly when in 1946 and 1947 he took fifteen children, some of them black, to the Stone Theatre every Monday afternoon, and when increasing numbers of even younger blacks began spending a good part of the day at the storefront. There, at age sixteen, Irving was running the game room. "It was almost like day-care," he recalled.

Beginning in 1947 Irving Levine ran all the BBC league competitions as athletic director. "Some of us," Irving said, "became even

Irving ("Hooker") Levine being sworn in as president of the BBC by Trustee Nat Azarow in 1950. (Courtesy of Irving Levine.)

more aggressive in recruiting blacks, as black basketball became prominent. Speed, one-handed shooting and the more open style promoted blacks in the game. And we wanted our teams to win. This desire reinforced a trend already established in a number of us by our social welfare ideology and our progressive, even 'left' politics."

It is important to remember that in the 1940s activist integration was a radical position. "Separate but equal" had been the legal order of the day; separate and unequal was the reality, North and South. Even the United States government had fought the Second World War with segregated troops, and it was not until the summer of 1948 that Harry S. Truman issued an executive order barring separation of the races in the armed forces. One understands in such a context why the boys, according to Irving Levine "were not only proud to be the first Jewish-led boys club, but also the first boys club to integrate."

Irving ("Hooker") Levine, now head of the American Jewish Committee's Institute for American Pluralism said,

The Brownsville Boys Club for me was all-consuming. At first I was preoccupied by sports; [he still remembers that he led the Bombers with thirty points in a basketball game against the Hawks] then social work became an obsession. . . . For me, work at the Brownsville Boys Club became preprofessional social work and practically a full-time job. I began to do poorly in college [Irving entered Brooklyn College in the spring of 1947]. There was *nothing* in college as exciting as this.

Irving was also doing poorly because he spent almost as much time on campus protesting the conservative policies of Brooklyn College President Harry Gideonse as he did in class (progressive students were particularly irked by the fact that Gideonse crossed a line of pickets protesting Woolworth's racial policies). Hooker Levine did eventually "drop out." At that point, Doc Baroff in whom Irving "saw a parental personality," intervened.

Doc somehow, in connivance with my mother, got me to come to lunch with Esther Hilton, the head of New York University's undergraduate Social Work Program, within which Doc was studying. She convinced me to go back to school. She said she would use her influence to make some arrangement for me to do Brownsville Boys Club work and to go to school at the same time.

Enrolled at New York University, Irving continued as athletic director at the Brownsville Boys Club. He grew increasingly disenchanted with sports, however, as he witnessed behavior that "violated [his] ideals," and made him question the value of sports as a *primary* vehicle for changing social consciousness.

Rules were violated by recreation leaders in the leagues almost with impunity. The sports "code" was broken every day. I was shocked by the "hustlers." I even witnessed corrupt behavior by priests in the Catholic Youth Organization Leagues, when I was a boxing coach. The brutalization inherent in boxing also began to get to me. All of this reinforced my moving from the emphasis on sports, to an emphasis on the intellectual and political.

While he was completing his degree at New York University, Hooker Levine, in 1950, gave up directing athletics and became a part-time paid social worker for the Brownsville Boys Club. Along with a number of other professionals, whom Levine describes as having been "the best of the 1940s non-Communist left," Irving brought the "group work" orientation to the Brownsville Boys Club. And for all intents and purposes they made the "recreational model" of Robert Moses and the Park Department peripheral. "We were going to be 'scientific humanists,' " Levine said. "We were going to make teams into clubs. Through serious supervision of social work interns, by senior professional staff and program directors, we were going to help develop *all* aspects of the boys' lives and personalities."[58]

The new group of professionals, hired with funds raised by Abe Stark, included several like Baroff, Levine, and Lenny Dryansky, who were former members and officers of the Brownsville Boys Club in its preprofessional era. Having recognized that "recreation" was "necessary" but hardly "sufficient," they would try to do social work on all the "tracks"—group work, case work, community relations, and community organizing. They were encouraged in their work by major figures in social welfare, many of whom visited the storefront and eventually the building. Nathan Cohen, the dean of Columbia's School of Social Work, and James McCarthy, head of the New York City Youth Board, came to praise and advise, as did Dan Dodson, head of the New York University Center of Intergroup Relations.[59]

Much advice and encouragement came from the left. Professional social workers, especially in New York and Brooklyn, were heavily represented in the social service unions associated with the "Office and Professional Workers of America." This organization is reputed to have contained a higher proportion of Communists than any other trade union.[60] Other militant unionists and social activists, like Bertha Reynolds, added their support and particular perspectives, as did radical community organizer Saul Alinsky.[61] Reinforced, the Brownsville Boys Club professionals and the volunteer staff continued to do creative social work and community organizing in the face of the increasing difficulties of neighborhood change.

There were other difficulties too. Funds raised by Abe Stark and the board had allowed BBC alumni and others to work as professionals, and facilitated their movement toward a deeper, more political understanding of gang problems and recreation. That understanding would soon come up against the more traditional outlook and conventional politics of Stark and the board of directors.

CHAPTER 5

Politicians, Professionals, and Philanthropists: Sell-Out or Trade-Off?

Somehow, somewhere . . . I will be in politics because . . . everything in this city—business, health and the home—is based on politics.[1]

—ABE STARK,
APRIL 23, 1949

In the minds of many, the Brownsville Boys Club is associated with the name Abe Stark, Brooklyn politician and community activist. The club, over a seven-year period, with the conspicuous aid of Abe Stark, raised thousands of dollars to pay a growing professional social work staff, and well over one million dollars for a modern building. In October of 1953, the Brownsville Boys Club opened an impressive and extensive recreational facility on Linden Boulevard. Less than one month later Abe Stark was resoundingly elected president of the city council. He ran well ahead of the Democratic ticket which had swept the citywide elections, and he even received more votes than the head of the ticket, victorious mayoral candidate Robert F. Wagner.[2]

Several of the Brownsville boys and at least one contemporary observer have suggested that Stark's interest in helping the club was as a steppingstone toward political place and power.[3] Stark had, after all, shown an active interest in politics as early as 1945 when he success-

120

The scoreboard at Ebbets Field. To the left of the name Abe Stark, the advertisement reads, "Hit Sign, Win Suit." To the delight of the Brownsville Boys in the left-field seats, the Brooklyn Dodgers are beating the Pittsburgh Pirates 3 to 2 in the bottom of the fifth inning. (Courtesy of Joseph Feldman.)

fully directed William O'Dwyer's mayoral candidacy. At the same time he first demonstrated interest in the Brownsville Boys Club. It would be unfair, however, to assume that Abe Stark's political and personal ambition, while real enough, were not joined by an honest and energetic commitment to philanthropy and moderately liberal reform. Born in 1894 to impoverished Jewish immigrants, Stark had been deeply immersed in Jewish philanthropic affairs, and in organized civic and business activities well before 1945. He was extraordinarily successful in raising funds for charity, was active in seeking improved public services for Brownsville and Brooklyn generally, and he served as president of the Pitkin Avenue Merchants' Association for many years.[4]

One of eight children, the energetic Abe was a newsboy at six; at eleven he worked as a soft-drink vendor at Ebbets Field, and by the time he was twenty-one, he was in the retail clothing business where he would prosper for over forty years. Abe Stark's elite men's clothing

The cartoonist's less-than-generous version of Abe Stark at Ebbets Field. (Drawing by Geo. Price; © 1938, 1966 The New Yorker Magazine Inc.)

store on Pitkin Avenue was not only an emporium, however. It also "came to have the reputation of a political and social welfare office to which hundreds, regardless of political party, race or color, came with requests for help."[5] The location of the store was well-known even beyond the immediate Brownsville neighborhood. In the days when the Brooklyn Dodgers played at Ebbets Field (until 1957), the name Abe Stark and the address of the clothing store were constantly on commercial display before the public. A sign at the concrete base of the right-field scoreboard there proclaimed that any batter who hit the advertisement—on the fly—would receive a free suit.

One famous cartoon (see above) depicting a merchant, glove in hand, backing up the outfielder in front of the sign, implied—in at least an obliquely anti-Semitic manner—that Stark was a tight-wad.[6] The cartoon, worth a chuckle, is nonetheless mean-spirited. Although no one remembers if any batter ever hit the sign—particularly difficult in the era of Dixie ("the peepuls cherce") Walker (1939–47) and Carl ("emperor of right field") Furillo (1946–57)—many recall Abe Stark's general openhandedness. He personally contributed funds to all of the many causes and organizations for which he helped raise money, and he was very generous with his time. Stark served on the Brownsville Chamber of Commerce for well over a decade, and persisted in seeking increased and improved public services—parks, playgrounds, schools and transportation facilities.[7]

After Abe Stark launched his formal political career he continued to evince a philanthropic and reform orientation. In 1945 he supported William O'Dwyer for mayor partly in the hope that the Brooklyn district attorney's rhetoric about adequate housing, schools and recreational facilities could be implemented upon his election to higher office. In 1948 Stark accepted from the mayor appointment as commissioner of commerce. The position, generally considered an honorary one, carried a one-dollar annual salary. But Stark in 1949 made an effort to convert the Department of Commerce into more than a token agency, and submitted plans for a $500,000 public facilities expansion program. The proposal, blocked according to Stark by Brooklyn Borough President John Cashmore, who "feared my getting too big in politics," never found its way into the formal request filed with the budget director. Stark resigned saying "I don't want to be just . . . a rubber stamp" with "a car, and a chauffeur and an office."[8]

Several months after his resignation Stark charged that Brooklyn was controlled by "a machine more powerful and corrupt than Tammany," and he called upon Cashmore to resign as the Democratic leader of Kings County (Brooklyn). At the same time, Stark announced his own candidacy for borough president, saying "Franklin Delano Roosevelt, Jr. beat the bosses in Manhattan and we can do it in Brooklyn."[9] Although Stark had said earlier, at the time of his resignation, that his political ambitions were far from serious, and that "politics" had been little more than "a hobby of mine for twenty-five years," the Pitkin Avenue clothier's's desire for social mobility and personal advancement were becoming manifest.[10]

Stark had only an elementary school education, was not a fluent speaker, and was neither a member of the inner circle of the city's Democratic leaders nor in control of a strong or "regular" political organization. As a Republican-Liberal Fusion candidate, Stark, the political "outsider," challenged Democratic incumbent Cashmore in 1949. Although he lost, he made an impressive showing in the strongly Democratic borough of Brooklyn. In 1950 after Mayor O'Dwyer's resignation during the corruption scandals of that era, Stark had apparently offered to back Vincent Impellitteri's mayoral candidacy in re-

BBCers including Mendy Bacall (Baklachuck) (left), Joe Feldman (third from left), and Sheiky Lenowitz (third from right) in storefront rented for the Abe Stark campaign in 1949. (Courtesy of Joseph Feldman.)

turn for an appointment as Deputy Mayor.[11] Disappointed here, Stark, in July 1953, announced that he would accept "a major nomination for a position on the City government from any party or parties with whose principles of good government," he could agree.[12] In September 1953 Abe Stark, helped by his demonstration of popularity in the 1949 contest for borough president, received the Democratic nomination for city council president.[13] Beginning in 1949 Stark pursued public office. He continued to do so relentlessly through the rest of his life.

Abe Stark no doubt saw politics as a vehicle for personal promotion, but he had apparently come to believe too, that in order to implement more effectively his ideas for political and humanitarian reform, formal power was necessary. Some of the BBCers may have resented Stark's use of the club for what they saw as "personal political purposes." And some like Abe Gerchick may have resented the disproportionate influence of "the Great White Father." But many more recognized, with Stark, the utility of politics and vigorously campaigned for him in 1949 and again in 1953. In January 1954 the boys and young men held a victory celebration for him in their new building, and had their own "swearing-in ceremony" for the new city council president.[14] Even many of those boys who continued to hold Stark's motives suspect agreed, then and now, that they had achieved "a valid exchange"— some loss of control for a significant gain in visibility and funding.[15]

In office, Stark surrounded himself with people possessed of reform and philanthropic credentials. He appointed Leonard Stavitsky, a Long Island University professor of history and government as his chief assistant, and he chose for his secretary, Dorothy Michaels, the president and founder of the Assembly of Brooklyn Jewish Women's Organizations.[16] This last was not only a shrewd political move on Stark's part (the assembly represented 250 Jewish women's groups); it reflected his political "ideology" as well. The groups represented in the assembly were actively involved in philanthropic and humanitarian endeavors. Over the years Stark received recognition for his efforts in these spheres. He won the Franklin Delano Roosevelt Award for Combatting Bigotry and Intolerance, the Man of the Year Award from the Council of Jewish Organizations in Civil Service, and the Alfaro Medal for "distinguished humanitarian and public service."[17] Less than a year after his election to the presidency of the city council, Stark who had called for a complete revamping of the existing laws regarding unemployment insurance and workmen's compensation, was honored by the Citizen's Committee for Government Planning and was lauded by Mayor Wagner for his "leadership efforts to improve the lot of the underprivileged."[18]

One group of the underprivileged in Stark's view since at least 1945, were the Brownsville boys who were deprived of adequate recreational facilities. In 1946 Abe Stark and a number of others organized the 46 Club and a Board of Directors for the Brownsville Boys Club to raise money for a modern clubhouse. The 46 Club and the Board consisted, with significant overlap, of local manufacturers, bankers, lawyers and merchants. These included many Brooklyn Jewish boys who had "made it," and who were, according to one social activist, "truly sympathetic towards the needs of the residents, lending a helping hand, not only with the club, but with scholarships and business loans."[19] Allen Beck, a furniture manufacturer, Jack Holland of Holland Steel, and U.S. Pencil Company President David Teitelbaum served in this way, as did florist Thomas Atkins, jeweler Ben Fabrikant, and attorney Hyman Barshay. Particularly active were Samuel Abrams of Esquire Shoe Polish, Samuel Rubin of Levy's Bread, and Paul Bluth, the owner of the Famous (dairy) Restaurant on Utica Avenue and Eastern Parkway.[20]

In 1947 Stark and the Board initiated a major drive for funds. Mayor O'Dwyer and Governor Thomas E. Dewey were named honorary chairmen of a $200,000 campaign to build a clubhouse for the Brownsville Boys Club.[21] Pledges were sought from various social agencies and private organizations, and the drive was supported by local publications, particularly the *Brooklyn Eagle*. In a promotional editorial the *Eagle* stated that "no community in the city is more desperately in need of a permanent clubhouse for youths, than is Brownsville."[22] There were generous donations including $14,000 from the Hebrew Butchers' Union which was $4,000 over their pledge.[23]

This initial fund-raising drive was climaxed by a $100-a-plate dinner at the Hotel St. George in Brooklyn on November 23, 1947. More than fifteen hundred people attended to honor Abe Stark, the head of the Club's Board of Directors. Attorney Hyman Barshay served as the dinner chairman, and William O'Dwyer, though "forbidden by his physician from making night appearances," gave the major address. He could not stay away, O'Dwyer said "because of my close friendship with Abe Stark," an "outstanding citizen and great humanitarian," and because of the need "to spur the construction of a new clubhouse for the boys."[24] Many Democratic notables appeared including State Attorney General Nathan Goldstein, City Council President Vincent Impellitteri, Superintendent of Schools William Jansen, and Kings County District Attorney Miles F. McDonald. The diners were entertained by Lena Horne and Milton Berle among others. Jack Leavitt, the sixteen-year-old president of the club, presented Stark with a plaque purchased with boys' pennies, nickels and dimes. "We can never repay him," said Leavitt; "all we can do is say thanks."[25] Leavitt and six other officers of the club sat at a table with Jacob Baroff, Irving Forman, Norman Goroff, George Schmaren, Isidore Lesovoy, Joe Feldman, Harold Radish, and Jacob Deutch, all of whom were former members of the Brownsville Boys Club and most of whom were now volunteer staff. At the same table were Harmon Putter, the recently hired executive director of the club, and one of his program directors, Vincent Tibbs.[26]

At table eighty-two, halfway across the enormous ballroom sat Harry Gross and "guests"—five high-ranking police officers. Gross was the kingpin in a $20 million-a-year bookmaking and gambling operation in which at least $1 million a year was paid to police to "look the other way."[27] In 1950, three years after this first Brownsville Boys Club dinner of 1947, Miles F. McDonald who sat at the dais would arraign Gross who sat at table eighty-two. McDonald charged Gross with innumerable counts of bookmaking. Shortly after his arraignment Gross pleaded guilty and agreed to become key witness in the criminal trial of dozens of police brass, whom he had identified behind a grand jury's closed doors. Gross, however, changed his mind at the last moment and sabotaged the trial. He was convicted of contempt and later of bookmaking, but District Attorney McDonald was forced to dismiss the indictments against the accused cops. The police conducted their own investigation. Many higher-ups were forced to resign, some retired early, and a small number took their own lives.

After a few months' experience with jail life, Harry Gross decided he had better make a deal to shorten his sentence and he agreed to testify at special hearings. He named those police brass who were the beneficiaries of his bookmaking enterprises, four of whom were personal political appointees of William O'Dwyer.[28] Earlier in these same hearings, John P. Crane, president of Local 94 of the International Association of Fire Fighters, said he gave $10,000 (which he "withdrew" from the association treasury) to O'Dwyer in 1949 to cement his commitment for firemen's pension legislation. He also claimed to have given $55,000 in three payments from 1946 to 1949 to James J. Moran, the deputy fire commissioner, a close friend of O'Dwyer and a "great influence" on him. Subsequently O'Dwyer appointed Moran, an intimate associate of mobster Frank Costello, as commissioner of water supply, a well-paid lifetime job.

Mayor O'Dwyer who had been on the dais at the Boys Club dinner in 1947 as a guest speaker, and who had resigned in August of 1950 for an appointment as ambassador to Mexico, testified that he had placed underworld "associates" in city jobs. He denied foreknowledge in some cases and cited "political expediency" in others. He also admitted that there could be no large-scale bookmaking operation in New York City without police protection and political connivance.[29]

These facts are included here not only to reveal how closely criminals, politicians, and law enforcement agents could cooperate in Kings County but to indicate why there was suspicion among some that Abe Stark had underworld connections. Several figures from that underworld were, after all, at the Brownsville Boys Club dinner in 1947, as were cops later convicted of perjury and "conduct unbecoming an officer." And Stark was a staunch supporter of the heavily implicated O'Dwyer until 1949. In Abe Stark's building above the clothing store was a billiard parlor, within which a major bookmaking operation was carried on by one Louis Katz. In 1949 when Stark broke with Democratic Mayor O'Dwyer and chose to run for borough president as a Fusion candidate against the Democratic incumbent, the poolroom was suddenly raided and Louis Katz arrested![30]

While some of the Brownsville boys thought that Stark may have had at least "a finger in the world of gambling and political payoff, nothing worse," the connections are tenuous. Harry Gross summed up his career as Brooklyn's bookmaking czar by saying, "I paid everybody. Everybody."[31] Yet Abe Stark's name surfaced only twice during the more than year long hearings, once in discussions of the Louis Katz incident and a second time when Gross said he paid for a small number of suits purchased from Stark by plainclothesmen. Gross also said he paid for the table of police brass at the 1947 Brownsville Boys Club dinner at which he had some drinks and had a "lovely time."[32] Firefighter representative John Crane also mentioned the Brownsville Boys Club dinner. He admitted taking $500 from his association's fund and giving it to Deputy Fire Commissioner James J. Moran to purchase Boys Club dinner tickets. But Stark's name was never mentioned by either Moran or Crane in their lengthy testimonies.

Given what was going on around him and the obvious opportunities and temptations facing him, Stark appears to have been relatively untouched by corruption. He was certainly deemed "innocent" by the more than one million voters who elected him to the presidency of the city council in 1953, soon after the hearings ended, and by the respectable donors he so successfully continued to solicit. The dinner in 1947 brought in over $100,000 and Abe Stark could use this base to promote confidence in other potential contributors.

In 1949 Stark, campaigning for the Brooklyn borough presidency and looking for more money for the Brownsville Boys Club, spoke to the Assembly of Brooklyn Jewish Women's Organizations. Here Stark met Minnie Weingart, the executive secretary of the assembly. He was so impressed with Weingart's knowledge of Brooklyn social agencies and the contacts she had through the assembly with 180 different organizations representing almost 100,000 women, that he offered her a position with the Brownsville Boys Club. This appointment was a stroke of genius on Stark's part. Minnie Weingart, who would come to be known as the "Angel of Brownsville," was a brilliant fund-raiser for the Brownsville Boys Club and an extraordinarily resourceful representative of the philanthropic and humanitarian dimensions of BBC work.[33] Minnie organized dinners in 1949 and 1950 which brought in more than $150,000, and she formulated a public relations program that elicited contributions from other more well-endowed organizations. Through her many speaking engagements, Minnie attracted dozens of women volunteer workers for the Women's Division of the Brownsville Boys Club which she initiated. These women solicited funds, helped with outings for the boys, and ran bazaars and raffles that netted between $3000 and $5000 every year.

At her desk in Stark's clothing store, often more than eight hours a day, Minnie served not only as the executive secretary of the Brownsville Boys Club, but as Stark's political assistant and a community social worker. With her vast knowledge of the borough's social welfare organizations, her background of service on a number of agency boards, and as the executive secretary of the Assembly of Brooklyn Jewish Women's Organizations, Minnie was able to give effective advice, and to make the appropriate contacts and referrals for people in need.[34]

Minnie (née Levine) was born on the Lower East Side in 1901, to Jewish immigrants. Her personal and social history prepared her well for her role as the Boys Club's "Angel of Brownsville." Minnie de-

Minnie Weingart in 1949 at her desk in Abe Stark's store, no doubt involved in one of her innumerable conversations about social welfare or politics. (Courtesy of Joseph Feldman.)

scribed her family as "relatively observant." Her mother kept a kosher home and her father, while a "scholarly man" who wrote occasionally for the Jewish Socialist *Daily Forward*, was also an active union organizer in the garment trade.

In an era when only very small percentages of Jewish youngsters, particularly girls, went beyond elementary school, Minnie was encouraged to continue her education and she earned a high school diploma in 1916.[35] The family moved to Bridgeport, Connecticut in 1917 where they had the "only kosher restaurant in town." After a time with the women's suffrage movement, Minnie, like her father, and like a disproportionate number of her Jewish contemporaries, joined the Socialist party. She took an active part in antiwar demonstrations in 1917 and 1918. Minnie Levine believed that her commitment to peace through the international solidarity of workers, and her commitment to women's rights were part of a coherent whole. "We demonstrated against war," she wrote, "and were sure that there would never be another

Boys, in August 1949, ready to go off for a two-week summer vacation at a camp in the mountains, courtesy of the Brownsville Boys Club, and Minnie Weingart (second from the left in the rear row) *with other members of the club's women's division. (Courtesy of Joseph Feldman.)*

one, if women got the right to vote."[36] Though she married Edward Weingart, a Democrat, Minnie remained a Socialist until 1936 when she voted for Franklin Delano Roosevelt whom she thought was moving toward socialism. Minnie's father died in 1933 and her mother moved in with the Weingart family which now included three children. Still Minnie found the time and energy to do volunteer social work with the Red Mogen David (Brooklyn Chapter of the Jewish Red "Cross"), the National Council to Combat Blindness, and the Dora Scher League for Handicapped Children.[37]

In 1939 she had an operation for breast cancer and this remarkably energetic woman was told that she had just five years to live, a prognosis that turned out to be considerably off the mark. "I decided to keep busy," Minnie said, and she rededicated herself to even more intense social welfare activity. Minnie Weingart volunteered to work full time at the Brooklyn Women's Hospital, eventually becoming its board's vice-president. She represented the hospital at the Assembly of Brooklyn Jewish Women's Organizations, and soon became the assembly's executive secretary, her first paid job.

When the Brownsville Boys Club offered Minnie her second professional position, she "resigned from the Assembly, but with great regret. I loved the concept, and working with a world of wonderful women. But I felt that the Brownsville Boys Club project was what I was born for."

Some of the Brownsville boys and particularly the alumni's volunteer staff had mixed feelings about Minnie Weingart and her role: "The Alumni youths didn't know my past performance, or my other world, or my knowledge of the entire borough. All they could see was that an old lady with graying hair (I was 48 at the time) was getting paid for a job they had been doing."[38] Since 1947 and before Weingart came aboard in 1949, the boys and the alumni had been active, effective fund-raisers. They had helped organize the very successful $100-a-plate dinner in 1947, an alumni dance which netted $13,000 in 1948, and an even more lucrative set of raffle drives, awarding a Buick donated by board member and auto dealer Aaron Bring, and a house contributed by builder William Levitt.

Minnie Weingart recognized the value of the work of the boys and young men:

The Alumni boys did a wonderful thing in organizing and working with kids . . . and in getting the community interested in a building. . . . I felt their resentment but it turned out that we became a family of friends and I loved them; they were like my children—and I honestly felt as time went on that most of them loved me.[39]

Despite this love there continued to be at least some ambivalence toward Minnie Weingart, and to the general "intrusion" of professionals and the influence of "big donors." The club from 1940 to 1945 had been an authentic mutual-aid society, or what might be called today a "natural helping network." Whatever funds were required to conduct the all volunteer organization were raised by members paying token dues. After 1946 contributions were generated by the adult board as well as by the boys. And the monies received enabled the Brownsville Boys Club not only to create a building fund, but to hire a number of professional social workers. Although the boys and the alumni were often consulted and apparently exerted some influence on who was hired—Doc Baroff was the very first paid worker—many believed that the donors quickly got "larger and larger voices."

In 1947 Abe Stark hired, along with several professional program directors, twenty-eight year old Harmon Putter as full-time executive director of the Brownsville Boys Club. He had a Master of Social Work (M.S.W.) degree from Columbia's School of Social Work and replaced Doc Baroff who became Putter's assistant. Putter, relatively inexperienced, and an "outsider," seemed "to want nothing to do with the boys," BBC President Jack Leavitt said. "He just wanted to be a boss."[40] Putter was resented and resisted by the boys and by the volunteer staff of former BBCers. This became evident to Stark and Putter who wrote in their annual report: "Because of the 'free flowing' structure of the boys club in which it is often impossible to distinguish membership and staff or staff and board it is difficult to arrive at clear cut policies and responsibilities. We must try to remedy this situation in the year to come."[41] It was the boys, however, who took the most aggressive action. The combination of Baroff's "demotion" and Putter's intrusion moved the Boys Club officers led by Leavitt, and the volunteer staff led by Norman Goroff to pressure the new executive director to resign. The day after a grueling two-hour interrogation by the boys, Putter failed to show up for work and was never seen again.

Adult control was resented. The boys had built the BBC virtually on their own, and there was a great deal of pride in this achievement. Moreover, it was precisely because the boys, through self-government, had successfully made their own policies and supervised their own recreation and other activities, that the club was so effective in attracting members. The experience of the Brownsville Boys Club in this regard closely parallels that of the Boys Brotherhood Republic. Begun in Chicago in 1914 as a democratic organization in which teenage "citizens" made and enforced their own laws, the BBR came to the Lower East Side during the depression. One of its "boy mayors" explained the attraction of the Boys Brotherhood Republic over settlement houses with adult social workers. The settlement houses "have nothing lasting to interest their members. There is no responsibility. . . . The amazing part of [the BBR] is that there are no adults whatsoever connected with the organization. The boys do everything.

The boys have responsibility, they create and carry out their own activities."[42]

In many cities since the beginnings of mass immigration to the United States, settlement house workers, educators, clergy, and reformers had campaigned for supervised play space for street children.[43] It was often difficult, as we have seen in the case of Brownsville, to raise funds needed to build playgrounds and clubhouses. Even when successful in building and staffing recreation centers, reformers were often unable to keep "street boys" in attendance and in line. Social workers spent most of their time trying to build a stable membership.[44] Boys continued to drop in only sporadically despite the exciting sports and games and equipment offered. They apparently would not commit themselves full-time to clubs with so much adult supervision. In Roy Rosenzweig's study of workers and leisure in Worcester, Massachusetts, children's interviews indicated disdain for following orders and pre-established adult rules. "I can't go to the playground now," complained one eleven-year-old. "They get on my nerves, with so many men and women around telling you what to do."[45]

The Brownsville boys wanted play space, but they also did not want to be told what to do. No executive director hired by the adult Board before 1951 lasted very long. Putter was in the job little more than a year; Sidney Winnick for fifteen months, and Benjamin Lambert, who had been executive director of the East New York "Y," held on for the first eleven months of 1950. Minnie Weingart, as Stark's executive secretary and director of community relations, had a great deal of authority in this fluid situation.[46]

But Baroff, continuing as assistant director, retained significant influence too. "We fought for our independence," he said, "and didn't let the big contributors push us around."[47] Jack Leavitt agreed. "We tried to maintain self-government," he said, and at a board meeting, Jack went so far as to remark, "We want your money, but we don't want to be controlled."[48] Stark, impressed with Leavitt's nerve and eloquence, and perhaps seeing the need to coopt him, used Jack thereafter as a speaker at fund-raising events and hired him to help in the clothing store.

Leavitt was in this way at least temporarily diverted from criticizing the board. Baroff would be dealt with somewhat differently. When

Doc in 1949 applied for admission to the Columbia School of Social Work, to try to earn an M.S.W., he was rejected, four votes to three, by a faculty review committee. The social work professors said it would be better for Baroff's career if he furthered his social work education outside New York City and if he separated himself from the Brownsville Boys Club to which they thought he was too closely attached. Several of the former BBCers, including Schmaren, Lesovoy, Feldman, and Goroff, continue to believe that Harmon Putter, a graduate of the Columbia school, and Abe Stark, to whom Doc was "not sufficiently deferential," influenced the faculty committee. In any case, Baroff soon went off to the University of Pennsylvania School of Social Work in Philadelphia, and while he wrote from there often, he returned only occasionally to Brownsville.[49]

In November of 1950, Reuben Bennett, a graduate of City College of New York and holder of an M.S.W. from Columbia, was hired as executive director. He, in turn, hired several assistants including Program Director John Snypes, a black man, and Teen-Age Program Supervisor Norman Adelman. Two other paid workers under Bennett's supervision, Junior Program Director Irving Levine and Educational Director Leonard Dryansky, were former BBCers.

Despite the increase of professional supervision in the BBC, the tension between the paid social workers on the one side, and the boys and the volunteers on the other, dissipated by 1951–52. Time had softened some of the resentment at Baroff's removal; the volunteer staff continued to maintain an effective presence; familiar former BBCers were conspicuous among the professionals; and the professionals generally came to be respected for their vision, integrity, and commitment as they directed meaningful programs, did case work and reached out to the wider community.

Although the boys had to modify their principle, "No adult supervision," the operation continued to be marked by characteristics that, more than a decade later, would become the buzzwords of social welfare: indigenous leadership, extended facilities, and maximum feasible participation. Sociologist Herbert Gans's 1962 prescription for settlement house activities, based on his participant-observer study in Boston, is remarkably similar to what the BBC was already doing in the late 1940s and early 1950s:

[S]ettlement houses can step up their recreation programs for children, espe-cially the younger ones, in order to provide a kind of day-care facility for mothers who have to work, or who have many children underfoot in a small apartment. They can offer "hanging out" places for adolescents and can pro-gram movies and social activities to reduce the drain on their pocketbooks. . . . Another important function is that of counseling. . . . Many settlement houses already program such activities, but they do it in such a way that only [already aspiring] people use them. . . . One solution is to staff [the house] with some internal informal caretakers from the neighborhood. While these persons may lack professional certification, they are much more likely to be successful in communicating with their neighbors, and in attracting them to the settlement house in the first place.[50]

Recreation, hanging-out, movies, and counseling—formal and infor-mal, were long-standing traditions in the BBC. Internal caretakers, and "natural helpers" from the neighborhood had also long been asso-ciated with the club. In 1940 older boys were already nurturing and guiding slightly younger boys, literally "kids helping kids." And as early as 1945 former BBCers, some of them returning veterans, volun-teered their services, or took jobs with the club, as program coordina-tors, athletic coaches, camp counselors, case workers, and teachers of crafts.

Irving Levine who went from volunteer staff to professional in 1950 and former BBCer Lenny Dryansky, hired in 1951, were key figures in the process of promoting indigenous leadership and maximum par-ticipation. Dryansky, like Levine, represented most fully the profes-sionals' general concern about "doing more than keeping the kids off the streets," and he would change arts and crafts from "busy work," to a "vehicle for discovery."

Born in 1927, Lenny was a member of the Atoms and a wartime president of the Brownsville Boys Club before he himself entered the merchant marine in 1947. His Russian-born father came to the United States in the early 1920's, was a member of the carpenter's union and of the I.W.O. "We were poor," Lenny said with no hesitation, "on welfare, on relief, as it was called then, and my father was unemployed until the WPA. He was outspoken, voted the American Labor party and sent me to Yiddish *kindershul*." Lenny had a model in his carpenter father who recognized "the aesthetic of everyday life," but the elder Dryansky did not really encourage his son to pursue an artistic career.

Leonard Dryansky, former BBCer and, in 1951, arts and crafts director, making a point at a Friday night meeting at the Brownsville Children's Library. (Courtesy of Leonard Dryansky.)

Lenny's aesthetic interests, however, were greatly stimulated and reinforced by the *kindershul* and by his increased access, through his membership in the Brownsville Boys Club, to the Stone Avenue Library and its librarians. Dryansky's Brownsville youth apparently helped implant in him what Irving Levine dubbed the "non-communist left aesthetic vision." Lenny as a professional brought this vision back to the Brownsville Boys Club in 1951 where it was further reinforced and where he tried to pass it on.

With a degree from Michigan State University, Lenny Dryansky began as the arts counselor for the day camp. He travelled, always carrying a large pack of art supplies, with the youngsters on one of the five buses used daily to transport children to beaches, parks, and hiking fields, as well as to ballgames and museums. One of his main goals, Dryansky said, was to "make kids more aware of their environments." On the beach it could be sand sculpture; on the street, sketches of houses that Brownsville children actually lived in, and not the conventional and artificial isolated boxes so often drawn or painted. In the fields Dryansky would encourage the use of natural materials:

leaves, pine cones, branches, and flowers. His programs were popular, and Bennett recognized Dryansky's talent and effectiveness. At the end of the summer of 1951, he hired Lenny as full-time education director of the Brownsville Boys Club.[51] A short time later Lenny said, "I intend to stay in social work. There's a lot of room for artistic expression in this field. You can reach children in a special way through the arts. Call it a projective technique, if you will. It's one of the best educational media available."[52]

Dryansky continued to try to "give back" some of what he received from the club by nurturing aesthetic sensitivity. Before the new building was ready he had a piece of the Christopher Avenue storefront converted into studio space, hired a music director, and went to work helping children discover a "sense of place and a sense of self" through the arts. He also tried to develop a program for adults, particularly for the parents of children he saw almost daily. He occasionally got the two generations involved in working together.

Lenny Dryansky viewed himself as a teacher of arts that were not isolated phenomena, but were part of human growth and development. The arts, Dryansky believed, could play a vital role in the community, building self-esteem, fostering latent talents, stimulating creativity. He has carried this perspective and commitment with him into his work at Syracuse University where he has been professor of theatre arts since 1967.

Men like Levine, Adelman, Snypes, Bennett, and Dryansky helped develop very positive relationships between the social workers on the one side and the volunteers and children of the community on the other. Whatever residue of tension might have remained was buried under the joy of extensive athletic, artistic, and community activity and under the euphoria of the increasing possibility of a *building*.

Athletic activity, no longer viewed as the primary vehicle of "salvation," nonetheless continued to be important. Although Brownsville Boys Club teams were forced to use the facilities of Thomas Jefferson High School, the East New York Y, and Betsy Head Park, and continued to feel the sting of having no home courts or fields of their own, they competed enthusiastically and successfully in citywide tournaments between 1948 and 1953. In these years, too, the club initiated, under Minnie Weingart's encouragement, what would become the

Abe Stark dispenses the goodies at the Annual Christmas-Hanukkah party sponsored by the Brownsville Boys Club. This one in 1951 drew ten thousand children to the 106th Regiment Armory. (Brooklyn Public Library, Brooklyn Collection.)

tradition of Christmas-Hanukkah parties for large numbers of youngsters. In 1951, in fact, ten thousand children between the ages of seven and fourteen crowded into the 106th Regiment Armory (on Bedford and Atlantic avenues) where the Brownsville Boys Club entertained them. There was food donated by restaurant owners, prepared gratis as sandwiches by the Cooks' and Countermen's Union and served without charge by the Waiters' Union. The Fire Department Band played and the Police Department Glee Club sang on a stage adorned with a Hanukkah menorah. Five hundred Brooklyn merchants contributed shopping bags "crammed with toys, clothes, candy, shoeshine kits and comic books."[53]

Each year between 1948 and 1953, the Brownsville Boys Club sent five hundred young people to summer camp; and in 1951, when the Brownsville Boys Club had an operating budget of close to $35,000, even younger children, seven to nine years old, could go the Club's very own day camp at Alley Pond Park in Queens. There Joe Feldman worked as a counselor. Other kids could join what Lenny Dryansky called "the rolling Brownsville Boys Club Day Camp," with its five buses and extensive array of outings.[54] The Brownsville Boys Club, still operating out of its three rooms on Christopher Avenue, Minnie Weingart's desk in Abe Stark's clothing store, and a small office on Sackman Street continued to do what it always had done. In addition the club worked at improving community relations and it did case work and case work referral. Many thought if the Brownsville Boys Club could do all of this with such limited facilities, how much more it could do with a modern clubhouse. "With [a] new building," George Schmaren said, "the possibilities are unlimited."[55]

By July of 1948, the club had raised $130,000 for the building fund, had become a provisional member of the Boys Clubs of America, and had purchased from the city at nominal cost a piece of tax-liened property that filled the entire block on Linden Boulevard from Stone to Christopher avenue and back to Hegeman Avenue. This was three blocks south of the Brownsville Boys Club's Christopher Avenue storefront. With these resources in hand and with the promise of more to come, Abe Stark and Sidney Winnick, the executive director, wrote to the Charles Hayden Foundation, noted for its interest in boys clubs and asked for help in building a $500,000 clubhouse.[56] Stark's application for funding was strongly supported by Edward J. Lukas, executive director of the Society for Prevention of Crime. Less than a month later, however, with no written explanation, the Hayden Foundation Trustees denied the Brownsville Boys Club request.[57]

The club then turned to the New York Federation of Jewish Philanthropies at the end of 1948, and again at the beginning of 1949. But, according to Lesovoy and Schmaren, federation representatives said that Brownsville's declining Jewish population made that neighborhood a low priority for them.[58] There were at the same time some negotiations with officials of the YMHA. The East New York Branch of the Y had since 1946 been supporting a number of Brownsville Boys Club activities.[59] But it became clear to the boys and to the volunteer staff, who prided themselves on having built an interethnic and inter-racial organization, that what the YMHA wanted was a *Jewish* Community House, a place that created "good citizens and good Jews." Even if the Brownsville Boys Club had agreed to this new, narrower identity, it would have been unlikely for the Y to agree to build in Brownsville. For one of the key grounds considered by Y sponsors in choosing a location for a new building was, "Does the area have a *substantial*, and more or less *permanent* Jewish population?"[60] Brownsville no longer fulfilled the latter criterion.

Undeterred by three consecutive strike-outs, the Brownsville Boys Club Board, Abe Stark, the alumni, and the boys themselves continued, relatively successfully to seek incremental resources elsewhere, and in October of 1949, a year after they were turned down by the Hayden Foundation, the Brownsville Boys Club broke ground for a new clubhouse at Linden Boulevard and Christopher Avenue. Abe Stark, having initiated his campaign for borough president on the anti-O'Dwyer Fusion Ticket and eager to publicize his ability to get to this stage in the plans for the new building, told reporters that Mayor O'Dwyer did not attend the ceremonies because, "He's afraid to face the facts."[61] Presumably Stark was referring to his superior ability to get things done. Of course, Stark on the eve of the election, may have "manufactured" the facts. Despite the "ground-breaking" actual construction did not begin for more than two years.

Early in 1950 Abe Stark wrote again to the Hayden Foundation explaining that the Brownsville Boys Club with a functioning Board, land, a property survey, increased funds and a new Executive Director (Benjamin Lambert), was now truly ready for outside help.[62] A meeting was arranged for February 16 between J. Willard Hayden, Abe Stark, and Benjamin Lambert. Also attending at Stark's request was Edward A. Richards, president of the East New York Savings Bank. Richards had been a municipal court justice for ten years in the Brownsville—East New York district, and he had been one of the managers of the Highland Park YMCA. He knew Brownsville and the Hayden Foundation well, and soon after the conference in Hayden's office he sent a strong letter in support of the Brownsville Boys Club, concluding that the building will help "underprivileged boys, without regard to creed or color, to become loyal American citizens."[63]

Hayden Foundation Trustees characterized the Brownsville Boys

Club as "a real aggressive outfit which owns a fine piece of property outright. . . . The sponsors are a young, energetic group who know what they want and will work like the devil to get it."[64] The Hayden Foundation Projects Committee recommended a conditional $300,000 grant to the Brownsville Boys Club and suggested another meeting of Stark, Lambert, and Richards with Edgar A. Doubleday to discuss the matter further.[65] One of the items to be discussed was the Brownsville Boys Club's need to affiliate fully with Boys Clubs of America in order to qualify for Hayden Foundation funding. To join the Boys Clubs of America, an organization had to have an adult governing board responsible for property, administration, management policies, personnel, programming, and financing. Members, limited to boys eight to fifteen years old, could participate in program planning only in an advisory capacity.[66]

The Board of the Boys Clubs of America in the early 1950s was dominated by bankers, lawyers, publishers, college presidents, stock-brokers, government officials and corporate executives.[67] The credo of the organization, to which the boys apparently pledged, included a belief in the American way, the Constitution and the Bill of Rights, fair play, honesty, sportsmanship, and a belief "in my Boys Club . . . which supports all of these."[68] Abe Stark, looking at a grant of $300,000 practically in hand, was not about to be put off by the generally conservative orientation of the Boys Clubs of America. He agreed to bring his board members to a meeting with David Armstrong, the BCA's executive director.

Armstrong came away from the meeting satisfied. He was pleased by the fact that the Brownsville Boys Club was "raising $20,000 annually for present operations." The BCA offered services in promotion and planning of buildings, and in the training and placing of club workers, but gave no direct aid for costs of buildings or for day-to-day management and programming. And the Hayden Foundation grants were given on the condition that upon completion of a building there be no further requests for funding *for any purpose*. Armstrong was impressed by the "largely Jewish . . . thoroughly interested, . . . sincere, capable," Brownsville Boys Club Board. He was particularly taken with Stark who he characterized as a "great leader and a considerable influence," and he recommended that the foundation formalize the $300,000 grant on the usual condition that the Brownsville Boys Club raise a nearly equal amount on its own.[69]

The Brownsville Boys Club had taken one giant leap closer to a clubhouse, but a considerable step away from the concept of mutual-aid and self-government. The possibilities inherent in the building and its projected facilities were so attractive, however, that many believed accepting the "constraints" of the BCA was another "valid exchange." In any case, by June of 1950, after four years of soliciting donations, the Brownsville Boys Club had raised $275,000, and was awarded the $300,000 Hayden Foundation grant.[70] Construction began a year later, but funding continued to be a problem. The board was persuaded by Minnie Weingart, cerebral palsy administrators and by parents, to add a special play room for cerebral palsy children and additional facilities for the handicapped.[71] As the plans for the building grew more elaborate and more expensive, general costs also rose, and original estimates had to be significantly modified.

Another $100-a-plate dinner was organized for September 23, 1951, at which William Levitt, "the builder of homes for men, and of men for homes," was honored. Stark continued to pump his close associates for more donations, and he wrote again in April 1952 to the Hayden Foundation for an additional $270,000 subsidy. He talked about increasing costs of day-to-day operations and he explained that a rise in construction costs and the expansion of the building to serve boys living in the Breuklen and Van Dyke Houses (low-income public housing projects) that were being built in the Brownsville Boys Club catchment area, had pushed the price of the clubhouse to $950,000.[72]

This new request shook several executives at the Foundation. Edgar Doubleday now believed that the Brownsville Boys Club "people are getting in way over their heads, not only on initial building costs but on maintenance costs as well. . . . Our commitment of $300,000 . . . was based on a building to cost about $500,000 [with] maintenance costs of $75,000 a year." And at least one trustee recommended that the foundation "pull out" of the Brownsville project entirely.[73] Stark, hoping to reassure Doubleday wrote: "The Brownsville Boys Club assumes full responsibility for the operating costs which are estimated will amount to *$75,000* per year. Should the annual operating costs exceed this amount, we are fully confident that we can raise it from

Site of the BBC building on Linden Boulevard and Stone Avenue, three blocks south of the Christopher Avenue storefront. (Courtesy of Joseph Feldman.)

our Board, Alumni, Women's Divisions, and friends of the Club."[74]

The Foundation Trustees, ultimately recognized the reality of rising construction costs and were impressed by the fact that the Brownsville Boys Club had, as of April 1952, raised close to $360,000 on its own. They voted an additional $100,000 grant. Stark, a year later, when the building was nearly complete, managed to get one more $75,000 grant from the foundation. It was approved after yet another fund-raising dinner honoring the Charles Hayden Foundation and major supporter and contributor William Levitt. The grant was to be paid after the completion of the building and only on condition that "it is to be distinctly understood that this is our final grant and they are not to come to us for further assistance."[75]

Once again Abe Stark had demonstrated his considerable talent for charitable fund-raising. "I don't believe any other man," J. Willard Hayden wrote to Stark, "could accomplish what you have done."[76] The building was completed and all construction bills were paid by September 21, 1953. David Armstrong and Edgar A. Doubleday said

Breaking ground for the new BBC building in 1951. Board members and boys look on. (Courtesy of Joseph Feldman.)

Brownsville Boys Club, under construction in February 1953. The building opened officially in October 1953 with a final cost of $1,250,000. (Courtesy of Joseph Feldman.)

the building with its pool and gyms and clinics and library and roof garden was "the finest boys club" they had ever seen.[77]

Residents in the vicinity of the building were delighted: "This new building is what we've been waiting for," said one mother of three. "I've been living in the same house close by, for 29 years, so I really know what this neighborhood needs. Up till now, we've always gotten the bottom of the heap. The Brownsville Boys Club is the most wonderful thing that has ever happened to Brownsville."[78]

The boys and volunteer staff who had helped raise money for the building were proud and optimistic. Dudley Gaffin, already practicing law in 1953, told a reporter "Being proud of your environment makes you a lot more secure. That's about the way I've doped it out. I pass the new building every morning, and it's hard to believe my eyes." Isidore ("Red") Karbel, who chose teaching as a career because of his experience with the Brownsville Boys Club, explained that "completion of [the] new building with [its] magnificent facilities . . . enable[s] the club to reach out further in the community in its task of developing better children."[79]

To this task, the professionals and volunteer staff, supervising fifty undergraduate students, dedicated themselves. Reuben Bennett, Norman Adelman, John Snypes, Minnie Weingart, Irving Levine, Lenny Dryansky, and a number of others in the new environment intensified their efforts to do social work on "all the tracks." Levine and Adelman concentrated on interracial cooperation and understanding. Dryansky, who had helped design the interior of the building, its decor, its furnishings and its spaces, included a gallery for the display of children's art, hired five new arts teachers, and developed new programs in music and dance for adults as well as children. Weingart continued her work with women's groups and helped organize community Parent Teacher Associations in an effort to get more summer programs in schools. And Executive Director Bennett developed closer ties to other neighborhood organizations. He served as president of the Brownsville Neighborhood Council, and then as one of four vice-presidents of the Brownsville Neighborhood Health and Welfare Council (a merger of the Brownsville Neighborhood Council with the Brownsville Health Council). He worked very closely too with John Newton, a black man who was president of the Brownsville Housing Project Tenant's Council.[80] For a time it looked as if a viable set of relationships had been put in place, linking self-help initiatives, human service professionals, and quasi-governmental agencies.

In March of 1954, however, five months after Abe Stark witnessed the opening of the new building, and less than three months after he was sworn in to his first elected office as president of the city council, he without notice fired Snypes, Dryansky, Levine, Adelman, and seven other workers from the Brownsville Boys Club. Bennett was released several months later.[81] "Reasons of economy" were cited, but Stark was apparently moved by fears having little or nothing to do with funding. The Brownsville Boys Club was becoming something that far exceeded Stark's "recreational" outlook and his noblesse oblige approach. The new professionals with their quest to educate the whole boy, indeed the whole family, and with their aggressive integrationist direction and involvement in community organizing, were going well beyond "keeping kids out of trouble" and dispensing turkeys at Thanksgiving, or crammed shopping bags at the Christmas-Hanukkah parties. Stark apparently failed to understand much of what the staff was doing and felt it was too much for him to handle and control. It was very likely, too, in 1954, still the tail end of the era of Joe McCarthy and the "Red Scare," that Stark was frightened by the professionals' progressive activism and their left-leaning ideological orientations.

The majority of the directors and supervisors were left-liberals. Bennett, who, several of the boys recall, had frequent parties at which "left-wing" songs were sung, and Snypes, were active democratic socialists, as was the vigorous and outspoken Norman Adelman.[82] Levine and Dryansky described themselves as having been on the left but not members of any left party.[83] BBC professionals naturally brought their "ideology" to their work but none were, even indirectly, *political* proselytizers. "There *was*," however, as Dryansky said, "something revolutionary about our work. Arts and crafts was no longer something that came in a kit; group work was more than outings and dances, and we were getting more deeply into integration, community outreach and community organizing."[84]

Abe Stark, though he was relatively unsophisticated, had complex motives in releasing many of the social workers. It was clear that Stark was very ambitious. A master coalition builder, Stark had connections to the business community, to Democratic organizations, both regular and reform, to gamblers, and to the vast networks of Jewish philanthropy. Fearing that a connection to the left might dry up the contributions necessary to run the Brownsville Boys Club (with an operating budget in 1954 of $150,000 per year), and fearing that a charge of sympathizing with, and employing "leftists" might damage, if not destroy, his political career, Stark fired the bulk of the Brownsville Boys Club senior professional staff.

The staff, however, did not quite fade away. They made it clear in a letter to the board that they were angry at being abruptly released— fired "without notice or prior discussion, without consideration of seniority or competence," and without coverage by unemployment insurance. Not only was the mass firing a blow to the workers "as human beings with families to support;" the dismissals, they argued, would drastically reduce service to the children and to the community. The staff asked for a hearing by the full Brownsville Boys Club Board and in the meantime they mounted a demonstration outside the five-month-old building.[85] In an attempt to break this "strike," Stark contacted Doc Baroff and asked him to return from Detroit where he was doing social work to become again a director for the Brownsville Boys Club. What a cruel choice for Doc. The BBC was his second home but, "My whole life was against strike breaking," Baroff said, "it was against my entire ethic. I was very homesick, but I wasn't going back for this!"[86]

The fired staff, having gone public and onto the streets, received strong support from the community, members of which joined the picket line, with signs like "Bring Back 'Hooker' Levine." All were rehired, but ultimately each was terminated as soon as individual contracts ran out. Dryansky, for reasons that were unclear to him at the time and which are just as unclear now, was asked to stay on as executive director when Bennett was released. But Dryansky could not work under what he presumed would be much more restrictive conditions. He left for a job with Karamoor Art Institute in Cleveland, Ohio.

With the building completed, and Stark in office, the new city council president may have determined, consciously or otherwise, that the Brownsville Boys Club had served its purpose in terms of his political career. Certainly Abe Stark no longer looked at the Brownsville Boys Club—at least the Brownsville Boys Club the way it had recently operated—as a powerful political asset. The "leftist" demonstrations and the publicity surrounding them had made him and other board members nervous. So did the continuing integrationist activities of club workers. In 1954 approximately 15 percent of the active membership of the teenage division of the BBC were black. An additional 5 percent were Hispanic, Italian, and other non-Jewish whites. Irving Levine continued his commitment to making the Brownsville Boys Club racially and culturally heterogeneous. So did Norman Adelman, who in 1954 was completing a master's thesis at Columbia University's New York School of Social Work entitled "Factors to be Considered in the Development of Intercultural Teen Age Programs."[87] Aggressive integration was still widely seen as radical in the early 1950s.

Although pursued by a variety of progressive groups, desegregation was also clearly an American Communist party cause. And large numbers of people continued to perceive the attempt to "mix the races" as a Communist conspiracy. The integration "problem," for Stark and the board was undoubtedly further complicated by the fact that with the completion of the BBC building there were larger numbers of girls in attendance for social and athletic activities, including swimming and dancing. Fear over the reaction to "mixing the races" was intensified by fear over the consequences of "mixing the sexes."

The Brownsville Boys Club had become less and less useful to Stark's political ambitions. Brownsville, too, would not much longer serve as a "natural" solid political base. By 1954 the Brownsville Jewish population—the masses of Jews as well as the older Jewish business and professional establishment—which had been Stark's traditional constituency, was thinning out rapidly, replaced by blacks. Housing projects with apartments going only to low-income families hastened the out-migration of Jews. It was time for Stark to jump ship. Claiming virtual "bankruptcy" in terms of the ability to maintain a viable budget, Stark and the board, ten months after the building had opened and five months after the "strike," turned the Brownsville Boys Club over to the City of New York. Stark wrote to the Hayden Foundation, whose funds were granted only for projects of private initiative, to justify the transfer:

I know that you must share with me some feeling of sadness over the transfer of the Brownsville Boys Club to the City of New York. But I know too that your thoughts, like mine, will always be guided by the principle of doing what is best for the children involved, irrespective of our personal preferences. The acceptance of the gift by the City guarantees the future of the Brownsville Club and assures its continued operation for years to come, long after you and I may not be around to give it the loving care which it deserves. We realize that no-one is indispensible, but from experience we also know that work of this sort is done by a handful of people who donate their money, their health and their lives to a cause such as this.

One third of the money which built the Club was the generous gift of your Foundation; the remaining two thirds, in addition to the maintenance costs over the years, were raised through voluntary contributions from people whose hearts were often bigger than their pocketooks. Two of the principal backers of the Club have serious financial problems today and economic conditions in general are bad, so that money is becoming harder and harder to raise for charitable purposes. As you know, there is no foundation to subsidize our annual operating budget which exceeds $150,000. All of the money comes from private contributions. It would be tragic indeed if, at some future date, there would not be enough funds to keep the doors open. . . .

I want to assure you that the Board of Directors of the Brownsville Boys Club, even though it is under City sponsorship, will continue to serve in an active capacity. We will be on hand to advise in policy making. In addition we will continue to raise money to help the Club undertake new programs and facilities which otherwise might not have been possible. In the long run, everyone in the community will benefit and the Club will become an even greater tribute to your confidence in its work.[88]

Clearly Stark and the directors were not completely deserting the Brownsville Boys Club. Indeed the board stayed quite active and raised more than two million dollars in less than two years. With this money they eventually erected two entirely new buildings, adjacent to the Brownsville Boys Club, one housing a Golden Age Center for "senior citizens," and the other an enlarged Cerebral Palsy Pavillion.[89] Obviously raising money was not the real problem. Stark and others could still solicit funds for traditional philanthropic purposes: the care of the elderly and the handicapped, for example. He could no longer, however, raise money, he thought—correctly or not—for activities for which he and potential donors had little understanding or sympathy and through which they thought they could derive little in the way of social and political advantage.

In addition to claiming "bankruptcy," Stark also justified the "gift" to the city by suggesting that it would serve as a model and stimulate the administration to open youth centers across New York in its many deprived areas.

It is my belief, and yours, I am sure, that a Boys Club of this type should be built in every problem community as part of a long-range, preventative approach to the problems of juvenile unrest. By offering the Boys Club to the City of New York for use as a pilot study, I have been able to interest the city administration in this most important work. This action will pave the way for similar clubs and youth centers to be opened throughout the city in places where they are needed most. When this is completed, then we will have made an even more meaningful contribution to young people on a basis broader than anything which a single club can accomplish alone.[90]

Unfortunately, although Mayor Robert F. Wagner "gratefully accept[ed] the Brownsville Boys Club" for "the people of New York City," and expressed a "hope that beginning in 1955 we shall undertake a program for playgrounds and recreation centers which will constitute a basic attack on our youth problems," little was done.[91] In fact the Brownsville Boys Club *replaced* the recreation center planned by the Department of Parks for Betsy Head Park, "resulting in a substantial saving to the City," and a loss to Brownsville youth.[92]

J. Willard Hayden and Edgar Doubleday received the news of the transfer from Stark with little comment, and the tone of their respective responses could be characterized as cool.[93] Even Minnie Weingart, Stark's "Gal Friday," said many years later, "The one thing I felt was wrong was turning the Brownsville Boys Club over to the City. The [Board] said this would serve as a pilot project, and that other such facilities would be built by the City in deprived areas. But I never knew whether or not any were in fact built."[94] At least through 1960 none were.

Even if several facilities had been erected by the city eventually as a result of the Brownsville Boys Club model, they likely would have been run primarily as recreation centers. This was implied in Mayor Wagner's thank-you letter, quoted above (with its reference to playgrounds as the solution to "youth problems,") and in the general long-standing recreational philosophy of Parks Commissioner Robert Moses. In January of 1955, the Brownsville Boys Club building itself was reopened, under the supervision of the Department of Parks, as the Brownsville Recreation Center; and the city's primary contribution came two years later in the form of a large adjacent playground for outdoor games. The general emphasis would continue to be recreation.[95]

The range of Abe Stark's political vision and imagination was unfortunately no more than ordinary. His decision to turn the BBC over to New York City's recreation program was part of a failure of understanding and nerve. The sell-out had begun with the firing of the progressive professionals who conceived of social work in broader terms than traditional charity and recreation.

This is not to say that recreation, in and around the city-run building, did not continue to help some boys, particularly when they were exposed to former BBCers. "My whole life changed when I attended the Boys Club in the 1950s," said Lenny Zeplin, now a high school principal:

I came in contact with teachers who were working second jobs. They were excellent role models. One, "Whitey" [Dave] Diamond, a former BBC member, was like a father to me. These people influenced my decision to devote my life to education and to children. I also won trophies for sports and developed a sense of self-worth. I went on to work in the BBC summer day camp when I was older and I also worked in the winter program. I love my life and I can actually say, "I owe it to the Boys Club."[96]

Zeplin, working at the camp and at the center, very much followed in the BBC tradition of giving back and passing on. George Benitez wrote from California that Len Zeplin was an important influence on him when he attended the Recreation Center in the late 1950s and early 1960s. Zeplin and others "kept us off the streets," George said. "Many were kept straight by the BBC [as the center continued to be known despite the name change]. I myself never got into trouble because I was a gym rat at the BBC."[97]

As we see here and have seen in earlier examples, recreation remained an important force in boys' lives. It could even operate, in combination with sensitive nurturing, especially by "peers" as a "solution" to the "youth problem" in individual instances. But recreation was not by itself going to be a general "solution" to Brownsville's increasing social difficulties, particularly racial tension, youth crime and juvenile delinquency. What the BBC professionals, volunteer staff, and boys themselves had been trying to do in the late 1940s and early 1950s might not have been a "solution" to Brownsville's problems either; but creative social work done "on all tracks," including community organizing, and the potential recruitment of new "indigenous leadership" from within the black population, might have had at least a chance.

CHAPTER 6

Fright, Flight, and Failure: Brownsville After the Boys Club

No other area . . . speaks more to a visitor of the sense of loss and waste.
. . . Brownsville is a disgrace to this city and to this country.
—PETE HAMILL,
JUNE 1970

When the Brownsville Boys Club was transferred to New York City, a hope was expressed that it could serve as a model for ways to combat juvenile delinquency. Stark claimed that "contrary to the general [large city] trend, the area served by the Brownsville Boys Club has experienced a 17 percent decrease in youthful offenses over the past two years."[1] Seizing this statement, Mayor Wagner repeated it—with no accompanying statistics—in a public letter to Abe Stark and to two thousand people attending the Brownsville Boys Club dinner in September 1954. The change in Brownsville's "rating," from a problem area in the 1940s, to one now "better than average" in juvenile delinquency, said Wagner, was "a miracle."[2] However, as with most alleged "miracles," there was little if any corroborating evidence. There may have been a decrease in youthful offenses for the age group six to twenty in Brownsville between 1952 and 1953, but between 1953 and the end of 1954, Brownsville experienced a 25.4 percent increase in juvenile delinquency, while at the same time New York City was showing a slightly smaller 23 percent rise and Brooklyn only 16.7

154

percent. Moreover, starting from at least as far back as 1951 (a period for which relatively reliable statistics are available), Brownsville exhibited a marked increase, absolute and relative, in youth crime and delinquency (see table below). There were 13.3 cases of juvenile offenses per one thousand youngsters aged six to twenty in Brownsville in 1951, 16.8 in 1952 and 19.7 by 1954—a 48 percent increase in three years. Brownsville late in 1954 was once again chosen as the "target" for an "intensified concentration of police strength to stamp out crime."[3]

The figures rose even more dramatically after 1955 so that by 1958 the rate for Brownsville was fifty-eight per thousand. This represented an increase of almost 200 percent since 1954 and well more than 300 percent since 1952. The Health Areas served most directly by the Brownsville Boys Club experienced equally startling increases. In fact, Health Area 60, within which the BBC building sat, had at least a 325 percent increase in juvenile delinquency between 1953 and 1957.[4]

Abe Stark's experience with the Brownsville Boys Club up to 1954 left a very positive impression on him. Moreover the club was so central to Stark's political persona and public identity that he needed to believe the BBC was a "success" by his definition. He could not get very much beyond the idea that recreation provided by the club had kept, and continued to "keep boys out of trouble." Stark knew that it

Delinquency Rates Per 1,000 Youths
Six to Twenty Years Old

	New York City	Brooklyn	Brownsville	H.A. 60	H.A. 59	H.A. 57
1951	17.5	14.9	15.3	18.2	22.1	28.7
1952	19.3	17.2	16.8	—	—	—
1953	23.6	20.9	15.7	15.9	31.1	34.5
1954	28.8	24.4	19.7	—	—	—
1956	33.5	30.6	35[a]	—	—	—
1957	35.8	33.4	43[a]	70[b]	70	70
1958	—	41	58	—	—	—

[a] Estimates based on the known figure 19.7 for 1954, and 58 for 1958.
[b] The rate in each of the Health Areas is at least 67.7 and may be as high as 85.5. The delinquency rates were, according to Bureau of Community Statistical Services "relatively low" only in Health Area 58.10 and 58.20, significantly higher in Health Area 56 (42.29) and Health Area 51 (44.2) and between 67.7 and 85.5 in all the others.[5]

was more than just inadequate recreation that got boys "into trouble." He pointed to the "resentment and frustration" caused by discrimination and exploitation. He understood the need to "spur equal opportunities in employment for all persons."[6] But Stark agreed with the president of the Boys Clubs of America that "as long as there are many boys roaming the streets seeking recreation and companionship, whatever the reasons, you are going to have a large amount of delinquency. I do not say a Boys Club is a cure-all for delinquency, but I do say it will lessen delinquency."[7] And he continued to place inordinate emphasis on the recreational solution for juvenile delinquency.

In August 1954, just as he was about to transfer the Brownsville Boys Club to the Department of Parks, Stark responded to Police Commissioner Adams's call for increased police forces. New York, according to the commissioner was on the verge of becoming little more than a "community of violence and crime." Stark eschewed the need for more cops and demanded more funding for "recreation centers and boys clubs". He cited figures from an FBI report to try to show that New York was relatively better off in many categories of serious crime than Chicago, Detroit, Philadelphia, and Los Angeles. And he warned that "undue" emphasis on crime in New York would frighten away business! The problem was serious, Stark said, but it could be dealt with over the long run through increasing athletic facilities. But Mayor Wagner said there should be "no sugar coating the unpleasant realities." The *New York Times*, while praising Stark for his emphasis on "corollary long-range action," agreed with the police commissioner that the "number one issue for immediate action was the considerable enlargement of the police force."[8] This might have been necessary in the short run, but it merely dealt with symptoms. Increasing the number of policemen promised no more true and enduring resolution to youth crime and juvenile delinquency than increasing the number of recreation facilities.

City Council President Stark may have been overly optimistic, or too enmeshed in his earlier political rhetoric. In either case he was unable to get off the "recreational train" he thought he could ride into even higher municipal office. But at least he understood that "each dollar we spend to prevent children from becoming criminals will be returned to us a thousand fold, not only in a healthier society but also in the actual saving of countless millions of dollars which are now lost throught vandalism, thefts and the cost of prison and reformatories."[9]

Others took a different approach and were at least indirectly critical of Stark including Judge Hyman Barshay, the BBC board member who hosted Stark's testimonial dinner in 1947. More recently Barshay had presided at the trial of four Brooklyn teen killers during which he criticized "the growing emphasis on long-range programs to cure juvenile delinquency." He said "immediate steps should be taken to open temporary jails for youthful offenders."[10]

Despite opposition, even from old friends, Stark persisted in touting the long-term solution. His concentration on prevention was healthy and useful, but Stark was naive about the redemptive powers of recreation and was wont to use his connection with the Brownsville Boys Club recreational facility for personal political promotion. Abe Stark wanted very much to be mayor of New York City. He had wanted this from as early as 1953 when he outran the entire Democratic ticket in winning the presidency of the city council, and perhaps from as early as 1949 when as the Republican-Liberal Fusion candidate for the borough presidency, he made a very impressive showing in Democratic Brooklyn.

In 1956 when Mayor Wagner was considering accepting a nomination to run for the United States Senate, Abe Stark said, "I see no reason why I shouldn't be a candidate if the Mayor doesn't run. I see no reason in the world why I shouldn't be considered a candidate at that time."[11] Were Wagner actually to win a Senate seat, City Council President Stark would automatically become Acting Mayor for a year, and it would be difficult to deny him the mayoral candidacy in 1957.

Some influential Democrats questioned Stark's qualifications to be mayor. When it became clear, in the summer of 1956, that Wagner *would* get the senatorial nomination, Stark wanted to begin to still doubts. He wanted to demonstrate—even before he might ascend to the position of acting mayor—that he had the stature, experience and ability to head the city.[12] An "opportunity" soon presented itself. In early August Police Commissioner Stephen P. Kennedy reported a 41.3 percent rise in juvenile delinquency for the first six months of 1956 compared with the same period for 1955. Stark very quickly called a major parley of public and private agencies to outline a plan to combat juvenile delinquency.[13]

In an address strongly resembling a campaign speech, Stark proposed a plan that "would be based in large measure . . . on the record of accomplishment of the Brownsville Boys Club." Stark, still strongly identified in the public mind with the club, reinforced the connection. He also indirectly inflated his own role in the club's history by implying that the club was founded in 1945, the year he first evinced an interest in it, rather than in 1940. Brownsville in 1945, Stark said, was a tough impoverished area with seventy-five gangs. "Today," he went on, repeating something beginning to resemble the "big lie," Brownsville "has one of the lowest delinquency rates in the city." This, he said, is a reflection of the fact that Brownsville also has a youth center, a youth center built privately with one and a half million dollars—raised mainly by Stark's efforts—and a youth center that he "handed over to the city free." [14]

In November 1956 Robert F. Wagner lost to Jacob Javits. Stark's mayoral ambitions and abilities became moot questions until the next election in 1961. In the meantime, Abe Stark continued to stick with boys clubs and recreation centers as the vehicles for his political career and the salvation of youth. In 1957 he asked for the city and the state to share in granting a $3 million subsidy to 150 youth agencies to help them strengthen their activities. By 1959 he turned to Congress to help stem the "rising tide of teen-age crime." He asked that $100 million be spent per year as "emergency subsidies" to boys clubs and settlement houses. [15] As limited as this proposed "solution" was, it appeared enlightened in the face of Mayor Wagner's narrow insistence on meeting the problem "with the full power of police, as many as we can put on the street," or compared with Police Commissioner Kennedy's simplified call for "stern justice in the Courts."

Stark also showed some courage when he responded to Judge Samuel S. Leibowitz's proposal for cutting crime. Citing the disproportionate numbers of Hispanics and blacks involved in crime, the judge had urged the Federal Government to restrict immigration from Puerto Rico and to significantly limit the migration of blacks from the South to northern cities. Along with Senator Jacob Javits and Congressman Emanuel Celler, Stark flatly rejected this "solution." The city council president scheduled a meeting at City Hall to canvass opinion on how to "smooth the social adjustment and cultural assimilation" of relatively recent Hispanic and black arrivals to New York. [16]

Many whites appeared to want to "smooth the social adjustment" of recently arrived nonwhites by moving away from them. In 1950, 90 percent of Brooklynites were white, 7.6 percent black, and less than 2 percent were Puerto Rican. Between 1950 and 1960, as blacks and Puerto Ricans arrived in larger numbers, almost one-half million whites left the borough. This resulted in a net population loss of over 160,000 and increased Brooklyn's black population to 14.1 percent and its Puerto Rican residents to 6.9 percent.[17]

It was not simply the migration to Brooklyn of Southern blacks and blacks from Harlem that spurred white flight. The borough had already suffered a significant decline in its population growth rate between 1930 and 1940, and an even more precipitous drop between 1940 and 1950. Immediately preceding and through World War II, Brooklyn appeared to be in relatively healthy condition economically. A Princeton University study serialized in the *Brooklyn Eagle* in 1942 depicted the borough as a leading center of foreign trade and demonstrated that its taxable real estate value was the second highest among the five boroughs of New York City.[18] Nevertheless, since the late 1920s the upwardly mobile or the upwardly aspiring no longer perceived Brooklyn as the end of the "great American trek." Moreover by the postwar period, Brooklyn experienced some of the same problems of other urban areas in America including an increase in the number of youth gangs and the escalation of gang brutality. There were other difficulties, too. As Pete Hamill pointed out, more youngsters died from overdosing on drugs than died in gang wars in the late 1940s and early 1950s.

The whole terrible period of the gangs, followed by the introduction of heroin, changed a lot of citizens' attitudes about Brooklyn. Those who had escaped the lower East Side now started talking about escaping Brooklyn. You could do the best you were capable of doing, work hard, hold two jobs, get bigger and better television sets for the living room, watch steam heat replace kerosene stoves . . . and still people in their teens were found dead in the streets of Prospect Park, their arms as seared as school desks. "We gotta get outa Brooklyn." You heard it over and over in those days. It wasn't a matter of moving from one neighborhood to the next; the transportation system was too good for that; it was out to the "island" or to California to to Rockland County. The idea was to get out.[19]

The most serious instability in the borough began with the development of the new freeways leading out of Brooklyn, and the relatively easy availability of automobiles in the early 1950s. Between 1950 and

1957 Brooklyn had a net loss in population of 135,000 inhabitants: the white population declined by 235,000 and the black population rose by slightly more than 100,000. Between 1957 and 1960 another 240,000 whites left; and an additional 208,000 blacks arrived.[20] In the ten years from 1950 to 1960 the white population of Brooklyn declined by almost 20 percent and the black population increased by 150 percent.

The in-migration of blacks to Brooklyn, represented the attempt by *relatively* mobile minority families and individuals to flee the South and to escape worsening conditions in Bedford-Stuyvesant or Harlem. "Black flight" had a significant impact on the racial and economic structure of the borough. Brooklyn became an area whose inhabitants were fearful. All groups, lower-middle and middle-class white residents and the newer more impoverished black and Puerto Rican Brooklynites were frightened by the pace of change and by the feeling of apparent decline.

One of the symptoms of that decline, and in turn one of the indirect contributors to further dcline was the folding of the *Brooklyn Eagle* in 1955. Although hardly a great paper, the *Eagle* had served an important purpose. It had helped to give some sense of community to a set of extremely heterogeneous neighborhoods.[21] Another factor hastening decline was the incremental closing of the Brooklyn Navy Yard, finally abandoned as a shipbuilding yard in 1966. The yard had employed over seventy thousand people. During and immediately after the war this meant paychecks that could be used to put down payments on row houses in Queens, and on automobiles to get there. But the navy yard also meant jobs for tens of thousands of Brooklynites. By the 1950s, however, the neighborhood around the dying Brooklyn Navy Yard was becoming one of the most depressed areas in the United States.[22]

The departure of the Dodgers for Los Angeles in 1957 was yet another blow. The loss of the Dodgers on top of the loss of the *Eagle* made Brooklyn the only American "city" with two million inhabitants not to have a newspaper or a ball team. A great source of pride for all Brooklynites, the Dodgers had held the borough together in a very special way. The team, its antics, and its perceived "invincibility" provided a common ground and "something to talk about" for a variety of ethnic groups and classes. There is endless argument over why the team left Brooklyn. According to Pete Hamill, the Dodger organization was still making money at Ebbets Field.[23] Dodger fans were nothing if not loyal, and between those crucial years 1950 and 1957, attendance was relatively constant each season, moving slightly up or slightly down between 1,020,000 and 1,280,000. "No team in all of baseball was more profitable," argues the Dodgers' recent historian Peter Golenbock.[24] Perhaps the Dodgers were just not making *enough* money for Club President Walter O'Malley, or perhaps, as Irving Rudd, the Dodgers' publicity director in the early 1950s, explained it, O'Malley was one of Brooklyn's fearful white middle-class residents.

O'Malley complained about the deteriorating atmosphere at Ebbets Field throughout his tenure as the Dodgers' president. He always worried about the unruliness in the stands, which he viewed as a manifestation of Brooklyn's changing social scene. He was also very concerned that Brooklyn might become a very poor community and that some day the money would not be there to support the ball club. You know, a lot of people call O'Malley a racist for leaving Brooklyn in the fifties, but, I say, he was just concerned about turning a profit. He did not care that the blacks were black, just that the blacks were poor.[25]

Rudd's comment is an indication of how difficult it is, often, to separate race and class in the analysis of white flight. On the one hand, substantial numbers of middle-class whites, as we have seen, left Brooklyn before blacks and Hispanics moved in in appreciable numbers. This suggests that class and economic status played a primary role. But white flight significantly intensified as the numbers of in-migrating nonwhites increased sharply from 1950 to 1957, and more dramatically between 1957 and 1960.

A similar dynamic animated Brownsville. The neighborhood was changing even more rapidly than Brooklyn as a whole. As late as 1950 the Puerto Rican population of Brownsville was negligible, less than half of one percent. By 1956, however, over twenty thousand Puerto Ricans made up 12 percent of Brownsville's general population. Even more visible was the growth in the number and percentage of blacks. In the 1940s, blacks had started to come North, men with cotton-baling hooks still in their pockets and women tired from holding their small children as they made their way in buses and railroad coach cars from South Carolina and Georgia and Florida.[26] This in-migration had already doubled Brownsville's black population between 1940 and 1950, and by 1957, thirty-eight thousand blacks made up 22 percent of Brownsville's overall population. At the same time, more than forty-six thousand white people left Brownsville, resulting in a net population decline and in higher percentages of nonwhites.

The nonwhite population, particularly blacks, in the 1950s were disproportionately represented among the youth who got "into trouble," some of it very serious trouble. The Health Areas in Brownsville with the highest rates of juvenile delinquency also had the highest percentages of black population and those areas with the lowest youth offender rates had the lowest percentages of blacks. Health Area 59, for example, with a black population of 33 percent had a juvenile delinquency rate of 31 per 1,000, and Health Area 58.20 with a black population of 3 tenths of 1 percent had a juvenile delinquency rate of 6 per 1,000.[27]

One explanation for this discrepancy was that by 1957, blacks in Brownsville were a good deal younger than whites. Between 1940 and 1950 the general six-to-twenty-year-old cohort in Brownsville experienced a 34 percent decline in population, while the decline for all ages was only 11 percent. This downward trend continued into the 1950s for the fourteen-to-twenty-year-old group. Apparently younger white families had been a disproportionate part of the general white exodus. By 1957 the median age of whites in Brownsville was twenty-nine, of blacks, fifteen. In the same year, when blacks were only 22 percent of the population, 32 percent of Brownsville's children were black.[28]

Equally important as the youth factor, was the class aspect. The Health Areas containing the largest percentages of blacks had the lowest median incomes. Almost 90 percent of Brownsville's blacks in the 1950s lived in Health Areas 57, 59, and 60. The median income in these sections was $2,600. In contrast, the almost all white Health Area 58.10 had a median income of $3,960.[29] In the middle 1950s the median annual income for families in the United States was approximately $4,500; in New York State it was closer to $5,000. An income of $3,900, then, might present significant financial problems, but it likely meant a family was at least viably working-class. Teachers and clerks in New York City, for example, earned median incomes of between $4,000 and $5,000 during the 1950s. On the other hand, the

$2,600 median income of black Brownsville represented significant, debilitating impoverishment, especially for larger families.[30]

Younger, poorer, more recently uprooted, and victims of historic oppression and deprivation, blacks in Brownsville were disproportionately the perpetrators and victims of vandalism and violence. In smaller proportions whites were perpetrators and victims, too. The general perception among the whites, however, was of their own victimization, or at least potential victimization, and this "race fear" helped some whites decide to move. "There was an influx of a new breed of people", one former Brownsville boy and BBCer said, "muggers, burglars, murderers and drug addicts. The decent citizen had to move away. The synagogues were closing. Older Jewish people retired to Florida. Children fled."[31] One Jewish woman, a veteran of reform politics and still infused with the social concern she had absorbed from the *Jewish Daily Forward* and from her active socialist brothers, stayed on as her Brownsville housing project turned blacker, poorer, and tougher. She tried to understand, reminding herself of her brothers' shibboleth, "Blacks are the last hired and first fired." But one day in the laundry room of the project building, she was beaten by a black girl. She gave in a joined the exodus.[32]

Race fear on the part of whites was not necessarily the primary motive for leaving Brownsville; but when added to a variety of other critical factors, race fear made leaving easier. Brownsville since the 1920s, before any appreciable nonwhite population had arrived there, was stigmatized as a "slum" and as a place to get away from. The upwardly-mobile could theoretically choose to remain in Brownsville and seek to revitalize the neighborhood. But too much history and culture operated against this possibility. As more than one analyst has suggested,

Generational turnover—the movement of potential second- and subsequent-generation residents away from their childhood neighborhood—constitutes one of the greatest problems for neighborhood preservation. In America it is "normal" for parents, relatives, and friends to convince the younger generation that their success in life will be demonstrated to others by their ability to move out (and presumably) upward via residential mobility.[33]

Jews were no exception to this "American" rule. Working-class Brownsville was a first step in the internal migration of Jewish immigrants. Second generation upwardly mobile Jews moved to more "sub-urban" areas including Flatbush and Borough Park even before signifi-cant black migration into Brownsville. Race fear intensified a steady flight of the upwardly mobile that was already in process. Whites had more than one motive for leaving Brownsville, and sometimes, as we saw in Irving Rudd's comment about O'Malley it is difficult to separate race from class.

A number of recent studies demonstrated that when nonwhites move in to a neighborhood, it is perceived as "bad" by the white inhabitants irrespective of the "character" of the arriving nonwhites.[34] This suggests that whites are after all more conscious of race than class. But race fear and fear of declining class status are as intricately entangled in the sociological analyses as they appear to be in the hearts and minds of whites. One study, for example, of East Flatbush (a neighborhood bordering the western edge of Brownsville) in the 1950s and 1960s contends that even when the blacks who moved in turned out to be "better neighbors" than the whites they displaced, whites still felt compelled to leave the neighborhood in order to prove to themselves and others that they had made it in American society.[35] Another study of the same neighborhood (with substantial pockets of middle class blacks, mostly from the West Indies and an appreciable number of Puerto Ricans) claims that while everyone talks about "how nice the newcomers are, and points to nonwhite neighbors they are fond of, a pervasive anxiety grips long-time residents about the neigh-borhood becoming another ghetto like Brownsville," poor *and* black.[36]

This same mixture of class and race fear, along with the more positive hope of "betterment," motivated white, mainly Jewish resi-dents of Brownsville in 1940s and 1950s. The vast majority of former BBCers left Brownsville between 1950 and 1956. Seventeen percent left before 1950, and another 15 percent left after 1957. There was, in response to the question "Why?" an almost perfectly even breakdown between those who said some version of "We wanted a better life," those who said "The neighborhood changed," and those who said both of those things. It was fairly clear in the interviewing process that some thought they were "running" and that others thought they were "aspiring." Several were quite explicit. One former Brownsville resi-dent living in Canarsie since 1956 said "The blacks were moving in;

we had no choice." Another, thinking of the increasing possibility of black "encroachment" in the area, said, with some bitterness, "We ran once; I guess the next step is a houseboat." Several used phrases like, there were "dangerous signs," or "deteriorating conditions." And one younger former Brownsville boy said, "My parents felt the neighborhood was changing dramatically, and it was time to try a new environment for their children."

However, the great majority of the respondents, thought that by leaving they were simply improving the "quality" of their lives or that they were, as Harold Radish put it, "moving to a 'so-called' better neighborhood." "Why did I leave?" said Ben Wernikoff in a tone implying that the answer was so obvious, the question need not have been asked, "To move up, of course. Just imagine: when we moved to East Flatbush we had a bathroom with a sink!"[37] "We were so poor in those days," said another former Brownsville resident who had joined the exodus in the 1950s,

We didn't have very much. We think back to those days a lot. Our children have no idea of what it was like. We didn't need much to make do. There was stoopball and checkers and hopscotch. The ice would melt on the ice wagon, and we'd watch it melt down and change shapes. The kids today would laugh at us. . . .

Most of us who live in Canarsie came from [Jewish] ghettoes. But once we made it to Canarsie, we finally had a little piece of the country.[38]

It is important to remember that for many of these "urban emigres" and for the BBCers particularly, we are looking at a group of men who were in their twenties when they left Brownsville. Dozens, in answering the question "Why?" simply said "I got married and we needed an apartment," or "My first son was born and we needed more room." Young, married, upwardly-aspiring fathers of small children, these men were not only or even primarily "fleeing." Nor were they simply preoccupied with "making it." By moving out of impoverished, cramped Brownsville and resettling in another "better neighborhood," these former BBCers did not think they had "hit the jackpot" but that they had gained a chance to live a life much less pinched by privation. "I moved in 1952 when my daughter was born," said Irving Forman. "I didn't feel like I was running, but moving up. I'd come back to Brownsville to play ball on weekends." Abe ("Lulu") Rubenfeld demonstrated in practically a single breath how "aspiring" and "running" could be combined. "I had an opportunity to buy a home in Canarsie! And the Brownsville I knew and loved was no more. It was time to go."[39]

Some whites left Brownsville because they were "pushed" by the "slum clearance" of the middle 1940s and early 1950s that preceded the building of public housing. Others were "channeled" out by public housing policy. No middle income developments were built in Brownsville though one was planned and soon scratched.[40] And some whites who managed to obtain apartments in Brownsville projects were later virtually evicted by rules requiring that any family earning more than a stipulated income must move out. In the second half of the 1950s, however, when black residents became increasingly visible, "running" was more likely to have been part of the cluster of white motives for leaving Brownsville. Race fear, "objectively" arrived at or irrational, was real. Many people, including 40 percent of the white BBCers, in the later 1950s, ran or were pushed by block-busters and real-estate speculators. Those white Brownsville residents who were not afraid of the idea of blacks as neighbors were forced to think about the responses of their panicky white neighbors, as well as the "character" of the new black arrivals. What if the stampede, touched off by white fear, emptied the neighborhood of whites, and a "bad element" of blacks moved in? "Tipping" (reaching that percentage of black residents that begins to turn an entire neighborhood or building complex black) was partly manipulated by hustlers, partly the result of clumsy government policies, and partly a self-fulfilling prophecy.

After 1963 no white BBCers of the generation of the founders and framers lived in Brownsville. They spread across some dozen states, but a significant majority remained in the greater New York area, more than 30 percent in Brooklyn. Most continued to feel connected spiritually to Brownsville, and maintained active membership in the Brownsville Boys Club Alumni Association that they had organized in 1948.[41] Two important goals outlined in the association's constitution kept the Brownsville connection explicit well into the late 1950s:

> As the founders of the Brownsville Boys Club, we support their activities and programs and will contribute to that program in any way that we can.
> As civic-minded adults of the community, we wish to foster a program of

charitable, social and cultural activities befitting our organization in an effort to further bind the ties among us.[42]

It is clear that the young men of the alumni association thought they would remain residents of Brownsville and continue to be "revitalizers" of the neighborhood at least for a time. We have already seen how active the alumni were in fund raising and as volunteer staff in the later 1940s and early 1950s. In the mid-1950s, as the Feldmans and Kronenbergs, Deutchs and Lesovoys moved out of Brownsville, they continued to try to play the role of revitalizers. "There was no real attention paid to trying to save the neighborhood by *staying on*," Sid Siegel remembered. "We were raising our families, trying to earn a living, moving out."[43] But there was real attention paid to helping, even when the former BBCers lived at a distance from Brownsville. In 1952 the association with over 165 fully paid members sent five boys to summer camp for eight weeks. From their headquarters in the new BBC building between 1954 and 1959, the alumni, despite the city takeover, ran fund-raising drives to support the center facility and its activities. In 1958 they sponsored a Boy Scout troop and a Little League baseball team. And each year they organized and sponsored an invitational basketball tournament.[44]

By the late 1950s, however, when 85 percent of these former BBCers no longer lived in Brownsville, the number of flyers and letters sent by the Alumni Association dwindled, and the stationery became increasingly chintzy. In 1959, with a bank balance of $142.34, the organization was for all intents and purposes defunct. The group, mainly through the efforts of Joe Feldman, revivified in the mid to late 1960s. Headquartered in a Queens YMHA, they were committed to "helping the club that meant so much to us in our youth." They also continued to do general "charitable" work. And, like the former Bruins and Comets and Stonedales, and other corner clubs that had been meeting continuously, they came together, too, in recognition of "the common interest inherent in our being former members of the community of Brownsville and [the] wish to perpetuate the memories of our earlier years in Brownsville."[45]

The Brownsville Boys Club Board of Directors also "stayed in business," even after 1954 when the building was placed under the control and supervision of the Department of Parks as the Brownsville

Recreation Center. No longer sponsoring innovative social welfare work and community organizing, the board did continue to raise money for charitable purposes. They ran a day camp and an orthodontal clinic. Under the directorship of Minnie Weingart, they provided senior citizens with entertainment in a new Golden Age Center paid for by the Board. There were theatre and birthday parties, holiday celebrations and Passover seders. By the late 1950s and early 1960s, as the alumni association withered, the Brownsville Boys Club, as represented by the board of directors, found that its traditional philanthropic activities were increasingly less relevant to Brownsville's mushrooming social problems, and less appreciated by Brownsville's largely nonwhite population.

The Jewish population had declined from over 175,000 in the 1930s and 1940s to less than 5,000, mostly elderly residents, in the late 1960s. The last synagogue in Brownsville, on Stone Avenue between Pitkin and Belmont avenues, closed in 1972. Earlier the Brownsville Synagogue on Riverdale Avenue near Herzl Street, built in 1905, had become the People's Baptist Church, and the famous "Amboy Street Schul"—Chevra Torah Anshei Rideskowitz—was converted to the St. Timothy Holy Church. In 1968 the Hebrew Educational Society moved to Canarsie. The building that housed the Society at Hopkinson and Sutter avenues was purchased by the Catholic Diocese of Brooklyn and the neighboring Hebrew Ladies Day Nursery was taken over by the Bethany Gospel Chapel. In 1969, after four years of sporadic disorders and riots in Brownsville by blacks over deteriorating conditions, lack of public services, and social welfare budget cuts, the Brownsville Boys Club Board of Trustees changed its name to the Abe Stark Philanthropies. Soon afterwards it, too, followed much of its constituency to Canarsie.[46]

The disorder and the riots continued to erupt in Brownsville in the 1970s and into the early 1980s, symptoms of a fractured community sinking in "fear and decay." Steadily declining in population from nearly 225,000 in 1940 to 125,000 in 1968, Brownsville, as one writer put it, went from being "a largely Jewish working-class community," to one "largely Negro and Puerto Rican and largely forgotten."[47] The neighborhood was, and would continue to be, impoverished and unstable. The median income in 1963 already sank below the accepted poverty line and it dropped further by 1970. The great majority of Brownsville's residents in the 1960s and 1970s attempted to eke out a subsistence by combining temporary jobs and welfare payments. During the mid-1960s, welfare aid was given to three hundred people out of every thousand—twice the city's average. And by 1970, four out of every five Brownsville families received welfare aid.[48]

The bulk of the welfare recipients were families without a permanent husband/father. Severely high unemployment, particularly among the young, but in any case double the average for New York City, ravaged the neighborhood. The men who were employed worked for low wages and were subject to frequent layoffs. Women were the main wage earners in many families, but they too, dependent on domestic work or antipoverty jobs, were rarely paid decently, or employed steadily. There was little growth of a black socioeconomic infrastructure in Brownsville. The black business sector that did exist was small, mostly service oriented and marginally profitable.[49] In the main, therefore blacks held jobs outside of the neighborhood. Those blacks that did succeed economically, inside or outside of the neighborhood, were often forced to leave Brownsville because they earned too much to stay in public housing. Unemployment, low-paying jobs often far from home, and shortsighted, insensitive public housing and welfare policy combined to produce an extraordinarily high instability of residence. More than half the 1970 population had lived in Brownsville less than ten years.[50] It is difficult, perhaps impossible to sustain a neighborhood under such conditions.

Deeply impoverished Brownsville was scarred too by other horrendous ills. Throughout this era and for at least another decade, Brownsville had the highest infant mortality rate in New York (four times the city average), the highest rate of narcotics addiction, the most juvenile delinquency, the lowest reading scores of any school district, and a skyrocketing rate of malnutrition and disease. In 1969, 45 percent of the children in the area had suffered from lead poisoning after eating paint and plaster from the cement walls.[51]

Brownsville, by 1970 may also have been the scene of the "worst housing conditions *to be found anywhere,*" conditions promoting the attendant dangers of fire, rats, and vandalism. Tenement landlords, including Jews and some West Indian blacks, provided few services to the poor and politically unorganized tenants. Rents for deteriorating apartments ran from $60 to $80 per month, but some landlords apparently charged double these amounts when they discovered the city would pay the higher rents for tenants on welfare. In 1965 the neighborhood, fueled by antipoverty grants began to organize itself with the help of the new Brownsville Community Center. Rent strikes were initiated, city agencies were pressed to inspect the worst buildings, and repairs were demanded from landlords. "We thought we could get action," said the president of the Brownsville Community Center, "but the landlords just ran. It all happened so fast." One black woman who moved to Brownsville from Alabama in 1964 said, "We pulled a rent strike [in 1967], but as soon as the landlord saw he couldn't get any more money out of us he disappeared. We all had to move out and now the building is abandoned."

By 1970 more than seven hundred buildings had been completely deserted. Some landlords stayed, made few, if any repairs, paid enough taxes to forestall foreclosure, and hoped the city would eventually condemn their properties for public use. This often happened but it did not do much that was positive for Brownsville residents. The vacant apartments became the dumping ground for many of the city's poor including welfare clients dislocated by redevelopment in other areas. The process fed on itself. Panic spread and led to a further exodus of the middle class, this time including blacks. Tenements emptied. More landlords walked away. The city government tried to make some emergency repairs. And with funds from Washington, New York made some efforts to relocate tenants, clear the worst blocks and build new housing.[52]

As early as 1961 parts of Brownsville were designated for urban renewal, and by 1967 Brownsville was part of Brooklyn's $29-million-a-year Model Cities Program. "The designation of an area as an urban renewal site," a major New York State Commission reported,

should have seen the neighborhood move progressively upward toward improvement in its physical condition. In Brownsville, the reverse occurred. Massive delays developed in the program and the City failed to meet its schedule for the renewal efforts. The City also seemed intent upon an outmoded plan for the area and as a result, physical deterioration in areas scheduled for rehabilitation occurred rapidly and irreversibly.[53]

The city's plan called for "conservation," i.e., the preservation of good and sound buildings, as well as for clearance and extensive redevelopment. Unfortunately, according to the state commission report, the program of conservation and rehabilitation had little city support and no city supervision. It was simply stricter enforcement of already existing codes, and only token rehabilitation took place.[54] Blocks originally designated for conservation were switched to clearance and redevelopment after inordinate delays which subjected tenants to long periods of landlord neglect, and the city engaged in widespread acquisition and extensive demolition. But by 1973,

not a single project ha[d] been fully completed since urban renewal began [in Brownsville] in 1961. Thousands of units of housing have been demolished by the City government and block after block has been left vacant for years, forming a wasteland of gutted carcasses of buildings and rat-filled rubble—*this* is unique. Nowhere else in the City has a 20 block renewal area existed, vacant and undeveloped, while excavation began of another 55 block contiguous area. In fact, the Planning Commission reports that "the City's demolition program has focused on Brownsville." The result is that nowhere else in the City is the gap between promise and delivery, *between the willingness to acquire and demolish properties, on the one hand, and the ability to relocate decently and rebuild, on the other, so grimly real.* Brownsville is a stark memorial of the delay and mismanagement of two City administrations.

The losers, beyond question, are the poor who live in the project area. The beneficiaries are property owners, demolition companies, bureaucrats, builders, a couple of favored industries within the project area, and a handful of community people whose selection for project sponsorship recruits them as local defenders of the renewal process.[55]

The city appears to have presided over a deal in which whites, including some Jewish landlords and a small number of black leaders benefitted, while the masses of blacks were victimized. The city had also apparently misstated relocation resources, and proceeded to demolish usable accommodations before replacement housing could be found for many tenants. Members of larger families even had to be relocated separately. The federal government finally intervened and acted to halt demolition of urban renewal properties on a citywide basis. But for large numbers of Brownsville tenants, the process had already delivered the worst of two worlds: tenants had suffered the psychological, social, and physical pain inherent in rapid dislocation, and they failed to end up with adequate housing.[56]

The Van Dyke low-rent public housing units rise above the Junius Street BMT elevated railway station in 1954. The promise of decent housing fairly quickly turned into the grim reality of shoddy, grim, barracks-like shelters. (Photograph by Ted Castle, Magnum Photos. Brooklyn Public Library, Brooklyn Collection.)

Even when public housing was completed, the projects were generally unsatisfactory. Between 1941 and 1955 at least four major public housing developments were built in Brownsville. The *New York Times* called them "impersonally cheerless barracks" that "have produced a terrifying new breed of slum." With little attention to aesthetics, light, general design, imaginative use of space, and possibilities for recreation, the desolate projects carried "the stigma of personal and environmental poverty and the seeds of despair." When in the middle 1960s the Federal Public Housing Administration sponsored a project design that did pay attention to attractiveness, the General Accounting Office condemned the plans, even though the costs came well within budgetary limitations. The GAO, to cut costs further, eliminated the "unnecessary" amenities. There appeared to be a "punitive intent" built into housing legislation—part of a larger guarantee that nothing too good shall be given to the poor.[57]

Abandoned apartment building on Powell Street, once the home of Joe ("Yussie") Feldman, the three Schmaren brothers, and several other BBCers. (Courtesy of BBC Alumni Association.)

Brownsville residents were very unlikely to get anything "too good." With the black middle class well on its way out and private enterprise virtually withdrawn, Brownsville was "dependent on government for nearly every basic need, from shelter to food and medical care."[58] This meant too that every fluctuation in state or city budgets and even often in the federal budget, would be felt by the people still living in the decaying ruin of Brownsville. Increased deprivation, especially after the hope generated by the march on Washington in 1963 and the promise inherent in the Civil Rights Acts of 1964 and 1965, could sometimes lead to riot. Two nights of arson were triggered, for example, in June 1970 by a reduction of garbage collection in the Brownsville area. In 1968 Brownsville community groups had demanded a clean-up drive by the city Sanitation Department, and in 1969 eighteen hundred youths were employed with federal funds, through the Neighborhood Youth Corps, to help the department keep the community clean. But there was a sizeable federal cutback in "poverty funding" in 1970 and Brownsville residents were again faced with five or six-day accumulations of garbage sitting out on the streets. Bad enough by itself, the rotting refuse aggravated another problem— rats. One Legion Street resident said, "You . . . see rats pecking in the garbage like chickens in a chicken yard." Houses had to have "rat guards"—family members who stayed awake all night to keep rats off sleeping children.[59] The frequency of rat bites did bring some money into Brownsville in 1968 for an antirat campaign, but that too dried up and in any case, as one antipoverty worker commented: "How can they really do a job on rats without doing a job on garbage?"[60]

In such a context of desperation, riot is hardly inexplicable. Even proposed cuts in funds could spark disorders. Sporadic arson and vandalism and bouts of robbery broke out in April of 1971 when the state budget called for decreased expenditures in public assistance, Medicaid and food stamps, and reduced educational and anitnarcotics programs.[61] Abandoned buildings were torched in protest of the cuts and because the buildings had become "festering dens of rats, narcotic addicts and criminals."[62] There was business property destruction and looting, the retributive and restitutive modes of "political" response available to the poor and virtually disfranchised. In the short run at least, the disorders brought little change. "When people riot and set fires, it draws a lot of attention," one black clergyman said, "but then things go back to the way they were before. The lives of the people here have not changed for the better despite all the attention Browns-ville gets from time to time."[63]

In fact in that same short run, things may have grown appreciably worse. The violence further hastened the decline in the number of small businesses and intensified the flight of working class and middle class blacks and Hispanics. The population that remained in Browns-ville represented the most severely disadvantaged segment of the urban black community. The few remaining whites who were not too old or disabled were also made more ready to flee. Leonard Wagner, white owner of a family liquor business that had been on Pitkin Avenue for seventy years, witnessed the wreckage of the front of his store and said: "We are pretty well-known in this neighborhood. . . . This is the first time this has happened."[64]

As futile as the short lived riots in the 1960s and 70s appear to have been, rent strikes, sit-downs, building occupations, and civil disorders were among the few political tools impoverished blacks had available to them. The protests, even the violent protests, can be seen as part of the effort to counter ghetto powerlessness.[65] Poor populations are always at a substantial disadvantage in the battle for "pieces of the pie." Brownsville's black residents were no exception to this rule. Unlike the poor working-class and small-business Jewish population which preceded it, Brownsville's poorer, less skilled black population with "almost no home ownership and very few commercial sources of sup-port" found it difficult to get political attention. Aside from money, communications, and legal assistance—the resources necessary for organizational effectiveness—black Brownsville lacked a stable social base and it was difficult to sustain pressure group action.

Housing conditions in Brownsville and the demolition of old buildings are partly to blame for its high transience, but city officials have done little to encourage population stability. Public housing officials for instance, require that any family earning above a stipulated income must move out. In effect this prevents upwardly mobile residents and those most likely to provide leadership from remaining in their community. A revolving door prevails in the social structure of the ghetto in which those persons most able to work for community betterment are soon shuttled into a middle-class world, leaving their compatriots to fend for themselves.[66]

Moreover, Brownsville as a result of the gerrymandering of East Brooklyn in the 1960s possessed no representative elected from the community. Political scientist Harold V. Savitch demonstrated that, "Canarsie with a population roughly comparable to Brownsville is able to elect, wholly or in considerable part, a councilman, a state senator, and an assemblyman. East Flatbush, though in a less enviable postion, does have an assembly seat within the district and shares state senatorial and council seats with communities of similar class and ethnic composition." In contrast Brownsville is "politically parceled out to the more affluent white communities which surround it."[67]

The bias against the poor is ideological and systemic, and is reinforced by the political system's mode of operation, especially when poor groups come into direct conflict with more affluent and more organized groups. Brownsville in the late 1950s and through 1966 had lost battles over busing, the location of new schools and the building of an educational park, in direct confrontation with other East Brooklyn communities, particularly Canarsie.[68] The educational park—a cluster of schools built in a campuslike setting in one large area—was recommended in 1964 by a New York State Commission as a way of facilitating integration in New York City schools. It was thought that racial balance could be more easily accomplished if white and black children commuted to a common location, rather than either having to be viewed as invaders in an alien neighborhood.

In Brooklyn, the Flatlands area, an enormous empty city-owned lot, lying directly between increasingly black and Hispanic Brownsville and largely white Canarsie looked like an ideal place to build an educational park. Brownsville residents formed a group named Parents for an Educational Park (PEP). They did research and field work and lobbied, and were delighted when a New York City Board of Education study revealed that of all sites examined, Flatlands had the best potential for an educational park. PEP's hopes were short-lived. White opposition, mostly Italian and Jewish, and particularly from local school board members and home owners associations, surfaced in East Brooklyn in a matter of weeks. Sam Curtis, formerly a Brownsville politician, and in 1964 a City Councilman from Canarsie, "accompanied delegations of real estate and homeowners groups to private meetings at the Boards of Education and Estimate. Curtis himself spoke at public hearings and took a public position against the park."[69] Curtis also visited Mayor Wagner and went to see Brooklyn Borough President and President of the Brownsville Boys Club Board of Directors, Abe Stark. Assemblyman Alfred Lama, another member of the BBC board, also interceded and spoke with Stark against building an educational park.

Backing for the educational park crumbled. When the commissioner of commerce said he wanted an industrial complex in Flatlands rather than an educational park, and went so far as to hint to some members of the board of education, that its budget might be cut if they pushed for the park, politically empowered support disappeared.

Even when not in *direct* political conflict with more powerful groups, Brownsville generally lost. Neighborhood leaders in 1971, for example, in the days after the riots had subsided, tried, unsuccessfully, to get state budget cuts restored. According to the head of the Brownsville community council, residents "knew" this would happen. "They didn't feel," he said, "that this is going to be any different than any other time when they've been disappointed."[70]

When the Brownsville black community, despite its inherent disadvantages in organization, *was* able to build some semblance of group activism through the community council, the rent strikes, the antipoverty work,. and PEP, it found that it continued to meet with failure, and many concluded, temporarily at least, that conventional political activity was useless. Periods of activism, including civil disorders, were often followed by even longer periods of quiescence, a cycle which resulted in little enduring or effective political organization. Black residents of Brownsville can not, however, be seen as simply apathetic. What they demonstrated was "political antipathy," an aversion to a "conventional politics that does not work for people who have lost before they have begun."[71]

In the late 1960s, a less conventional politics began to emerge from Brownsville. Recognizing the bias in the system which prevents victory in head-on contests with groups in positions of greater power, black leaders "narrowed" goals to the revitalization and rehabilitation of the neighborhood and its institutions through black power and community control.

If integration was doomed by a nearly monolithic white resistance and by the maldistribution of power inherent in the system, perhaps decentralization and local control were viable options. There was also a growing conviction that the rhetoric and ideology of the integration movement—e.g., black children can achieve academically only when they go to school with whites—actually heightened the stigma attached to blacks. This conviction reinforced the quest for decentralization and informed the struggle over community control of schools in the Ocean Hill–Brownsville District in 1968.[72] The local control idea also moved a number of Brownsville residents to involve themselves in planning and shaping neighborhood agencies. A $1.6 million multiservice community center proposed by the city's Human Resources Administration, with two-thirds of the funding coming from the federal government, was expected to be approved for Brownsville before the end of 1968. At the urging of Brownsville residents, the plans for the center were changed to include outpatient clinics for alcoholics and drug addicts, a twenty-four hour emergency welfare office and a small library. One of the goals was to overcome the "hurdle problem" of city services, services for which needy residents had to take long bus and subway rides from their neighborhoods to widely separated city agencies. The center was planned for a site on Hopkinson and Atkins avenues, eight blocks from J.H.S. 271, the hub of the school controversy. According to a neighborhood coordinator for the Brownsville Community Center, "many of the same residents involved in the school struggle, took part [beginning in late August of 1968] in the weekly planning meetings for the new center."[73]

The community control movement had some success. But in regard to schools it was a political failure. It was perceived by the "establishment" as a threat—a vehicle for "black nationalism and racial separatism." The leaders of the community control movement also resorted to antiwhite and anti-Semitic rhetoric (educators, teachers' union leaders and administrators were disproportionately Jewish). By doing this they attacked the very interests whose cooperation black leaders needed. After the fiery rhetoric had cooled, however, the community control movement did leave a positive legacy. Increasing numbers of people and political actors, black and white, were convinced that "blacks must not be seen as an inferior caste, to be pitied and dispersed, but as an ethnic group asserting its demands and interests like others in a pluralistic society."[74] Black power, furthermore, remained a rallying cry and a stimulant for community activism and enterprise which could "help rouse the ghetto out of its quiescence,"[75] collective and individual. In the 1970s some Brownsville blacks took the cue.

In the urban renewal and Brooklyn Model Cities area where the city government had contributed to regression in the housing situation, a third-generation Brownsville resident, Joseph ("Brother Joseph") Jeffries-El, succeeded in 1973 in providing decent shelter for 185 low and moderate income families. Born two blocks from the federally aided development he sponsored and managed, the minister and social worker Brother Joseph attributed much of the success of the project to his close ties with the neighborhood and his rapport with residents. "Tenants have a natural distrust of landlords," he said. "That's something we've got to change, and it's very important to have black management to do that." The five buildings that make up the Nobel Drew Ali Plaza are, according to the *New York Times*, "an island of cleanliness and order in the sea of decay and desolation that spreads out in all directions in Brownsville."[76]

Joseph Richardson, a Brownsville community activist, in 1974 persuaded the city to install high-intensity lights on his block. He also set up a walkie-talkie patrol system with the aid of Banker's Trust. Evidence of hunger in the community prompted Richardson to contact the Department of Agriculture from whom he obtained bag lunches—650 of which he distributed every day from sidewalk tables to children. Looking for some indoor space to expand and rationalize his program, Richardson was directed by the mayor's office to the Crown Heights Office of Neighborhood Government, some distance from his own Brownsville section. He was unsuccessful there, and turned to the New York Urban Coalition. According to Richardson they never responded to his letters. Undaunted, he continued to dispense lunches from his "makeshift cafeteria" every day, and he and fellow block workers went on to arrange outings for neighborhood youths.[77]

Richardson also persisted in remaining, after all the other tenants had moved, in a landlord-neglected building on Park Place in an effort to get the owner to make repairs. The landlord claimed he had no money and was willing to sell the building to Richardson for $1,000. "I wouldn't have any trouble raising the $1,000," Richarson explained, "but the building has a $7,500 mortgage plus it would take another $100,000 to make this place liveable again." Despite Richardson's efforts and appeals to the city throughout 1974, and despite professional advice that in the long run "it would be cheaper to rehabilitate that property than to turn it over to the dogs and demolition teams," little was done. The buildings along Park Place continued to decay as tenants left them, landlords abandoned them, and vandals destroyed them.[78]

Individuals, community associations, and tenants' groups accomplished some positive things, not the least of which was a reinforced group consciousness. But they could not gain an inch on those most basic issues—jobs and housing. By the end of 1975, in the face of continued deterioration, Brooklyn's Model Cities program, mandated to develop viable urban communities, had its annual operating budget cut drastically from $29 milliion to $12 million. Early in 1976, City Housing Administrator Roger Starr said that it was a positive thing that tenants were leaving buildings and neighborhoods like Brownsville and the South Bronx. This would decrease already shrinking populations, he said, and allow the city to concentrate its services. Starr defended this policy as "planned migration," not forced resettlement.[79] Insensitivity, inertia, euphemistic rationalizations, political and bureaucratic complexities continued to keep the crucial problems of employment and housing virtually intractable. In 1981, twenty-four projects involving job training, new housing construction and old housing rehabilitation, which had been in the planning stages for years, were all still "held up."[80]

A coalition of thirty-five churches in East Brooklyn, most of them in Brownsville, determined late in 1981 to do what many experts had told them was impossible: build affordable housing for low and moderate income families. The Nehemiah project, aptly named after the biblical prophet who rebuilt the walls of ancient Jerusalem, broke ground in October 1982 for the first home—a three-bedroom brick town house that sold for $39,000. To qualify, families had to have incomes of $20 to $40,000 a year, and a $5,000 down payment. The church coalition amassed an $8 million revolving fund to finance construction through loans from the Roman Catholic Diocese of Brooklyn and the Episcopal Church. Brownsville congregations taxed them-

selves at a rate of $12 per year for each family. The state guaranteed
low-interest loans and the city donated the land. "It was an idea whose
time had come," said an organizer for the East Brooklyn churches.
"People who were previously locked out of owning equity in this
economy now have a piece of the pie." By the end of 1987 there were
1,050 Nehemiah houses in Brownsville.

Given the fact that Nehemiah construction can only produce 14.6
new dwellings per acre in a city with a severe housing shortage, and
given the fact that families earning under $20,000 are excluded, there
was and still is some concern over how appropriate these suburban-
type developments are for all of Brownsville. But the Nehemiah houses
are apparently helping make Brownsville once again a working-class
and lower middle-class neighborhood rather than exclusively poor.
"The neat brick Nehemiah homes," the *New York Times* reported recently, "have made Brownsville a neighborhood of hope reincarnated."[81]

Hope was reincarnated, too, in Public School 332 in Brownsville
between 1981 and 1987. Inheriting an unstable, nearly chaotic school
situation in 1981, Hispanic principal Anthony Amato helped turn P.S.
332 into "the pride of Brownsville." The school at 51 Christopher
Avenue is in "one of the poorest neighborhoods in the city." The
students all qualified for free breakfasts and lunches at school and
fewer than a dozen in 1987 had two parents at home. "When I got
there, I had only one ace in the hole, Amato said, "a sixth grade with
large students. So I started with physical achievements. We made a
basketball team, the 332 All-Stars. And they were the champions in
the first year." Amato was opting for the classic "recreational solution,"
but he did not see it as a panacea. He recruited a science teacher who
set up a zoology center, and he brightened the place with bulletin
boards filled with student work. The new principal also established a
daily ritual of morning line-up and silent procession to class. He put
"unabashed emphasis on test-taking skills." The stress, Amato said,
"which is frowned on by some educators, was essential for the credibility of the students and the school." By 1986, education officials
labeled Brownsville's P.S. 332 "a model school."[82]

One other "success story" needs telling here not only because it
suggests another hopeful possibility for Brownsville but also because it

bears some extraordinary resemblances to the story of Doc Baroff and the Brownsville Boys Club.

When Christopher Armstrong, a resident of Amboy Street in Brownsville, was fifteen years old in 1977, he organized a softball team. "I was fed up with being bored," Armstrong said in a 1985 interview. "Everybody was bored and getting into trouble. The crime rate here [was and still] is sky high. The police statistics show the crimes [were] committed by young men—boys, really." There was nothing else for poor Brownsville boys to do: no Boy Scouts, no YMCA, no park activities. In 1979 at the age of seventeen, Christopher Armstrong decided it would take more than a softball team to help neighborhood boys. After long hours of study in the library, he drew up the papers to form the Brownsville Youth Organization, a nonprofit group. He recruited teammates and other boys to fix up the playground behind Public School 183 and to make it usable for softball. Six years later it still had its problems: innumerable sink holes, and an old handball wall standing conspicuously and inappropriately in left-center field. After forming the Brownsville Youth Organization, Armstrong sought contributions of money and material from local businesses. The softball team became a league, then two leagues.

Armstrong developed a public relations group of several of the ballplayers. They attended dinners and ceremonies at which they accepted donations and gave speeches. "You meet a lot of important people," said Kemah Jones, a fifteen-year-old player. The food is great, too. But you have to play it off a little, you know and not pig out." The organization receives contributions from two hundred businesses ranging from Chase Manhattan Bank to Rudy's Coffee Shop and a board of directors has been assembled including officers of corporations, banks and utility companies.

Three hundred youngsters were playing in the softball league in the summer of 1985, and the organization said it had had two thousand participants in all of its programs, playing ball, putting out a newsletter, videotaping games, and running a youth theatre. Armstrong, who accepts no money for his work, has also secured space in two basements across the street from the schoolyard, and he furnished them for a school tutoring program. He checks everyone's report card. One night in the summer of 1985, after softball practice, an adult from the neighborhood stopped by and said, "I thank God for this. It gives the kids something to do and keeps them from getting into trouble and getting hurt. These boys didn't ask to be born here."[83]

The self-help, peer-group dimensions of the Brownsville Youth Organization, the fundraising, the selfless commitment of the leadership, and the sports, are direct reminders of the boys of 1940s Brownsville. Community activists like Christopher Armstrong, Joseph Richardson, the staff of P.S. 332, the East Brooklyn Coalition of Churches, and the Brownsville Community Center are among the individuals and groups who represent the resilience, imagination, and mutual-aid orientation of some of Brownsville's largely black and Hispanic residents. These are important similarities between the activists in today's Brownsville, and the Jewish organizers who preceded them.

There are, however, many differences which continue to make the task of the nonwhite, non-Jewish leaders and doers much harder. They face, of course, a radically different cultural and class constituency. Blacks, particularly, have had a history, especially in the twentieth century, which moved against family stability. Anthony Amato's students and Christopher Armstrong's ballplayers, unlike the Jewish youngsters of 1940s Brownsville, were more often than not members of households without fathers. The current consensus in social science scholarship is that strong, stable families have been characteristic of "successful" minorities. The Jewish experience and more recent examples of several Asian immigrant groups, with tightly knit family structures providing both secure environments for children, and distinct economic advantages, tend to reinforce the findings of the scholarly studies.[84]

Family history made a difference. So did religious culture. Black Christianity, a viable and coherent synthesis of African tradition, white Christianity, and the experiences of everyday black life, helped adherents cope; and it did nourish, through the black church, civil rights activism; but black Christianity did not have at its center the dynamic secular messianism of modern Judaism which moved many twentieth century Jews to act upon the belief that change, even revolutionary change, was possible.[85]

Jews, in the old countries, in the 1880s and 1890s, often impelled by secular messianism and the injunction of *tikn olam* (the repair or improvement of the world) were disproportionately represented in trade unionism, radical politics, and revolutionary movements. Although the vast majority of Jews, including those who come to the United States, were not radicals, they were very much influenced by radicals. And in America they were particularly politically active.[86] Blacks had had some experience of political participation, too, beginning dramatically as free persons recently liberated from slavery in the era of post–Civil War Reconstruction; but the socioeconomic realities of life in the South forced blacks into long periods of quiescence.[87]

Jews also had more experience with organizing self-help. Transients everywhere in the diaspora before the mass migration to America, Jews in Eastern Europe were forced to live apart from "host" societies, and forced to develop modes of self-government. Their *shtetlekh* (small towns) were run by *kehillot* (community councils) and were permeated with committees devoted to specific collective responsibilities. In America, almost immediately, Jews reestablished their organizations and created new ones—*landsmanshaftn*, mutual-aid and burial societies, free loan associations, and institutions for helping those more recently arrived.[88]

A significant percentage of Jews had come to America after having taken a series of steps toward modernization and urbanization in the old countries. Almost all Jews in those countries had also been prohibited from owning land and were channeled into towns, some into cities. Whether Jews came from cities or from *shtetlekh*, they brought with them experiences and attitudes acquired in crafts and petty commerce and even light industry. These would serve them relatively well in the urban Northeast where in the late nineteenth and early twentieth centuries, the skills they possessed were in great demand. Exploited and buffeted by the vicissitudes of seasonal garment work, Jews nonetheless were relatively consistently employed. Many with commercial backgrounds, were also self-employed. They built small businesses through self-exploitation, the help of family, and free loans from communal organizations. They sustained themselves in what constituted an ethnic economy.[89] Moreover, despite a strained relationship, the East European Jews ultimately received significant support and aid in the process of acculturation from the German Jews who had established themselves here earlier, and had become a moderately prosperous community by the mid-nineteenth century.[90]

Some East European Jews from the Lower East Side came to Brownsville at the turn of the century as a small move up the socioeconomic ladder. Others after "failing" elsewhere, came looking for new opportunities, and still others came directly from Europe. Although by the 1930s, Jews who stayed in Brownsville were mainly working class and relatively impoverished, they continued to maintain the ethnic economy, living and working in the same neighborhood, employed in Jewish enterprise and industry. The worst off were rescued economically to some extent by communal *tsedaka*, New Deal programs, and war work.

Unlike the Jews, blacks (as well as Hispanics) migrated in the main from agrarian economies and brought with them few commercial or industrial skills. Moreover, by the time the great masses of blacks— four million between 1940 and 1970—reached the North and Brownsville, the war work boom was over. Not only less experienced in commerce and industry than the Jews, these unskilled rural blacks were also more disadvantaged than the immigrant peasants who preceded them between forty and ninety years earlier. The newcomers faced a much more urbanized and industrialized setting, with a much more intensified demand for skilled and semiskilled labor.

In addition to facing a less favorable economic environment, blacks experienced severe prejudice and discrimination. Though anti-Semitism was a powerful sentiment (particularly in the 1920s and 1930s) which imposed significant social and economic barriers for Jews, blacks faced a racism more endemic, more virulent, more deeply institutionalized and more disabling.

Late arrival, lack of skills, and pervasive race discrimination were all factors that contributed to the continuing incarceration of disproportionate numbers of blacks in the lower class, with all of its attendant problems. Herbert Gans and other sociologists have argued persuasively that there is an "absolute qualitative difference between the lower-class subculture and all the others." People in the lower class try, like people in other classes, to cope with existing structural realities and to make life as bearable as possible. That they fail to succeed is "largely the result of the intense deprivations," particularly occupational, with which they are saddled. Unskilled jobs, sporadically available work, and long-term unemployment add up to economic insecurity and instability, and produce a "subculture overlaid with pathology."

The consequences of intense deprivation—alcoholism, desertion, drug abuse, crime and the stigma of criminal records—in turn have consequences which make it even more difficult for lower-class people to take advantage of opportunities for improvement, even if they become available.[91] The easy accessibility to drugs, for example, partly produced by organized crime's systemic role in heroin distribution, and the availability of crack and other crime-causing substances is a new pathology, a new element of urban unhappiness with which earlier immigrant groups did not have to cope.[92] This is not an argument that there is an incorrigible "culture of poverty." Many in the lower class, particularly the vast majority of its women, have working-class aspirations. They do not appear to be content, in the least, with the lower-class subculture or the female-based family and they try to see that their children escape it.[93] As we have seen, they are up against very heavy odds in Brownsville, as elsewhere in urban America.

There are some blacks who have demonstrated significant degrees of economic and social mobility in areas of the United States, including Brownsville and neighboring East Flatbush. These blacks are, in the main, West Indians, most of whom are descended from persons who moved from the islands to the American northeast between 1900 and 1924. Unlike native-born blacks, 80 percent of the West Indian blacks came from cities. Their experience in slavery was also different from that of slaves in the American South. West Indian slaves had been assigned land and some unsupervised time to raise their own food. They sold surpluses in the markets and bought amenities for themselves. It appears too that they were able, in this "free space," to continue to employ the traditional West African "rotating credit association." Later they used this device, as did other immigrant groups from southern China, Japan, Korea, and Vietnam, as a principal means for capitalizing small business.[94] American-born blacks apparently did not maintain a comparable institution.

The disproportionate success of the West Indian blacks suggests that race discrimination is not necessarily an *absolutely* fatal handicap in the American economy. But it needs to be pointed out that the good fortune of the West Indian businessmen, landlords, doctors, lawyers, grocers, and tailors in the United States is dependent on a large black clientele and market. West Indians who migrated to England with its much smaller black population are not nearly so successful.[95] Race discrimination can still play a role in retarding economic mobility. Blacks in Brownsville continue to be burdened with the consequences of race discrimination, past and present, including lack of job training and general political neglect. Brownsville, as we have seen, shows some signs of resurgence. But it has a long way to go to recover from its slide into a lower-class neighborhood, and to regain its working-class character. "The decline of Brownsville started," one black minister declared in 1968, "when the Jews began moving out." The "Jewish population moved," added a black teacher with seventeen years of service in the local schools, "and took all their institutions with them."[96] With more commercial experience and economic stability, more experience in politics and in the organizing of communal mutual-aid, more employability and social acceptability, a long-standing, more complex religious culture permeated with ethical injunctions, and a more stable family structure, the Jews were indeed a rare breed. Given this background, it is understandable that Jewish Brownsville produced more upward mobility and many fewer serious social problems than black Brownsville, or for that matter, than many white ethnic neighborhoods.

Class was, and is, important in impeding or enhancing occupational and social mobility. Ethnic culture, too, was and is important. "There are different heritages with certain common experiences and aspirations" and, as more than one interpreter of American ethnic history has told us, "some are better adapted to certain circumstances than others."[97] Mobility and acculturation were never as rapid or as sure for the vast majority of ethnic Americans, black or white, as has been traditionally believed.[98] That disproportionate numbers of the children of Jewish immigrants were able to succeed in a class system which, in effect, is "moderately restrictive and fundamentally segregationist," is explained in part by an extraordinarily fortuitous constellation of Jewish experiences and values.[99] These experiences and values also help us understand why Jews in Brownsville, when they felt the need, were able to produce the nurturing, activist Brownsville Boys Club, an extensive, long-lasting, authentic self-help community in microcosm.

In 1988 New York City undertook what it saw as an attempt to increase the possibility of black mobility in Brownsville. Noting inordinate rates of crime, drug addiction, and unemployment in the area around the Brownsville Recreation Center, the Parks Commission initiated a $7.5 million restoration of the facility.[100] Refurbishing was in order. A visit in 1987, and a talk with William Hurley, the director of the center since 1956, revealed a physically deteriorated, underused and inadequately staffed building and program.[101] In January of 1989 Mayor Edward Koch and Parks Commissioner Henry Stern, wielding a large hammer and symbolic golden nails, marked the start of the renovations which will include the pool, gymnasium, locker rooms, and rooftop recreation area. Although the Center will also house pre-school and day care programs, the emphasis, apparently, will continue to be recreation.[102] In the 1950s this emphasis proved inadequate, if not tragic. Perhaps by this second time around, more has been learned, and farce will be avoided.

An upgrading of recreational facilities, without accompanying "renovations" in job training, income levels, health care, housing and education, will not solve the problems of Brownsville's black population. Moreover, where poverty has led to what sociologist William J. Wilson calls a "clustering and concentration of social casualties," societal intervention is required to deal with the *consequences* of the poverty as well as the causes.[103] Here evidence from many parts of the world suggests that agencies and government programs do best in terms of improving the material and moral quality of people's lives when they tap into the existing informal helping networks of a community.[104] Even in impoverished, transient Brownsville there is still evidence of self-help initiative. Agencies that take advantage of this, that recruit internal caretakers and informal "natural" peer helpers, like Christopher Armstrong or Doc Baroff, are likely to be more effective. Social care delivery systems that develop nonpaternalistic approaches, that lighten the heavy hand of bureaucracy, and use at least part of their resources to support self-help groups, appear to have the best chance of succeeding.[105] The residents of black Brownsville need a refurbished recreation center. They also need more basic benefits (jobs, housing, health care), as well as resources to support self-help networks. Such a combination has at least a chance of avoiding "rotten outcomes," a chance of promoting increased self-esteem and the kind of economic and occupational mobility that allows the recovery of dignity and social health.

CHAPTER 7

Livelihoods, Longings, and Legacies: Brownsville Boys Now

Immigrants arrived, with weddings soon after
And Brownsville grew louder with our children's laughter.
Beachclubs, vacations, were out of our sphere
Concrete, open hydrants, so very near.
This was our beach, I wish to make clear.

Our interests were simple, hang-ups so few
Baseball, food, an occasional brew.
Coke was a drink, grass was just green
No way, no wish, to wind up unclean.

We all were liberals, with an unflinching passion
Democrats were flawless, that was the fashion.
One day we awoke, little boys no more
Families of our own, ambitions galore.

We moved to the suburbs, but just never the same
So, now to our kids, we do hereby proclaim,

Take your beaches, camps, vacations and all
Oh to be on Powell Street hearing the cry

"Play Ball"[1]

—AL APTER,
UNPUBLISHED POEM

The Brownsville Boys of the 1940s moved "up" and out to the suburbs, but their lives are still deeply informed by the values and simple
pleasures of the old neighborhood. And their attitudes, activities and

189

rhetoric continue to reflect the indelible experiences of their adolescence—saturation in *yiddishkayt*, intense peer-group togetherness, and participation in the Brownsville Boys Club.

The boys rarely rose from rags to riches but they did move, at least, from rages to respectability. Nearly 22 percent are social work professionals, lawyers, engineers, college professors, dentists, and accountants. More than 30 percent own their own small businesses, and 23 percent are teachers, principals, educational supervisors, and civil servants. Another 20 percent are corporate executives, managers and salesmen.

Moderately prosperous and often in work they enjoy (or enjoyed—approximately 20 percent are retired) these men have also managed to build fulfilling, enduring marriages. Many have done this with women who had grown up in Brownsville or neighboring East New York. "After all," as Bernie Stuffer put it, "who had carfare?" Nine percent have been divorced. That is three times higher than their parent's rate, but it is disproportionately low compared to the rate for their non-Jewish peers. Several BBCers echoed Carl London who said, "as of this date none of us [former teammates] has divorced, and the rewards are great."[2] They take satisfaction too in the fact that their children have also done well. Eighty-three percent of the sons and daughters have completed college and 44 percent have at least one graduate degree. More than 30 percent are doctors, lawyers, dentists, engineers, college professors, and accountants, and another 22 percent are in educational or social work.

The former BBCers have good jobs, meaningful marriages, and successful children. But out there in Jericho and Douglaston, in Bellmore and East Meadow, and even in Canarsie and Howard Beach, there is a longing. Dealing with taxes and crabgrass, and neighbors, few of whom ever shared a common social or childhood experience with them, these former Brownsville residents feel the need to come together with one another often to socialize and especially to talk, mostly about the old neighborhood. From "the corner of Powell and Riverdale," one BBCer wrote, "where seven of us, Good Friends [and members of the Mustangs], used to hang out, came a life-long bond. We have been getting together socially for thirty years." Brownsville was hardly utopia or "Green Pastures." But a childhood marked by

intense friendships, on streets filled with play and laughter and challenge, and outside the candy stores on corners where the games and
kibbitzing went on for hours, is an experience not easily discarded.
Nor is the experience of having together created the BBC.

At annual reunions of the BBC Alumni Association in the Catskill
Mountains, at occasional breakfasts in New York City, and throughout
the year at innumerable social gatherings of former sets of teammates,
they meet to talk. The conversation lasts late into the evening and even
into the early morning hours and ranges from how Arthur Caplin's
jaws would bulge chewing on a penny's worth of "shoe leather," to
how Harold Reisman and Sam Guber got caught stealing Heinz pick-
les at the 1939 World's Fair. Somehow year after year there are always
enough stories to avoid repetition, and some that deserve retelling.
Who wouldn't want to hear again about the vicious slow ball of "One
Pitch" Charlie, two-hand touch with cereal boxes, Hymie Shapiro's
laugh, the fight between Dutch and Dubby, or those great pickup
basketball games in Nanny Goat Park?

The memories are long and deep. Few can forget the stickball
fanaticism of Stan ("Wee Wee") Shapiro, or how "Frenchy" Resnick
did play-by-play reenactments of the Brooklyn Dodger games, with
his lively descriptions and that unique "knock" he could make with his
tongue to simulate a base hit. Some still tell the story of how Stan
Shapiro became Wee Wee. Every day at noon Stan left P.S. 184 and
ran home to "walk" his mutt Popsie. Needing to get back to school
quickly, Stan coaxed loudly, "Wee-wee, wee-wee." Inevitably the
older boys tagged him with that name, and for years, together with
Stan, they continued to laugh about it.

And how about the time in the P.S. 184 school yard that "Lefty the
Lob" Ribakowitz belted a "spaldeen" so far that it hit above the statute
on the Walkins Street side? Or the many times that cabbages destined
to become sauerkraut at Leibowitz's Pickle Works on Newport Street,
rolled off the delivery ramps and ended up instead in soup pots on
Stone Avenue or Sackman Street? George Berch still remembers the
circus elephants in the freight yard on Junius Street, and Murray
("Injun") Rosen, the telephone number of Gorgeous Gus's candy store
on Powell and Lott, where the boys discussed everything from girls to
the D-day invasion. They are still talking at every chance they get.

The Siegels, the Schmarens, the Feldmans, the Pinchuks, and the Rosens have never quite left Brownsville. A part of them wants to be there still, fourteen years old and playing basketball or stickball. But when they are confronted with the realities of present day Brownsville, they wince or shrug or sigh. A small number react as if they have been cheated by what happened to *their* neighborhood—as if Brownsville had been "stolen" from them. BBCer Morton Werbel continued to maintain a lucrative law practice on Rockaway Avenue long after he had moved to Nassau County in 1955. In 1979 it was "necessary" for him to shoot two of five armed holdup men who invaded his office.[3] Gerry ("Sheiky") Lenowitz moved to Far Rockaway partly because of the "dangerous conditions" in Brownsville. So did college basketball star Sidney Tanenbaum. Twice winner of the Haggerty Award as the outstanding player in the metropolitan New York area, Tanenbaum opened a small business in Far Rockaway, in a section that fairly soon began to "run down." Described by his son as an "unofficial social worker" and by the police as "something of a benefactor in the neighborhood," Tanenbaum made frequent handouts and "loans" to street people. He turned down a woman one day in 1987 whom he had helped too many times in the past. When Tanenbaum turned his back, she plunged a knife into him. The recipient of the 1947 Bar Kochba Award as America's Outstanding Jewish Athlete was dead. Sheiky Lenowitz moved to Florida.[4]

Although there is some rancor, most often when the men talk about Brownsville, they talk about the old Brownsville, and it is without bitterness or resentment. Rather it is with warmth and fondness. Beneath the occasional sentimentality that surfaces when the men talk, lies a basic sincerity, the willingness to share—even to reexamine. And there is, too, the expression of wonderment at how so many boys from such pinched circumstances were able to "be good" and to "make good."

Some neighborhood boys, even BBC boys, were, of course, not so "good." Beyond the handfuls who broke windows, gambled, "acted out" at school, or shoplifted at Woolworth's, there was an even smaller number who committed more serious offenses and continued as adults to live at the edges of the underworld. At least four former BBCers are directly involved in organized crime. One, "Herbie," as a youngster was almost killed when he tried, rashly enough, to stick up some neighborhood bookmakers. He was badly beaten up, but apparently, the mob admired his moxie and recruited him as a collector. In 1948 Herbie was charged with assault and robbery, but was not convicted. More recently he has been involved in the underside of professional boxing, and in mob control of product distribution for concessions at race tracks and sports complexes.[5] Another former BBCer, with many friends in professional sports, for a time managed boxers. The FBI photographed him having dinner with Gaspar di Gregorio, head of the Bonnano "family" and Tommy Eboli, one of the acting bosses of the Genovese clan.[6]

Exceptionally distressing to a community permeated with progressive political ideologies and militant unionism was the case of two former BBCers who were indicted in 1954 on charges of conspiracy, bribery, and forgery committed against union workers. Employed by the International Ladies Garment Workers Union as accountants, these men allegedly kept two sets of books; one set consistently understated wages paid by at least five dress manufacturers, thereby allowing the manufacturers to pay less into the welfare and retirement fund maintained by the union's Dress Joint Board.[7]

An equally painful example of a Brownsville boy "gone bad" is the case of Long Island University basketball star Jack Goldsmith. If unions and progressive politics were important in Brownsville, basketball, as Arthur Spetter and others put it, "was next to God in our neighborhood." Yet the Brownsville-born-and-raised Goldsmith was at the center of the metropolitan area college basketball bribery scandals in the late 1940s and early 1950s. The third of a series of these scandals over a five-year period erupted in 1951 when student players at Manhattan College were charged with accepting bribes to shave points or throw games.[8] District Attorney Frank Hogan's investigation soon disclosed that New York University, City College of New York, and Long Island University players were also implicated in what appeared to be widespread corruption. When Sherman White of LIU reputed to be the number one college player in the nation, admitted, in February of 1951, receiving several thousand dollars for his involvement in seven fixes over a two-year stretch, he rocked the world of college sports. His confession forced an intensification of the investigation.[9]

Soon the newspapers were filled with the names of Jewish boys like

Alvin Roth of CCNY, Harvey Schaff of NYU, and Louis Lipman of LIU, charged or indicted or convicted for bribery or conspiracy. Jews in the 1940s and 1950s were still very much "overrepresented" in college basketball in the Northeast, and it was highly improbable that a scandal there would leave them untouched. Some college officials and coaches, however, apparently anxious to find scapegoats pointed to the "problem of unsupervised basketball during the summer months in the 'borscht circuit,' [as] one of the primary causes of the scandals." Phog Allen, the University of Kansas (Lawrence) coach said, smugly and prematurely, "out here in the Midwest, this condition of course doesn't prevail, but in the East, the boys, particularly those who participate in the resort hotel leagues during the summer months are thrown into an environment which cannot help but breed [this] evil."[10] Several months later Allen's self-assurance would wither as charges were brought against players at the University of Kentucky, Oregon State, and Bradley University—in the center of Peoria, Illinois.

On April 21, 1951, Jack Goldsmith—Jackie, to the Brownsville boys he played with in Nanny Goat Park and P.S. 184—was arrested as he stepped from his apartment at 683 Stone Avenue. He was charged with bribing four LIU players in the 1948–49 season. Jackie had graduated from Thomas Jefferson High School and gone on to LIU after three years in the Coast Guard. Standing only five feet, seven inches, Goldsmith had an excellent set shot and could bring the audibly gasping LIU fans to their feet by scoring from as far "outside" as forty-five feet. As a sophomore in the 1945–46 season he put in an astounding 395 points, becoming the school's leading scorer.[11] At the very height of that season Goldsmith spoke at the Stone Avenue Library to a BBC meeting of "seventy five of his admirers." You "boys out here," Goldsmith told them, "should learn how to take the one-handed set shots up the middle instead of hook shots. The Western teams have had quite a success with it."[12]

Jack Goldsmith that same night agreed to help the club by coaching the 150-pound BBC basketball team. The boys were ecstatic. Unfortunately, Goldsmith, who is remembered by Stan ("Wee Wee") Shapiro as "able, easily, to shoot 250 to 300 baskets in a row, especially when he was betting money on it," spent precious little time coaching the boys. He played erratically as an LIU Junior and did not play

basketball at all in his Senior year. He had become in the district
attorney's words, "a well-known associate of gamblers and bookmakers
in the Brownsville section of Brooklyn." After Goldsmith's arrest it
became clear that the "Brownsville Bomber," as he was affectionately
known, had been involved in fixes since his outstanding sophomore
year. Goldsmith was indicted on April 23, 1951, and though he showed
only defiance and apparently no remorse, he finally admitted his guilt
after a year.[13]

These instances of boys "gone bad" are, as we have seen, not
reflective of the behavior of those who were part of the BBC or even of
Jewish youth generally in Brownsville. Max Stavitsky undoubtedly
exaggerated, when he bragged that "ninety-nine percent of us turned
out good," but his point is nonetheless valid. The Jewish street-corner
boys of Brownsville not only "turned out good," they, as indicated
earlier, "made good." It is instructive to compare that experience with
the experience of corner boys in other depression-era communities.
When Gilbert Sorrentino was growing up in Italian South Brooklyn,
for example,

People lived lives as inevitable as those in a tribal society; from street corners
to the corner candy store, to the poolroom and neighborhood saloons, the
haphazard and frustrating "dating"—and thence to marriage. In those days of
the thirties and forties, young couples settled in to the trap of the neighborhood. . . . It was a kind of deadly life which spawned . . . "characters." They
were merely normal denizens of the place, their eccentricities ragged flutter-
ings of the ego in the face of the vast ennui in which they were caught.[14]

And in sociologist William F. Whyte's "Cornerville," the Italian
North End of Boston,

The gangs grew up on the corner and remained there with remarkable persistence from early boyhood until the members reached their late twenties or
early thirties. In the course of years some groups were broken up by the
movement of families away from Cornerville, and the remaining members
merged with gangs on near-by corners; but frequently movement out of the
district does not take the corner boy away from his corner. . . .
   Home plays a very small role in the group activities of the corner boy. . . .
And his friends always go to his corner first when they want to find him. . . .
The married man regularly sets aside one evening a week to take out his wife.
. . . Some corner boys devote more attention to their wives than others, but,

married or single, the corner boy can be found on his corner almost every
night of the week.

One leader of corner boys told Whyte: "Fellows around here don't
know what to do except within a radius of about three hundred yards.
That's the truth, Bill. They come home from work, hang on the
corner, up a show [go uptown to see a movie], and they come back to
hang on the corner."[15] The corner boys of Jewish Brownsville, most
often, did not feel trapped in ennui. Through creating and running the
Brownsville Boys Club, Jack Leavitt remembered, "we got a sense that
we had control over our destinies. Everything we did seemed to count.
And what we did affected other people's lives."[16]

In Arthur Granit's novel *The Time of the Peaches*, on one extraordinary Brownsville block during the Depression, a peach tree grew up
miraculously out of the dirt between the cracks of the cement. The
tree was poisoned by a madwoman. But it eventually bloomed again.
The young protagonist, Usher, discovers that one of the peaches had a
thumbtack for a pit, and came to believe that the tree was nourished
by a box of tacks thrown into the street earlier. Usher was delighted
with the beauty and mystery and hopefulness of this miracle and tried
to gladden the hearts and minds of his downtrodden neighbors. But
his friends lost faith in his story and nothing on the block changed.
Usher himself grew disenchanted with flowering thumbtacks and concluded that misery is irreparable and unending and that acts of goodness are irrelevant.[17] Many of the young founders and framers and
1940s members of the Brownsville Boys Club came to a different
conclusion. They were aware that "damage" could and would continue
to be done, and that goodness could be poisoned; but these boys
influenced by Jewish spiritual injunctions believed it was possible to
make repairs and even improvements.

When energetic and creative Doc Baroff, the single-most important
catalyst in the founding of the club, insisted that it was a duty "to do
good on earth," he was reflecting the prophetic dimensions of the
Hebrew Scriptures. Similarly, when Norman Goroff, whose dedication to the club and its role in social justice, talked about "building a
better world," he was invoking the Jewish concept of *tikn olam*. And
Abe Rubenfeld drew on the Talmudic teaching that "to save even one

life is to save the world," when he said simply: "We wanted to help the younger kids coming up behind us." These sons of Jewish immigrants and political progressives had wanted to play ball, but they also had talked about "mission," and about "making a difference," for themselves and for others. They did not merely talk. They built a club that was a successful mutual-aid society and an authentic nurturing community in microcosm. In doing this on their own, the boys came to feel empowered and responsible. The club brought them benefits and desired "privileges," and enabled them to develop and reinforce particular sensitivities and talents. They used these in entertaining and nurturing other younger boys, and in community work, and later in pursuing careers. The process intensified a sense of commitment to the welfare of others at the same time that it reinforced the self-esteem and ambition of individuals.

The boys continued to carry what they had learned—the combination of individual aspiration and community orientation, as part of their cultural baggage. As businessmen, professionals, and civil servants, these former BBCers, having won a fair portion of the American prize, credit Brownsville and the BBC for their direction and achievement. Most still feel an obligation to "give something back." A great many try to sustain community in their post-Brownsville locations and in their lives generally. As early as 1948 they had founded an alumni association that performed a variety of community services, including fund-raising for the Brownsville Boys Club for ten years until most of the founders and framers had removed from Brownsville.[18] In 1966 when they revived the alumni association, the BBCers were anxious to do two things: to see and talk with one another again on some regular basis, and "to help the club that meant so much to us in our youth."[19] Over 350 people, some from as far away as Atlanta and Los Angeles, arrived at the Congress Hotel near Kennedy Airport for a reunion/reorganization meeting in March. "It was super," said George Levine, "Just like being back on the corner or in Nanny Goat Park."[20] Almost immediately the alumni, led by Joe Feldman, began again to raise funds for the Brownsville Boys Club and for "worthy community projects" elsewhere. In 1967 they contributed to the Annual BBC Interfaith Holiday Party and set up a scholarship fund to send youngsters with developmental problems to camp. At the suggestion of Vice-

Martin Kronenberg being sworn in as president of the BBC Alumni Association in 1956, along with executive officers, Isidore ("Red") Karbel, Joseph ("Yussie") Feldman, and Jacob ("Yankel") Deutch. Judge Nathaniel Kaplan (left) presided over ceremony in the gymnasium of the two-year-old Brownsville Recreation Center. A buffet dinner for over two hundred guests followed. (Courtesy of Martin Kronenberg.)

President Sid Siegel, the alumni in 1970, "adopted" as its special charity, the Brooklyn School for Special Children. Headed by Rabbi Morris A. Block, the school was designed for developmentally disabled youngsters. By 1976, the wives of the former BBCers had formed the Women's Philanthropic chapter of the Alumni Association, to do their own fund-raising for charities, most of them related to disabled children[21]

The process of receiving and passing on had always been part of the Brownsville Boys Club ethic. Sometimes the getting and giving was quite direct: Baroff, for example, nurtured Kronenberg, Kronenberg helped Kushner; Diamond influenced Zeplin, and Zeplin aided Benitez. Often the "giving back" took the form of working for the BBC as volunteers or professionals. Dozens including Sheiky Lenowitz, Joe Feldman, and Lenny Dryansky did it this way. Jack Oventhal served for a time as the playground director at Nanny Goat Park and went on to work for the Police Athletic League under the supervision of yet another former BBCer, Irving Forman.

It is no accident that ultimately a significant number of the boys— approximately 25 percent—chose the helping professions. The BBC youngsters like so many college educated, second generation Jews were culturally predisposed in this direction.[22] They had been raised in a politically progressive Jewish community, in a context of Jewish ethical teaching and behavior, and they were surrounded by institutions for mutual-aid. These boys were virtually primed to be attracted to social work and teaching. In the late 1940s both of these careers emphasized a connection to social action and social change. Their intense involvement in the BBC reflected and reinforced this attraction. "Looking back on my experience," said Isidore ("Red") Karbel in 1953, "I now realize how greatly the Club's activities influenced my choice of a career. . . . Working and playing together with children of varied backgrounds was a rich democratic experience. The enjoyment and interests I developed led me to choose working with children as my life's work."[23]

Instructing "tough kids in arts and crafts [also] inspired [Harold Radish] to become a school teacher"; and educator Sid Gerchick, who was sworn in as a principal by Abe Stark in 1966, named six other boys on his Brownsville block who had become principals, superintendents, or deputy superintendents of schools. Gerchick in assessing this remarkable outcome correctly pointed to the influence of parental emphasis on education, the Jewish cultural environment and the club. Irwin Millman who "gave back" by working as a day camp supervisor at the BBC in 1953 also went on into education. He carried the BBC tradition with him. Millman is now the Brooklyn Borough Superintendent for Afterschool Sports Activity.[24]

Those who became policemen like Milt Kirschner, Fred Feit, Leo Yedin, and Irving Forman, also saw *that* choice as "giving back." Forman, Kirschner and Feit worked directly with youth through the Police Department's Youth Division and Juvenile Aid Bureau. The Brief brothers also chose to minister aid directly, Seymour as a social worker, and Neil as a Rabbi. Bernard Berman, the director of Jewish Family Services on Staten Island is certain his vocational orientation came from Brownsville and the BBC, "the career training ground," as he called it, "for an awful lot of people."[25] Norman Goroff, professor of social work, and Irving Levine, director of the American Jewish Committee's Institute for American Pluralism, both of whom lived in the same building on Christoper Avenue with the Brief boys, are emphatic about the BBC–social work connection in their lives. Levine said directly that his experience with the Brownsville Boys Club from the time he was fifteen was "preprofessional social work." And he is described by Doc Baroff as "using in his American Jewish Committee work, Boys Club techniques with fancy names."[26]

Technique, of course, is only a very small part of what these boys who went on to be educators and social workers learned in Jewish Brownsville and in the BBC. They "learned," as Lulu Rubenfeld put it, "what life is all about—what you can do for other people."[27] BBCers who chose the helping professions were not the only ones who demonstrated that they had learned this lesson. Significant numbers stayed active in philanthropic endeavors, lodges, local civic associations, and synagogue work. Several like Jack Ergas continue to volunteer their time to coach recreation center basketball teams. Lenny ("Bee Bop," for his love of jazz) Cohen, who is president of an electronics corporation which serves the television industry, has been officially cited, twice, for his commitment to hiring handicapped workers. Al Bart, the owner of a growing printing enterprise, also hires handicapped and minority workers, "at every opportunity. It comes from my upbringing in impoverished Brownsville. Actually we were 'wealthy' because we had each other. I was there, I needed, I received. Now I try to give back."[28]

When the Brownsville Boys Club Alumni Association in October of 1984, honored Jacob ("Doc") Baroff, who had done so much of the giving in the 1940s, he said that although he "never shot one basket in the 'promised land' of the new building, the *journey* was worth it." He thanked the assembled hundreds for "taking the trip" with him. It was a special trip. The boys had helped one another in innumerable ways. They had sustained each other and derived dignity from their working and playing together. They were reinforced in their understanding of human interdependence. They had experienced the joy of mutual-aid and commitment to community. Baroff, ever the director, concluded his talk by saying that the former BBCers ought to work hard to

*Jacob ("Doc") Baroff about to receive a plaque from Joseph ("Yussie") Feldman,
naming Baroff the BBC Alumni Association Man of the Year, at Brown's
Hotel in the Catskill Mountains of New York, October 1984. (Courtesy of
Jacob Baroff.)*

continue to "stay together and to continue to give to charity and to promote social welfare. This is our heritage."[29] The BBC Alumni Association between 1984 and 1988 contributed an average of $3,000 per year to the Brooklyn School for Special Children. And by 1989, the former BBCers were in the process of creating a foundation that would enable the organization to increase substantially its charitable giving, and to fund scholarships for deserving and needy youngsters.

If one had not gotten to know these men and the lives they had lived in Brownsville, one might be tempted to characterize their talk as mere *unreflective* nostalgia—an odd mix of present discontents, yearnings, and a sense of small paradises lost. Some writers, in fact, have pointed an accusing finger at urban America's nostalgia for the "old ethnic neighborhood." Sociologist Gerald Suttles, for example, complains that this kind of longing for "a past in which interpersonal relations and territorial solidarities were more fixed," blinds people to present realities and squelches the possibilities for a "creative, democratic reconstitution of the American city."[30]

Such complaints miss the positive, creative element in nostalgia. It need not be mere yearning or reminiscing. Nostalgia can also be an insistence that there are some things about the past worth recovering and preserving. We must surely agree that nostalgia *is* a looking back, that it signals some uneasiness about the present and the future, and that it represents a quest for continuity and relative certainty. And this kind of nostalgia did play a role in the renewal of interest in the Brownsville Boys Club Alumni Association. The men were, after all, explicit about the "wish to perpetuate the memories of our earlier years in Brownsville."[31] And it was significant that the association, after having dissolved in the 1950s, revived in the late 1960s. The Brownsville "boys" had become, by then, men in their forties, a significant transitional phase in the life cycle.[32] They had also experienced some rude transitions rendered by history. The widespread, long-term, racial upheavals in America's cities, the confusions, complexities, and moral challenges of the Vietnam War, and the general social disarray of the 1960s, promoted a powerful sense of cultural discontinuity and a longing for stability.

The Boys Club Alumni Association, reborn in a context of perceived disorder, was in part, an exercise in nostalgia—a link with the more stable "good old days." Dozens of men, Jewish and in their forties, who had never even been BBCers, some never even residents of Brownsville, poured into the Alumni Association looking for that link. But this nostalgia is not necessarily "false consciousness." Karl Marx, who presumably first used that term, complained, after all, that the speed and power with which the future overtakes us makes "all that is solid melt into air, all that is holy . . . profane."[33] Reflective nostalgia, the attempt to assuage apprehensions about what is to come by *retrieving* the value of what has been, can act as a temporary "brake on the headlong plunge into the future"—a brake that "influences some individuals and peoples to look before they knowingly leap."[34]

When the BBC men and their wives—who early on became an integral part of the camaraderie and interdependence—talk about family, friendship, self-help, a sense of mutual obligation, neighborhood, citizenship, coherence, commitment, loyalty, and spiritual rather than material riches, they are engaging in a dialog between their perceived past and the perceived future. They do not in this way reject the future; they try to bring to it some of what they see as worth salvaging from their past.

Their past in Brownsville had been powerfully influenced by Jewish religious culture, and by "the secret treasure of family and Jewish togetherness." No more than one of these boys chose the Orthodoxy of their grandparents, and few followed with any strict consistency the already modified ritual observances of their mothers and fathers. But virtually all identified strongly as Jews and continue to do so.

Rabbi Alter Landesman, the foremost historian of Brownsville, concluded that only a small proportion of Brownsville parents "were able to transmit to their American offspring a *full* appreciation of their rich Jewish cultural heritage."[35] No doubt. But parents had enveloped children in a Jewish community, a community of *yiddishkayt*, Jewish self-help institutions and ethical obligation—particularly *takhles*, *tsedaka*, and *tikn olam*. The boys in their peer groups, in the streets, on their teams, and sometimes at school, did develop a camaraderie and interdependence separate from the home. But they carried values absorbed in the context of family and Jewish community to their games and clubs and corners. Here the Brownsville boys forged a new *American* Jewish identity. They produced a viable and coherent synthesis of the Jewish culture they learned in the household and the culture and mores they learned in American streets and institutions. This new American Jewish identity was reflected in the behavior and lives of the boys who built the Brownsville Boys Club and fostered its social welfare activities. It continues to be reflected in the work and values of the men they became.

Interviews

Norman Adelman	June 18, 1989
Al Apter	April 4, 1988
Mendy Bacall	March 23,1988
Sol Bakalchuck	April 4, 1988
Jacob Baroff	July 6, 1987 and February 8, 1988
Al Bart	May 14, 1988
David Behar	May 4, 1988
George Berch	February 25, 1988
Seymour Berkowitz	June 14, 1988
Bernard Berman	April 3, 1988
Seymour Berman	May 10, 1988
Henry Brief	April 4, 1988
Neil Brief	October 13, 1988
Seymour Brief	March 10, 1987
William Brief	April 18, 1988
Martin Broschowitz	April 4, 1987
Al Cohen	October 11, 1987
Franklin Cohen	April 1, 1988
Leonard Cohen	April 12, 1987
Robert Cohen	April 28, 1988
Nathan Dassa	January 6, 1987
Jacob Deutch	October 19, 1986 and October 11, 1987
Leonard Dryansky	August 11, 1988
Alfred Eckert	November 20, 1987

Hyman Edelman	May 21, 1989
Joseph Feldman	September 22, 1986 and October 11, 1987
Irving Forman	June 27, 1987
Dudley Gaffin	June 20, 1987
James Vincent Genovese	May 21, 1989
Leonard Gerber	May 10, 1988
Sidney Gerchick	February 10, 1987
Irwin Gladstein	October 18, 1986 and April 10, 1987
Leon Glovsky	November 9, 1987
Norman Goroff	July 23, 1987
Herbert Grosswirth	February 10, 1987
Isidore Hertzberg	January 7, 1987
Ted Horn	October 18, 1986
William Hurley	January 27, 1988
Seymour Janovsky	August 9, 1988
Bernard Kaplan	February 8, 1987
Isidore Karbel	April 28, 1988
Reeba Karney	April 23, 1988
Milton Kirschner	March 9, 1987
Stanley Kirschner	April 3, 1988
Martin Kronenberg	January 13, 1987 and October 11, 1987
Lawrence Kushner	February 7, 1987
Jack Leavitt	February 25, 1988
Gerald Lenowitz	April 21, 1987
Isidore Lesovoy	November 4, 1986 and October 11, 1987
Irving Levenberg	May 21, 1989
George Levine (b. 1921)	October 25, 1986
George Levine (b. 1929)	January 24, 1988
Irving Levine	October 8, 1986 and April 11, 1988
Morris Levine	June 5, 1988
Alvin Matsil	February 11, 1987
Eli Matsil	February 10, 1987
Irwin Millman	February 5, 1988
Stanley Moel	May 21, 1989
Ruby Nudelman	March 17, 1987
Jack Oventhal	April 19, 1988
Charles Pinchuk	July 7, 1987

Harold Radish	March 12, 1987
Jerome Reiss	August 24, 1988
Seymour Ribakowitz	January 5, 1987
Donald Rosen	April 23, 1988
Mel Ross	May 3, 1987
Abe Rubenfeld	January 12, 1987
Louis Rudowsky	January 6, 1987
Jesse Salit	July 7, 1987
Irwin Sandler	April 8, 1987
Bernard Scharen	October 12, 1987
Seymour Schlosberg	April 3, 1988
George Schmaren	October 18, 1986 and October 11, 1987
Jack Schmaren	October 12, 1987
Stanley Shapiro	February 18, 1989
Sidney Siegel	September 22, 1986
Irving Sikora	February 14, 1988
Sam Simon	May 18, 1988
Seymour Smolin	March 16, 1987
John Snypes	April 7, 1988
Arthur Spetter	January 5, 1987
Max Stavitsky	October 11, 1987
Irwin Steltzer	May 21, 1989
Bernard Stuffer	May 11, 1988
Herman Thalen	January 10, 1988
Charles Trester	May 4, 1988
Edward Werbel	May 23, 1988
Morton Werbel	March 13, 1988
Benjamin Wernikoff	May 7, 1987
Al Yarinsky	April 11, 1987
Leo Yedin	May 7, 1987
Abe Zaslofsky	April 4, 1987
Leonard Zeplin	October 8, 1987

Questionnaires

More than two hundred men returned questionnaires which contained useful biographical information and relevant facts about the social, economic, and physical conditions of 1930s and 1940s Brownsville. Those listed below were somewhat more expansive and their responses contained unusually interesting or pertinent material.

Sol Altman	Fred Levenberg
David Behar	Carl London
George Benitez	Alvin Matsil
Neil Brief	Eli Matsil
Martin Broshowitz	Harold Radish
Murray Cutler	Abe Rubenfeld
Nathan Dassa	Edward Sanders
Ralph Delitsky	Stanley Shapiro
Sam Geller	Irving Sikora
Herbert Grosswirth	Sol Silverberg
Harold Hershenson	Charles Trester
Ted Horn	Morton Werbel
Milton Kapp	Ben Wernikoff
Milton Kirschner	Leonard Zeplin

ℛotes

Prologue

1. Many members of the alumni association in addition to meeting at the reunions and breakfasts see each other socially as individuals and as members of their former street-corner clubs on a regular basis. The alumni will be discussed primarily in the later sections of the book.

2. The club was interethnic and interracial; the founding generation, however, was entirely Jewish. And the membership continued to be 90 to 95 percent Jewish until the postwar era. See chaps. 4 and 5 for more on this.

3. Juvenile delinquency is a complex social, personal, and ideological problem, hard to define, hard to measure, hard to analyze. I have done some defining and analyzing, but not a great deal; that is not the primary purpose of the study. Wherever I have tangled with juvenile delinquency in the work, particularly in regard to public perceptions, I *have* made use of some of the available statistics, but only in combination with other persuasive, even if impressionistic evidence, and in combination with, I hope, common sense.

4. Robert E. Park and Herbert Miller, *Old World Traits Transplanted* (1921; reprint, New York: Arno, 1969); Robert E. Park, "Human Migration and the Marginal Man," *American Journal of Sociology* 23, no. 3 (May 1928): 881–93; Louis Wirth, *The Ghetto* (Chicago: University of Chicago Press, 1928); William I. Thomas and Florian Znaniecki, *The Polish Peasant in Europe and America*, 4 vols. (Boston: Richard G. Badger, Gorham Press, 1918–20); Lloyd Warner and Leo Srole, *The Social Systems of American Ethnic Groups* (New Haven: Yale University Press, 1945). For very recent works that grapple with definitions of ethnicity and prognostications about its social "usefulness" and resilience, see Alan Kraut, "My Daughter Tells Me You're Ethnic," *Journal of American Ethnic History* 7, no. 1 (Fall 1987): 74–82.

5. Milton Gordon, *Assimilation in American Life: The Role of Race, Religion, and National Origins* (New York: Oxford University Press, 1964); Rudolph J. Vecoli, "*Contadini* in Chicago: A Critique of *The Uprooted*," *Journal of American History* 51, no. 3 (December 1964): 404–17. Vecoli initiated a critical onslaught

of Oscar's Handlin's beautifully written but seriously flawed study of immigrant life, *The Uprooted: The Epic Story of the Great Migration That Made the American People* (Boston: Little, Brown, 1952). Handlin, most historians now agree, placed far too much emphasis on disorganization and discontinuity in immigrant life. By 1985 John Bodnar had developed a very different set of conclusions from Handlin's, hence his title *The Transplanted*. See n. 7 below. Deborah Dash Moore, *At Home in America: Second Generation Jews in New York* (New York: Columbia University Press, 1981) persuasively challenged the earlier notion of dissolution of ethnicity from generation to generation, and made a strong case for the idea of the reformulation of ethnic identity.

6. Rudolph J. Vecoli, "Ethnicity: A Neglected Dimension of American History," in *The State of American History*, ed. Herbert J. Bass (Chicago: Quadrangle, 1970), 70–88; "The Reemergence of American Immigration History," *American Studies International* 17, no. 2 (Winter 1979): 46–66; "The Search for an Italian American Identity: Continuity and Change," in *Italian-Americans: New Perspectives in Italian Immigration and Ethnicity*, ed. Lydio Tomasi (New York: Center for Migration Studies, 1985), 88–112; Josef Barton, *Peasants and Strangers: Italians, Rumanians and Slovaks in an American City, 1890–1950* (Cambridge: Harvard University Press, 1975); Michael Karni, *For the Common Good: Finnish Immigrants and the Radical Response to Industrial America* (Superior, Wis.: Tyomies Society, 1977); John Bodnar, *Lives of Their Own: Blacks, Italians and Poles in Pittsburgh, 1900–1960* (Urbana: University of Illinois Press, 1982); Gerald Sorin, *The Prophetic Minority: American Jewish Immigrant Radicals, 1880–1920* (Bloomington: Indiana University Press, 1985). Much of the work of John Higham challenges the importance assigned to the role of culture in immigrant life. For an introduction to his work see "Current Trends in the Study of Ethnicity in the United States," *Journal of American History* 69, no. 2 (Fall 1982): 5–15.

7. John Bodnar, *The Transplanted: A History of Immigrants in Urban America* (Bloomington: Indiana University Press, 1985), 210 and xx, 54–55, 120–38, 184–209; see also Richard Hamilton, *Class and Politics in the United States* (New York: John Wiley and Sons, 1972), which argues that "There are distinctive patterns of training that are independent of class and that are shared across the class lines, but within the major socio-religious communities" (406).

8. Karl Marx himself left the definition of social classes open in his unfinished chapter in *Das Kapital*. For recent works which treat class not as a mere collection of attributes but as a historical force, i.e., a social process that evolves over time, see E. P. Thompson, "Eighteenth-Century English Society: Class Struggle Without Class," *Social History* 3 (May 1978): 146–50; Edward Pessen, "Social Structure and Politics in American History" [with rejoinder by Michael B. Katz and Robert H. Wiebe], *American Historical Review* 87 (December 1982): 1290–341.

1. Brooklyn's "Lower East Side"

1. William Poster, " 'Twas a Dark Night in Brownsville: Pitkin Avenue's Self-Made Generation," *Commentary* 9 (May 1950): 458–67.

2. Alter Landesman, "A Neighborhood Survey of Brownsville" typescript,

1927, Jewish Division, New York Public Library; *Brownsville: The Birth, Development and Passing of a Jewish Community in New York* (New York: Bloch Publishing, 1971), 50–56.
3. Deborah Dash Moore, *At Home in America* (New York: Columbia University Press, 1981), 20–23.
4. Ralph Foster Weld, *Brooklyn Is America* (New York: Columbia University Press, 1950), 110–11; Morris Horowitz and L. J. Kaplan, *The Jewish Population of the New York Area, 1900–1975* (New York: Federation of Philanthropies, 1959), 22, 49, 78; Florence Adamson; *A Study of the Recreational Facilities of the Brownsville Section of Brooklyn* (Brooklyn: Brownsville Neighborhood Council, 1941), 4.
5. Poster, " 'Twas a Dark Night in Brownsville," 460.
6. Alfred Kazin, *A Walker in the City* (New York: Harcourt, Brace, 1951), 11–12.
7. Herbert J. Ballon, "Brooklyn Neighborhoods: A Basis for Neighborhood Studies and a District Plan for a Neighborhood Council Program in Brooklyn," manuscript, June 1941, Brooklyn Collection, Brooklyn Public Library, Main Branch.
8. Louis Wirth, "A Bibliography of the Urban Community," *The City*, ed. Robert E. Park and Ernest W. Burgess (1925; reprint, Chicago: University of Chicago Press, 1967), 190.
9. Landesman, *Brownsville*, 375
10. Arthur Spetter, interview with author, January 5, 1987; Nathan Dassa, interview with author, January 6, 1987.
11. Martin Kronenberg, interviews with author, January 13, 1987 and October 12, 1987; Norman Goroff, interview with author, July 23, 1987.
12. Gerald Lenowitz, interview with author, April 21, 1987.
13. Gerald Green, "Brownsville," *New York* 20, no. 50 (December 21–28, 1987): 102–3.
14. *Brooklyn Eagle*, March 30, 1949.
15. Adamson, *A Study of the Recreational Facilities of the Brownsville Section*, 9; Horowitz and Kaplan, *The Jewish Population*, 49.
16. Moore, *At Home in America*, 31–33; Nettie P. McGill and Ellen N. Matthews, *The Youth of New York* (New York: Macmillan, 1940), appendix, table 3.
17. Landesman, "A Neighborhood Survey," 5–9.
18. Isidore Karbel, interview with author, April 28, 1988.
19. Arthur Granit, *I Am from Brownsville* (New York: Philosophical Library, 1985), 205.
20. Leonard Dryansky, interview with author August 11, 1988.
21. Adamson, *A Study of Recreational Facilities*, 31; Landesman, "A Neighborhood Survey," 9.
22. Bernard Berman, interview with author, April 3, 1988.
23. Larry Kushner, interview with author, February 7, 1987.
24. McGill and Matthews, *The Youth of New York*, 343.
25. James Vincent Genovese, interview with author, May 21, 1989.
26. Poster, " 'Twas a Dark Night in Brownsville," 461.
27. Adamson, *Recreational Facilities*, 10, 25–28; Moore, *At Home in America*, 95–103.

28. Landesman, "A Neighborhood Survey," 4.

29. Moore, *At Home in America*, 22.

30. McGill and Matthews. *The Youth of New York*, appendix, table 6.

31. Kazin, *A Walker in the City*, 38–39.

32. Nettie McGill, "Some Characteristics of Jewish Youth in New York City," *Jewish Social Service Quarterly* 14 (December 1937): 255.

33. Margaret B. Freeman, *The Brownsville Public Library: Its Origin and Development* (New York: Brooklyn Public Library, 1940).

34. Nathan Glazer, "The American Jew and the Attainment of Middle-Class Rank," in *The Jews: Social Patterns of an American Group*, ed. Marshall Sklare (Glencoe, Ill.: Free Press, 1958), 142–44.

35. Irving Howe, *World of Our Fathers* (New York: Harcourt Brace Jovanovich, 1976), 310.

36. Jacob Deutch, interview with author, October 19, 1986; Milton Kirschner, interview with author March 9, 1987; Ruby Nudelman, interview with author, March 17, 1987.

37. Adamson, *A Study of Recreational Facilities*, 4.

38. *Brooklyn Eagle*. Innumerable issues of this daily paper, beginning as early as August 1, 1920, carried stories and reports on Brownsville, and on housing problems in that section, right up until the folding of the *Eagle* in 1955.

39. Milton Goell, *Brownsville Must Have Public Housing* (Brooklyn: Brownsville Neighborhood Council, 1940), 5–14.

40. Community Council of Greater New York: Bureau of Community Statistical Services, *Brooklyn Communities: Population Characteristics and Neighborhood Social Resources*, vol. 1 (New York: Community Council, 1959), 164; New York City Youth Board, "Brownsville Youth Board Area Report" typescript, 1954, Brooklyn Collection, Brooklyn Public Library, 1.

41. Jacob Baroff, Interview with author, July 6, 1987.

42. "Brownsville Youth Board Area Report," 1.

43. *Brooklyn Eagle*, February 9, 1945.

44. Goell, *Brownsville Must Have Public Housing*, 9–23.

45. New York City Board of Health, "Statistics on Infant and Maternal Mortality, 1939," cited in Adamson, 15; *Brooklyn Eagle*, February 3, 1942; Milton Goell, *Better Health for Brownsville* (Brooklyn: Brownsville Neighborhood Council, 1942).

46. Goell, *Brownsville Must Have Public Housing*, 21, 24–25.

47. *New York Times*, February 4, 1940.

48. *Brooklyn Eagle*, May 14, 1940.

49. Granit, *I Am from Brownsville*, 9.

50. Ronald Bayor, *Neighbors in Conflict: The Irish, Germans, Jews and Italians of New York City, 1929–1941* (Baltimore: Johns Hopkins University Press, 1978), 41–45; For underworld figures' desire to attain social advancement and prestige see Daniel Bell, "Crime as an American Way of Life," *Antioch Review* (June 1953): 131–54.

51. Jenna Joselit, *Our Gang: Jewish Crime and the New York Jewish Community, 1900–1940* (Bloomington: Indiana University Press, 1983), 106–39; David Singer, "The Jewish Gangster: Crime as 'Unzer Shtik,' " *Judaism* 23, no. 1 (Winter 1974): 70–77.

52. Elliot Willensky, *When Brooklyn Was the World, 1920–1957* (New York: Harmony Books, 1986), 166.

53. Ibid.

54. *New York Times*, February 3, 1940.

55. Willensky, *When Brooklyn Was the World*, 167.

56. Sammy Aaronson, *As High as My Heart* (New York: 1959), 42–43.

57. Joselit, *Our Gang*, 150–52.

58. Ibid, 166–67.

59. Ibid.

60. Cited in Joselit, *Our Gang*, 166.

61. From 1940 on, leaders and organizations were caught up in the convolutions of trying to get their fair share of services and protection at the same time that they were trying to defend the name of their community and its residents. See *Brooklyn Eagle*, February 11, 1940, May 25, 1942; David Suher, *Brownsville Neighborhood Council* (New York: New York School of Social Work, 1948); *New York Times*, December 28, 1944, and further discussion of this in chaps. 3, 5, and 6.

62. Sophia Robison, "Delinquency Among Jewish Children in New York City," in *The Jews: Social Patterns of an American Group*, ed. Marshall Sklare (Glencoe, Ill.: Free Press, 1957), 535–41; Landesman, *Brownsville*, 324–28. For statistical information see Irving W. Halpern, et al., *A Statistical Study of the Distribution of Adult and Juvenile Delinquents in the Boroughs of Manhattan and Brooklyn, New York City* (New York: New York Housing Authority, 1939); "Children's Division of the Court: Statistics for 1940, New York," cited in Adamson, *A Study of Recreational Facilities*, 23.

63. Herbert Bloch and Arthur Niederhoffer, *The Gang: A Study in Adolescent Behavior* (New York: Philosophical Library, 1958), 107.

64. Joselit, *Our Gang*, 162–70.

65. Halpern, *A Statistical Study*, 159; and Landesman, "A Neighborhood Survey," 13

66. Aaronson, *As High as My Heart*, 43.

67. *Brownsville Boys Club News*, 7, no. 6 (July 28, 1947) (hereafter *BBC News*).

68. Jacob Baroff, interview with author, July 6, 1987; Jesse Salit and Charles Pinchuk, interview with author, July 7, 1987.

69. Ben Wernikoff, interview with author, May 7, 1987.

70. Norman Podhoretz, *Making It*, (New York: Harper and Row, 1967), 7, 51.

71. Daniel Bell, "Crime As an American Way of Life." op. cit.

72. Joseph Epstein, "Browsing in Gangland," *Commentary* (January 1972); 46–55.

73. Robert Warshow, "The Gangster as Tragic Hero," in *The Immediate Experience*, ed. Robert Warshow (Garden City: Atheneum Press, 1962), 127–33.

74. Aaronson, *As High as My Heart*, 12.

75. Jacob Baroff, interview with author, July 6, 1987.

76. David Dortort, *Burial of the Fruit* (New York: Crown Publishers, 1947).

77. Arthur Granit, *The Time of the Peaches* (New York: Abelard-Schuman, 1959).

78. Irving Shulman. *The Amboy Dukes* (New York: Doubleday, 1947).

79. *New York Times Book Review*, April 13, 1947, 5.

80. Alfred Kazin, "My New Yorks," *New York Times Book Review*, August 26, 1986, 29–30.

81. *Brooklyn Eagle*, April 29, 1937; November 17, 1940; November 18, 1940; March 14, 1941.

82. David Suher, *Brownsville Neighborhood Council*, 30; *Brooklyn Eagle*, January 7, 1941.

83. *Brooklyn Eagle*, March 19, 1941.

84. On Brownsville's liberalism see Landesman, *Brownsville*, 103–45; Moore, *At Home in America*, 203–8; and Irving Howe, *World of Our Fathers* (New York: Harcourt, Brace, Jovanovitch, 1976), 318. Also Bayor's *Neighbors in Conflict*, throughout, demonstrates disproportionate liberal to radical voting trends, 1930–40, among Jews in New York City generally. For progressive perspectives on delinquency, see reports in the *Brooklyn Eagle*, December 10, 1940; January 7, 1941; February 9, 1945; and April 21, 1946.

85. Adamson, *A Study of Recreational Facilities*, 48.

86. *Brooklyn Eagle*, April 29, 1937; May 14, 1940.

87. *Brooklyn Eagle*, February 11, 1940; December 10, 1940; January 7, 1941; March 11, 1941. *Brooklyn Eagle* "Series on Juvenile Delinquency," fifty-two installments from September 1943 to September 1944; *Brooklyn Eagle*, January 4, 1949; February 9, 1945; "A Post-War Plan for Brownsville," program leaflet, February 8, 1945; Brooklyn Council for Social Planning, "Report of Youth Activities Project," April 1946.

88. Adamson, *A Study of Recreational Facilities*, 2; Landesman, *Brownsville*, 205–6; *Brooklyn Eagle*, newsclipping, n.d.

2. Founders, Framers, and the Formative Years

1. Alfred Kazin, *Walker in the City* (New York: Harcourt Brace, 1951), 84

2. New York City Youth Board, "Brownsville Youth Board Area Report," typescript, 1954, Brooklyn Collection Brooklyn Public Library, Main Branch.

3. Ibid; and Florence Adamson, *A Study of the Recreational Facilities of the Brownsville Section of Brooklyn* (Brooklyn: Brownsville Neighborhood Council, 1941), 31.

4. *Brooklyn Eagle*, April 30, 1935.

5. Cary Goodman, *Choosing Sides* (New York: Schocken Books, 1979), 3. This book contains some interesting material, but the single-minded ideological attempt by the author to prove that play and sport were "colonized," i.e., that the "recreation" movement transformed an "autonomous cultural activity of workers [into] a mechanism for the efficient transmission of capitalist values," is so heavyhanded that the volume crumbles under its weight. Goodman overstates the class-consciousness of working-class boys and fails to see their resilience, and their resistance to manipulation by "reformers."

6. Abe Rubenfeld, interview with author, January 12, 1987; Sid Siegel, interview with author, September 22, 1986; Milt Kirschner, interview with author, March 9, 1987.

7. William Poster, " 'Twas a Dark Night in Brownsville: Pitkin Avenue's Self-Made Generation," *Commentary* 9 (May 1950): 459.

8. Gerald Lenowitz, April 21, 1987.

9. Max Zaslofsky in *Echoes from the School, Yard* Comp. Anne Byrne Hoffman (New York: Hawthorn Books, 1977), 9.

10. Mendy Bacall, interview with author, March 23, 1988.

11. Charles Trester, letter to author, 1987.

12. Hoffman, *Echoes*, 9.

13. Selma Berrol, "Immigrants at School: New York City, 1898–1914," (Ph.D. diss., City University of New York, 1967), 124; Adamson, *A Study of Recreational Facilities*, 28.

14. Alter Landesman, "A Neighborhood Survey of Brownsville," typescript, 1927, Jewish Division, New York Public Library, 13.

15. Adamson, *A Study of Recreational Facilities*, 41–42.

16. Jewish Welfare Board, *A Study of the Jewish Community of Brooklyn for the YMHA of Brooklyn* (New York: Jewish Welfare Board, 1935).

17. *Brooklyn Eagle*, March 2, 1935.

18. Adamson, *A Study of Recreational Facilities*, 50.

19. *Brooklyn Eagle*, March 8, 1935.

20. Adamson, *A Study of Recreational Facilities*, 51.

21. Ibid.

22. George Levine, interview with author, May 23, 1987.

23. Milton Kirschner, letter to author, 1987.

24. Irving Levine, interview with author, October 8, 1986.

25. WINS, radio broadcast transcript, August 11, 1945.

26. "Petition," n.d., BBC Files

27. Jacob Baroff, interview with author, July 6, 1987.

28. Isidore Lesovoy, interview with author, November 4, 1986; WINS, radio broadcast transcript, August 11, 1945.

29. Jacob Baroff, interview with author July 6, 1987.

30. Margaret Freeman, *The Brownsville Public Library: Its Origin and Development* (New York: Brooklyn Public Library, 1940); Adamson, *A Study of Recreational Facilities*, 30.

31. Jacob Baroff, interview with author, July 6, 1987; Irving Levine, interview with author, October 8, 1986; Irving Levenberg, May 21, 1989.

32. Arthur Granit, *I Am from Brownsville* (New York: Philosophical Library, 1985), 222.

33. Alfred Kazin, *Walker in the City*, 87, 91.

34. Freeman, *The Brownsville Public Library*, 104.

35. Minutes of Brownsville Boys Club weekly meetings, May 24, 1940 to December 19, 1941 (hereafter BBC meetings); Norman Goroff, "The Brownsville Boys Club," typescript, 1947, 6; Adamson, *A Study of Recreational Facilities*, 43.

36. William H. Whyte, *Street Corner Society*, (Chicago: University of Chicago Press, 1981), 247–249.

37. Ibid., 256.

38. Herbert J. Gans, *The Urban Villagers: Group and Class Life of Italian Americans* (New York: Free Press, 1962), 198, 37, 30.

39. Minutes of BBC weekly meetings, May 24, 1940 to December 19, 1941; dues records, March 1940.

40. Joseph Feldman, interview with author, September 22, 1986; Sol Altman, letter to author, 1986.

41. Jacob Baroff, interview with author, July 6, 1987.

42. Ibid., July 6, 1987 and February 8, 1988.

43. Ibid.

44. WINS, radio broadcast transcript, August 11, 1945.

45. Minutes of BBC weekly meetings, October 1940 to November 1941.

46. Ibid., January 9, 1942 to March 13, 1942.

47. New York World Telegram and Sun, September 22, 1951.

48. WINS, radio broadcast transcript, August 11, 1945.

49. Seymour Brief, interview with author, March 10, 1987; Jacob Baroff, interview with author, July 6, 1987.

50. Norman Goroff, interview with author, July 23, 1987.

51. Eddie Cantor, My Life is in Your Hands (New York: Curtis Publishing, 1928), 30–34.

52. Herb Grosswirth, letter to author, 1987; Jacob Baroff, interview with author, July 6, 1987.

53. Goroff, "The Brownsville Boys Club," 5.

54. George Levine, letter to author, 1987; Abe Rubenfeld, interview with author, January 12, 1987.

55. WINS, radio broadcast transcript, August 11, 1945.

56. Joseph Feldman, interview with author, September 22, 1986.

57. Jacob Baroff, interview with author, July 6, 1987 and February 8, 1988.

58. Dan Dodson, "Frederick Thrasher, 1892–1962," American Journal of Sociology 27 no. 4 (August 1962): 580–81.

59. Frederick Thrasher, letter to Brownsville Boys Club, November 13, 1941; minutes of BBC weekly meeting, November 20, 1941.

60. Jacob Baroff, letter to "Ma, Pa and Miriam," May 8, 1945.

61. Jacob Baroff, interview with author, July 6, 1987.

62. Norman Goroff, interview with author, July 23, 1987.

63. Aurora (Brooklyn: Thomas Jefferson High School, January 1943).

64. Deborah Dash Moore, At Home in America (New York: Columbia University Press, 1981) 20–23; Alter Landesman, Brownsville: The Birth, Development and Passing of a Jewish Community (New York: Bloch Publishing, 1971) 103–45.

65. New York Times, November 13, 1941; November 11, 1943; November 7, 1947.

66. Norman Goroff, interview with author, July 23, 1987.

67. Alfred Kazin, Walker in the City, 78.

68. Norman Goroff, "The Authentic Community," typescript, n.d., 5.

69. Nathan Glazer, The Social Bases of American Communism, 130–68; Roy Lubove, The Professional Altruist: The Emergence of Social Work as a Career, 1880–1930 (Cambridge: Cambridge University Press, 1965).

70. State of Maine, Senate, H.R.: SP768, January 27, 1986.

71. Norman Goroff, letter to Joseph Feldman, November 15, 1987.

72. Joseph Feldman, interview with author, September 22, 1986.

73. Jacob Deutch, interview with author, October 19, 1986.

74. *Aurora*, June 1942.

75. Isidore Lesovoy, interviews with author November 4, 1986 and October 11, 1987.

76. Werner J. Cahnman, "Attitudes of Minority Youth: A Methodological Introduction [investigation into the cultural interests of Jewish and Negro youth in the Brownsville District of Brooklyn]," *American Sociological Review*, 14 (August 1949): 543–48.

77. George Schmaren, interviews with author October 18, 1986 and October 11, 1987.

78. Gerald Green, *The Last Angry Man* (New York: Charles Scribner's Sons, 1956), 45.

79. George Schmaren, interviews with author, October 18, 1986 and October 11, 1987.

80. Joseph Adelson, "The Development of Ideology in Adolescence," in *Adolescence in the Life Cycle*, ed. S. E. Dragaston and G. H. Elder (New York: John Wiley, 1975), 71; and "The Political Imagination of the Young Adolescent," *Daedelus* 100 (1971): 1013–50.

3. Corner Kids and Cultural Cornerstones

1. William Poster, " 'Twas a Dark Night in Brownsville," *Commentary* 9, no. 5 (May 1950): 461.

2. George Berch, interview with author, February 25, 1987; Seymour Smolin, interview with author, March 16, 1987; Leonard Gerber, interview with author, May 10, 1988.

3. William Brief, interview with author, May 15, 1988; Isidore Karbel, interview with author, April 28, 1988.

4. Alfred Kazin, *Walker in the City* (New York: Harcourt Brace, 1951), 45.

5. Norman Podhoretz, *Making It* (New York: Harper and Row, 1967), 29–30.

6. Arthur Granit, *The Time of the Peaches* (New York: Abelard-Schuman, 1959), 10.

7. Arthur Granit, *I Am from Brownsville* (New York: Philosophical Library, 1985), 83–84.

8. Gilbert Sorrentino, "No Radical Chic in Brooklyn," *New York Times*, January 16, 1971.

9. Herbert Gutman, *The Black Family in Slavery and Freedom*, (New York: Pantheon Books, 1976), 461–519.

10. Moses Kligsberg, "Jewish Immigrants in Business: A Sociological Study," in *The Jewish Experience in America*, ed. Abraham Karp, vol. 5 (New York: KTAV, 1969), 249–84.

11. Jacob Baroff, interview with author, July 6, 1987.

12. Quoted in Thomas Kessner, *The Golden Door: Italian and Jewish Immigrant Mobility in New York City, 1880–1915* (New York: Oxford University Press, 1977), 97.

13. Samuel Tenenbaum, "Brownsville's Age of Learning: When the Library Stayed Open All Week," *Commentary* 6, no. 8 (August 1947): 174.

14. Herbert Grosswirth, interview with author, February 10, 1987; George Berch, interview with author, February 25, 1987.

15. Kazin, *Walker in the City*, 21.

16. Nettie McGill and Ellen N. Matthews, *The Youth of New York* (New York: Macmillan, 1940), 344; *Forty-Fifth Annual Report of The Superintendent of Schools* (Brooklyn: Board of Education, 1942–43), 47–56; *Forty-Seventh Annual Report of the Superintendent of Schools* (Brooklyn: Board of Education, 1944–45).

17. Deborah Dash Moore, *At Home in America: Second-Generation New York Jews* (New York: Columbia University Press, 1981), 95–96, 103.

18. Poster, " 'Twas a Dark Night," 463.

19. Nettie McGill, "Some Characteristics of Jewish Youth in New York City," *Jewish Social Service Quarterly* 14 (December 1937): 252–72.

20. Morris Levine, interview with author, June 5, 1988.

21. Deborah Dash Moore, *At Home in America*, 102–3; Theodore Saloutos, "Exodus USA," in *Trek of the Immigrant*, ed. O. F. Ander (Rock Island, Ill.: Augustan College Library, 1964), 199–201; Masakazu Iwata, "The Japanese Immigrants in California Agriculture," *Agricultural History* 36, no. 1 (January 1962): 25–37; Colin Greer, *The Great School Legend: A Revisionist Interpretation of American Public Education* (New York: Basic Books, 1972), chap. 5.

22. Thomas Kessner, *The Golden Door*, 98; Fred L. Strodtbeck, "Family Interaction, Values and Achievement," in *Talent and Society* ed. David McClelland, Alfred Baldwin, Urie Bronfenbrenner, and Fred Strodtbeck (Princeton: D. Van Nostrand, 1958), 135–94; Nathan Hurvitz, "Sources of Motivation and Achievement of American Jews," *Jewish Social Studies* 23, no. 4 (Fall 1961): 217–34.

23. Lucy Dawidowicz, *The Golden Tradition: Jewish Life and Thought in Eastern Europe* (Boston: Beacon Press, 1967), 28–30.

24. Leonard Covello, "The Social Background of the Italo-American School Child," (Ph.D. Diss., New York University, 1944), 467–537; R. F. Foerster, *The Italian Immigration of Our Times* (Cambridge: Harvard University Press, 1919); Joseph Lopreato, *Peasants No More* (Scranton, Pa.: Chandler Publishing, 1967); Richard Gambino, *Blood of My Blood: The Dilemma of Italian Americans* (Garden City, N.Y.: Doubleday, 1974), 233–35, 247.

25. Leonard Covello, "Social Background," 603.

26. Thomas Kessner, *The Golden Door*, 28–30; C. Bezalel Sherman, "Immigration and Emigration: The Jewish Case," in *The Jew in American Society*, ed. Marshall Sklare (New York: Behrman House, 1974); Miriam Cohen, "Changing Educational Strategies Among Immigrant Generations: New York Italians in Comparative Perspective," *Journal of Social History* 11, no. 2 (Spring 1982): 443–66; Richard A. Varbero, "Philadelphia's South Italians in the 1920's," in *The Peoples of Philadelphia: A History of Ethnic and Lower Class Life, 1790–1940*, ed. Allen F. Davis and Mark H. Haller (Philadelphia: Temple University Press, 1973), 255–75.

27. Leonard Covello, "Social Background," 467, 500–537.

28. Herbert J. Gans, *The Urban Villagers: Group and Class in the Life of Italian Americans* (New York: Free Press, 1962), 132–33, 139. Although Gans found a

value system and a "clearly identifiable social structure that has changed very little in the passage of time and place from Italy to America," he believed this persistence to be a result of "working-class structure," rather than "ethnic culture." Gans is not entirely persuasive, partly because of his insistence on an either/or conclusion.

29. Jonathan Rieder, *Canarsie: The Jews and Italians of Brooklyn Against Liberalism* (Cambridge: Harvard University Press, 1985), 36.

30. Andrew Greeley, *That Most Distressful Nation: The Taming of the American Irish* (Chicago: Quadrangle Books, 1972), 190.

31. Mary Gordon, " 'I Can't Stand Your Books': A Writer Goes Home," *New York Times Book Review*, December 11, 1988, 36.

32. Milton Kirschner, interview with author March 9, 1987; Jacob Baroff, interview with author, July 6, 1987.

33. Leo Yedin, interview with author, May 7, 1987.

34. Ruby Nudelman, interview with author, March 17, 1987.

35. Kazin, *Walker in the City*, 119.

36. Ben Wernikoff, interview with author May 7, 1987; Abe Rubenfeld, interview with author, January 12, 1987.

37. Seymour Schlosberg, interview with author, April 3, 1988; Jack Schmaren, interview with author, October 12, 1987.

38. John Bodnar, *The Transplanted: A History of Immigrants in Urban America* (Bloomington: Indiana University Press, 1985), 84.

39. Irving Howe, *World of Our Fathers* (New York: Harcourt Brace Jovanovich, 1976), 58; Samuel Joseph, *Jewish Immigration to the United States from 1881 to 1910* (New York: Columbia University Press, 1914).

40. Edward Banfield, *The Moral Basis of a Backward Society* (New York: Free Press of Glencoe, 1958), 85–110; Leonard Covello, "Social Background," 150–92; Rudolph J. Vecoli, "*Contadini* in Chicago: A Critique of *The Uprooted*," *Journal of American History* 51, no. 2 (December 1964): 404–17; R. F. Foerster, *Italian Immigration*, 51–75: quote from Mark Zborowski, *Life is with People* (New York: International University Press, 1952), 420.

41. Thomas Kessner, *The Golden Door*, 94.

42. Alter Landesman, *Brownsville*, 208–17; idem, "A Neighborhood Survey," typescript, 1927), 7–8.

43. Jack Oventhal, interview with author, May 19, 1988.

44. Landesman, *Brownsville*, 323–324; "A Neighborhood Survey," 12; Reuben Fink and Bernard Richards, eds., *Jewish Community Directory of Greater New York: A Guide to Central Organizations and Institutions* (New York: The Jewish Information Bureau, 1947).

45. David Suher, *The Brownsville Neighborhood Council* (New York: New York School of Social Work, 1948), 6–8.

46. Ibid., 49.

47. Landesman, *Brownsville*, 116–19; Florence Adamson, *A Study of the Recreational Facilities of the Brownsville Section of Brooklyn* (New York: Brownsville Neighborhood Council, 1941), 48; Rae Glauber, *All Neighborhoods Change: A Survey of Brownsville, Brooklyn, U.S.A.* (New York: n.p., 1963), 29–30.

48. Seymour Schlosberg, interview with author April 3, 1988; Harold Radish, interview with author, March 12, 1987.

49. Morton Werbel, interview with author, March 13, 1988.

50. Jonathan Rieder, *Canarsie*, 52

51. Ibid., 25.

52. Jacob Baroff, interview with author, July 6, 1987.

53. Edward Banfield, *Moral Basis*, 102.

54. Herbert Gans, *The Urban Villagers*, 160–73.

55. Jonathan Rieder, *Canarsie*, 38, 27.

56. Victor Greene, *American Immigrant Leaders, 1800–1910: Marginality and Identity* (Baltimore: Johns Hopkins University Press, 1987), 122–37; Donna Gabaccia, *From Sicily to Elizabeth Street: Housing and Social Change Among Italian Immigrants, 1880–1930* (Albany: SUNY Press, 1984); John Briggs, *An Italian Passage: Immigrants to Three American Cities, 1890–1930* (New Haven: Yale University Press, 1978); Joseph Lopreato, *Italian Americans* (New York: Random House, 1970); Edwin Fenton, "Immigrants and Unions, A Case Study: Italians and American Labor, 1870–1920" (Ph.D. diss. Harvard University, 1957).

57. Rudolph J. Vecoli, "Prelates and Peasants: Italian Immigrants and the Catholic Church," *Journal of Social History* 2, no. 3 (Spring 1969): 217–68; Richard A. Varbero, "Philadelphia's South Italians and the Irish Church: A History of Cultural Conflict," in *The Religious Experience of Italian Americans*, ed. Silvano Tomasi (Staten Island, N.Y.: American Italian Historical Association, 1975), 33–54.

58. Quoted in Gans, *The Urban Villagers*, 201.

59. On familism and fatalism see Edward Banfield, *Moral Basis*, 85–110; Joseph Lopreato, *Italian Americans*, 10; Fred Strodtbeck, "Family Interaction," 135–94. As a counter to these views see Micaela di Leonardo, *The Varieties of Ethnic Experience: Kinship, Class and Gender Among California Italian Americans* (Ithaca: Cornell University Press, 1984). She challenges many accepted ideas about Italian American families and makes class and environment primary in her analysis.

60. Max Stavitsky, interview with author, October 11, 1987; Irving Forman, interview with author, June 27, 1987; Don Rosen, interview with author, April 23, 1988.

61. Abraham Cahan, *Jewish Daily Forward*, August 6, 1903.

62. Louis Green, interview with Irving Howe, cited in Irving Howe, *World of Our Fathers* (New York: Harcourt Brace Jovanovich), 1976, 259.

63. Robert Slater, *Great Jews in Sports* (Middle Village, New York: Jonathan David Publishers, 1983), 121; Bernard Postal, Jesse Silver and Roy Silver, *Encyclopedia of Jews in Sports* (New York: Bloch and Sons, 1965), 42.

64. Slater, *Jews in Sports*, 166, 171–72.

65. Postal, et al., *Encyclopedia*, 138.

66. Slater, *Jews in Sports*, 10–12.

67. Ibid., 10, 59–62.

68. Ibid., 132–34.

69. Ibid., 56, 67–68, 202–3.

70. Ibid., xiii, 181–84.

71. Ibid., 83–86.

72. Ibid., 147–50.

73. Slater, *Jews in Sports*, 77–79; Landesman, *Brownsville*, 359.
74. Peter Golenbock, *Bums: An Oral History of the Brooklyn Dodgers* (New York: G. P. Putnam's Sons, 1984), 25, 448.
75. Jacob Baroff, interview with author, February 8, 1988.
76. Pete Hamill, "Brooklyn: The Sane Alternative," *New York*, July 14, 1969, 28.
77. Podhorets, *Making It*, 100–101.
78. Landesman, *Brownsville*, 362; Slater, *Jews in Sports*, 104–6.
79. Seymour Schlosberg, interview with author, April 3, 1988; Landesman, *Brownsville*, 363.
80. *Aurora* (Brooklyn: Thomas Jefferson High School, 1941–44).
81. Landesman, *Brownsville*, 361–62.
82. *Aurora*, January 1945.
83. Anne B. Hoffman, *Echoes from the Schoolyard* (New York: Hawthorn Books, 1977), 9.
84. *New York World Telegram and Sun*, September 22, 1951; *New York Daily News*, December 3, 1982; *New York Times*, October 17, 1985.
85. Hoffman, *Echoes from the Schoolyard*, 14–15.
86. Irving Levine, interview with author April 11, 1988; Jacob Baroff, interview with author, February 8, 1988. Irwin Sandler, letter to author, October 1987.
87. Irwin Gladstein, interview with author October 18, 1986; Nathan Dassa, interview with author January 6, 1987. *New York World Telegram and Sun*, September 22, 1951.
88. William Poster, " 'Twas a Dark Night," 461–62.
89. Jacob Baroff, *New York Sunday News*, November 23, 1947.
90. WINS, radio broadcast transcript, August 11, 1945.
91. *Brooklyn Eagle*, March 19, 1941.
92. Raymond Schroth, *The Eagle and Brooklyn: A Community Newspaper, 1841–1955* (Westport, Conn.: Greenwood Press, 1974); *Brooklyn Eagle*, September 29, 1943 to September 24, 1944.
93. Brooklyn Council for Social Planning, "Report of Youth Activities Project," pamphlet, April 21, 1946.
94. *Brooklyn Eagle*, December 28, 1944.
95. *New York Times*, December 28, 1944.
96. Irving Shulman, *The Amboy Dukes* (New York: Doubleday, 1947).
97. Dudley Gaffin, letter to author, June 14, 1988.
98. Shulman, *Amboy Dukes*, 63.
99. Ibid.
100. Ibid., 64.
101. *Brooklyn Communities*, vol. 1, 168–71; *Brownsville Youth Board Area Report*, 2–4.
102. Adamson, *Recreational Facilities*, 10, 11, 55.
103. "Report on Youth Activities Project," 2.
104. Golenbock, *Bums*, 429.
105. "Report on Youth Activities Project," 3.
106. Ibid., 6–7 (emphasis mine).
107. Flyer, "Sixth Anniversary Meeting," March 22, 1946.

108. Norman Goroff, "The Brownsville Boys Club," typescript, 1947, 5–8.

109. Ibid.

110. Ben Wernikoff, interview with author, May 7, 1987.

111. Mihaly Csikszentmihalyi, "The Pressured World of Adolescence," *Planned Parenthood Review*, 16, no. 2 (Spring 1986): 1–4; Csikszentmihalyi and Reed Larsen, *Being Adolescent: Conflict and Growth in the Teenage Years* (New York: Basic Books, 1984), 239–260.

112. Nathan Dassa, interview with author, January 6, 1987; Dudley Gaffin, interview with author, June 20, 1987; Irwin Gladstein, interview with author October 18, 1986, and dozens of others.

4. Soldiers, Storefronts, and Social Change

1. *New York World Telegram and Sun*, September 22, 1951.

2. Joe D'Antone, letter to *Brownsville Boys Clubs News*, 2, no. 4 (October 1943) (hereafter *BBC News*).

3. Alter Landesman, *Brownsville: The Growth, Development and Passing of a Jewish Community* (New York: Bloch Publishers, 1971), 321–22.

4. *BBC News* 7, no. 2 (March 1947): 3.

5. *New York Daily Mirror*, October 29, 1947; Franklin Cohen, interview with author, April 13, 1988.

6. Joe Skope, letter to *BBC News* 2, no. 4 (October 1943).

7. Hy Rabinovitz, letter to *BBC News* 2, no. 4 (October 1943).

8. Sid Siegel, letter to *BBC News* 2, no. 3 (October 1943).

9. Minutes of Brownsville Boys Club weekly meetings, December 12, 1941; March 13, 1942 (hereafter BBC meetings).

10. *New York Herald Tribune*, March 4, 1949; *BBC News*, March 1947.

11. Norman Goroff, "The Brownsville Boys Club," typescript, 1947, 5.

12. Martin Kronenberg, interviews with author, January 13, 1987, October 11, 1987.

13. Lawrence Kushner, interview with author, February 7, 1987.

14. *Brownsville Boys Club Alumni Newsletter*, October 1975.

15. Minutes of BBC weekly meeting, May 31, 1940.

16. "Report of Activities, 1940–1944," typescript, 1944.

17. Sid Siegel, letter to *BBC News*. 2, no. 3 (October 1943); WINS, radio broadcast transcript, August 11, 1945.

18. *New York World Telegram and Sun*, September 22, 1951.

19. *BBC News* 7, no. 1 (February 1947).

20. *BBC News* 7, nos. 11 and 12 (November 1947).

21. *Brooklyn Eagle*, November 2, 1947; *BBC News* 7, nos. 11 and 12 (November 1947).

22. Jacob Baroff, interview with author, July 6, 1987.

23. *BBC News* 7, nos. 11 and 12 (November 1947).

24. Gilbert Sorrentino, "No Radical Chic in Brooklyn," *New York Times*, June 16, 1971.

25. Bradford Chambers, "Juvenile Gangs of New York," *American Mercury* 62 (April 1946): 485–86.

26. "Report on the Brownsville Boys Club Program," flyer, 1947.

27. *New York Herald Tribune*, March 4, 1949.

28. "Juvenile Delinquency: War's Insecurity Lifts Youthful Crime 100 percent," *Life*, April 8, 1946, 83–93; Chambers, "Juvenile Gangs," 480; *Brooklyn Eagle*, February 1, 1946; Pete Hamill, "Brooklyn, the Sane Alternative," *New York*, July 14, 1969, 25–33.

29. *New York Times*, July 20, 1947; Brooklyn *Eagle*, July 20, 1947.

30. Ibid.

31. *Brooklyn Eagle*, January 23, 1946; November 18, 1946.

32. *Brooklyn Eagle*, January 23, 1946.

33. *New York World Telegram and Sun*, November 15, 1947.

34. *Brooklyn Eagle*, May 19, 1948.

35. New York City Youth Board, "Brownsville Youth Board Area Report," typescript, 1954, Brooklyn Public Library, Main Branch, 3.

36. *Brooklyn Eagle*, March 3, 1949; March 4, 1949; March 10, 1949; March 15, 1949; April 5, 1949.

37. *Brooklyn Eagle*, January 23, 1946.

38. *Brooklyn Eagle*, March 20, 1949.

39. *Brooklyn Eagle*, March 4, 1949; Brooklyn College *Vanguard*, March 18, 1949.

40. *Brooklyn Eagle*, March 4, 1949.

41. *Brooklyn Eagle*, March 3, 1949; March 10, 1949; March 15, 1949, March 20, 1949; April 15, 1949; May 11, 1949.

42. Milton Goell, *Brownsville Must Have Public Housing* (Brooklyn: Brownsville Neighborhood Council, 1940); Goell, *A Post-War Plan for Brownsville* (Brooklyn: Brownsville Neighborhood Council, 1944); *Brooklyn Eagle*, December 11, 1941; December 22, 1941; May 6, 1941; June 29, 1941.

43. Minutes of BBC weekly meetings, May 1940 to December 1945.

44. WINS, radio broadcast transcript, August 11, 1945.

45. BBC "Sixth Anniversary," flyer, March 22, 1946.

46. David Suher, *The Brownsville Neighborhood Council* (New York School of Social Work, 1948), 28–29, 46, 51, 64–65.

47. Werner J. Cahnman, "Attitudes of Minority Youth: A Methodological Introduction (Investigation into the Cultural Interests of Jewish and Negro Youth in the Brownsville District of Brooklyn)," *American Sociological Review* 14 (August 1949): 543–48.

48. *BBC News* 7, no. 1 (February 1947).

49. Minutes of BBC weekly meetings, May 1940 to December 1946.

50. Alfred Kazin, *Walker in the City* (New York: Harcourt Brace, 1951), 141.

51. Martin Kronenberg, interview with author, January 13, 1987; Irving Levine, interviews with author, October 8, 1986; April 11, 1988.

52. Minutes of BBC weekly meetings, March 1943 to December 1945.

53. *BBC News* 7, no. 6 (July 1947).

54. David Suher, *Brownsville Neighborhood Council*, 46–65.

55. Irving Levine, interviews with author, October 8, 1986; April 11, 1988.

56. *BBC News* 7, no. 6 (July 1947); *BBC News* 7, no. 9 (September 1947).

57. *BBC News* 7, no. 9 (September 1947).

58. Irving Levine, interviews with author, October 8, 1986; April 11, 1988.

59. Isidore Lesovoy, Jacob Deutch, Joe Feldman, George Schmaren, Martin Kronenberg, collective interview with author, October 11, 1987; Norman Goroff, interview with author, July 23, 1987; Jacob Baroff, interviews with author, July 6, 1987, February 6, 1988; Irving Levine, interview with author, October 8, 1986.

60. Nathan Glazer, *The Social Bases of American Communism* (New York: Harcourt Brace, 1961), 143–68.

61. See nn. 58 and 59 above.

5. Politicians, Professionals, and Philanthropists

1. *New York Times*, April 23, 1949.

2. *New York Times*, November 4, 1953.

3. Rae Glauber, *All Neighborhoods Change* (New York: Rae Glauber, 1963), 24–25.

4. *New York Times*, September 20, 1960; July 4, 1972.

5. Alter Landesman, *Brownsville: The Birth, Development and Passing of a Jewish Community* (New York: Bloch Publishers, 1971), 341.

6. *New Yorker: Twenty-Fifth Anniversary Album 1925–1950* (New York: Harper, 1951).

7. *Brooklyn Eagle*, February 14, 1935; December 28, 1944; Landesman, *Brownsville*, 320, 341–42.

8. *New York Times*, April 3, 1949;

9. *New York Times*, August 4, 1949; September 8, 1949.

10. *New York Times*, April 23, 1949.

11. *New York Times*, August 25, 1953.

12. *New York Times*, July 1, 1953.

13. *New York Times*, August 25, 1953.

14. *New York Times*, January 25, 1954.

15. Jacob Deutch, Joseph Feldman, Martin Kronenberg, Isidore Lesovoy, George Schmaren, collective interviews with author, October 11, 1987; Norman Goroff, interview with author, July 23, 1987.

16. *New York Times*, January 5, 1954.

17. *New York Times*, January 2, 1948; July 19, 1955; October 6, 1958.

18. *New York Times*, October 18, 1954.

19. Minnie Weingart, letter to author, April 6, 1988.

20. Ibid.; Seymour Berkowitz, interview with author, June 14, 1988; Landesman, *Brownsville*, 204–6.

21. *New York Times*, June 5, 1947; September 24, 1947.

22. *Brooklyn Eagle*, March 25, 1947.

23. *BBC News* 7, no. 6 (July 1947).

24. *New York Times*, November 24, 1947; *Brooklyn Eagle*, November 24, 1947.

25. *Brooklyn Eagle*, November 24, 1947.

26. Dinner program, November 23, 1947.

27. Elliot Willensky, *When Brooklyn Was the World 1920–1957* (New York: Harmony Books, 1986), 170; *New York Times*, May 9, 1952.

28. *New York Times*, May 9, 1952.

29. *New York Times*, March 21, 1951; May 9, 1952

30. Ibid; and William O'Dwyer, *Beyond the Golden Door*, ed. Paul O'Dwyer (New York: St. John's University, 1987), 271–78, 359–73.

31. Willensky, *When Brooklyn Was the World*, 171.

32. *New York Times*, April 9, 1952.

33. Minnie Weingart, letter to author, April 6, 1988; *Flatbush Life*, March 9, 1957; Glauber, *All Neighborhoods Change*, 24.

34. Reuben Bennett, memorandum to Abe Stark, April 17, 1951; Minnie Weingart, resumé, 1950; Glauber, *All Neighborhoods Change*, 24; *Flatbush Life*, March 9, 1957.

35. Minnie Weingart, letter to author, April 6, 1988.

36. Minnie Weingart, letters to author, April 6, 1988; September 25, 1988.

37. Ibid. and Weingart, resumé.

38. Minnie Weingart, letters to author, September 25, 1988; October 5, 1988.

39. Ibid.

40. Jack Leavitt, interview with author, February 25, 1988.

41. Abe Stark and Harmon Putter, "Report of Brownsville Boys Club Activities 1947–1948," typescript, n.d.

42. William Welling, *East Side Story: The Boys' Brotherhood Republic's First Fifty Years on New York's Lower East Side* (New York: Boys' Brotherhood Republic 1982), 95–99.

43. David Nasaw, *Children of the City: At Work and Play* (New York: Oxford University Press, 1985) 17–61.

44. Ibid., 35–37, 117.

45. Roy Rosenzweig, *Eight Hours for What We Will: Workers and Leisure in an Industrial City, 1870–1920* (Cambridge: Cambridge University Press, 1983), 150–51.

46. Times determined by interviews and changing rosters on the Brownsville Boys Club stationery.

47. Jacob Baroff, interview with author, February 6, 1988.

48. Jack Leavitt, interview with author, February 25, 1988.

49. Jacob Deutch, Joseph Feldman, Martin Kronenberg, Isidore Lesovoy, George Schmaren, collective interview with author, October 11, 1987; Jacob Baroff, interviews with author, July 6, 1987; February 6, 1988.

50. Herbert J. Gans, *The Urban Villagers: Group and Class in the Life of Italian Americans* (New York: Free Press, 1962), 271–72.

51. Leonard Dryansky, interview with author, August 11, 1988.

52. "Up from Nanny Goat Park," pamphlet, n.a., 1953.

53. *New York Times*, December 28, 1951.

54. *New York World Telegram and Sun*, September 22, 1951.

55. "Up from Nanny Goat Park."

56. Abe Stark, letters to J. Willard Hayden, July 1, 1948; July 21, 1948; Sidney Winnick, letter to Charles C. Hayden Foundation, September 21, 1948.

57. Edward J. Lukas, letter to Hayden Foundation, September 23, 1948; Edgar Doubleday, letter to Abe Stark, October 21, 1948.

58. Deutch, Feldman, Kronenberg, Lesovoy, Schmaren, collective interview with author, October 11, 1987.

59. *Brooklyn Eagle*, newsclipping, 1946.

60. Jewish Welfare Board, *A Study of the Jewish Community of Brooklyn for the YMHA of Brooklyn* (New York: Jewish Welfare Board, 1935), 50–76.

61. *New York Times*, October 24, 1949.

62. Abe Stark, letter to Edgar A. Doubleday, January 24, 1950.

63. Edward A. Richards, letter to J. Willard Hayden, March 13, 1950.

64. Memorandum to Doubleday, February 16, 1950.

65. J. Willard Hayden, letter to Abe Stark, March 21, 1950.

66. David Armstrong, letter to Edgar Doubleday, April 7, 1950.

67. William Hale, *100 Years and Millions of Boys*, (New York: Farrar, Straus, and Cadehy, 1961) 114–36.

68. Ibid., vii.

69. David Armstrong, letter to Edgar Doubleday, April 7, 1950.

70. Abe Stark, letter to Edgar Doubleday, May 31, 1950; Doubleday, letter to Stark, June 1, 1950.

71. *New York Times*, July 15, 1951; Seymour Berkowitz, interview with author, June 14, 1988.

72. Abe Stark, letters to Edgar Doubleday, April 4, 1952; April 18, 1952.

73. Edgar Doubleday, memorandum to J. Willard Hayden, April 7, 1952; E. Daveler, memorandum to Doubleday, April 14, 1952.

74. Abe Stark, letter to Edgar A. Doubleday, April 18, 1952.

75. Memorandum, June 8, 1953.

76. J. Willard Hayden, letter to Abe Stark, June 19, 1953.

77. Edgar Doubleday, letter to Abe Stark, September 22, 1953; Stark, letter to Doubleday, June 19, 1953.

78. "Up from Nanny Goat Park."

79. Ibid.

80. *Brooklyn Eagle*, June 19, 1953; Reuben Bennett, memorandum to Abe Stark, April 7, 1951; Leonard Dryansky, interview with author, August 11, 1988.

81. Staff, letter to board of directors, March 1954.

82. John Snypes, interview with author, April 7, 1988; Irving Levine, interview with author, October 6, 1986; Deutch, Feldman, Kronenberg, Lesovoy, Schmaren, collective interview with author, October 11, 1987.

83. Leonard Dryansky, interview with author, August 11, 1988.

84. Leonard Dryansky, interview with author, August 11, 1988; Irving Levine, interview with author, October 6, 1986.

85. Staff, letter to board of directors, March 1954.

86. Jacob Baroff, interview with author, July 6, 1987.

87. Leonard Dryansky, interview with author, August 11, 1988; Irving Levine, interview with author, April 11, 1988; Deutch, Feldman, Kronenberg, Lesovoy, G. Schmaren, collective interview with author, October 11, 1987; Norman Adelman, interview with author, June 18, 1989; Norman Adelman, "Factors to be Considered in the Development of an Intercultural Teen Age Program" (master's thesis, Columbia University, New York School of Social Work, June 1954).

88. Abe Stark, letter to Edgar A. Doubleday, September 7, 1954.
89. Ibid., January 3, 1956.
90. Ibid., September 7, 1954.
91. *New York Times*, October 5, 1954; November 16, 1954; December 9, 1954.
92. Robert F. Wagner, letter to Abe Stark, September 1954; *Brooklyn Eagle*, February 8, 1946; April 18, 1948.
93. Edgar A. Doubleday, letter to Abe Stark, September 9, 1954.
94. Minnie Weingart, letter to author, April 6, 1988.
95. *New York Times*, January 31, 1955.
96. Lenny Zeplin, letter to author, October 1987.
97. George Benitez, letter to author, May 1987.

6. Fright, Flight, and Failure

1. Abe Stark, letter to Edgar A. Doubleday, April 7, 1954.
2. Robert F. Wagner, letter to Abe Stark, September, 1954; *Brooklyn Eagle*, September 20, 1954.
3. *Brooklyn Eagle*, November 20, 1954.
4. New York City Youth Board, *Brownsville Youth Board Area Report*, typescript, 1954, 1–3; Community Council of Greater New York, Bureau of Community Statistical Services, *Brooklyn Communities: Population Characteristics and Neighborhood Social Resources*, vol. 1 (New York: Community Council, 1959), xxxviii, 168–70.
5. Ibid.
6. *New York Times*, January 20, 1954; June 26, 1956; August 25, 1959.
7. David Armstrong, quoted in *Boys Club Bulletin* 26, no. 1 (November 1953): 3.
8. *New York Times*, August 14, 1954.
9. *New York Times*, March 4, 1955.
10. *New York Times*, May 8, 1955.
11. *New York Times*, February 27, 1956.
12. *New York Times*, September 10, 1956; September 19, 1956.
13. *New York Times*, August 7, 1956.
14. Ibid.
15. *New York Times*, August 8, 1959; August 23, 1959; August 25, 1959.
16. *New York Times*, August 25, 1959.
17. *Brooklyn Communities*, xii–xvi, 164–65; Ron Miller, et al., "The Fourth Largest City in America—A Sociological Survey of Brooklyn," in *Brooklyn, USA*, ed. Rita S. Miller (Brooklyn: Brooklyn College Press, 1978), 25–27.
18. Ron Miller, et al., "The Fourth Largest City," 3–44; *Brooklyn Eagle*, several issues in May 1942.
19. Pete Hamill "Brooklyn: The Sane Alternative," *New York* July 14, 1969, 27.
20. Miller, et al., "The Fourth Largest City," 25–27; *New York Times*, February 18, 1962.

21. Ray Schroth, *The Eagle and Brooklyn* (Westport, Conn.: Greenwood Publishers, 1974).

22. *The Brooklyn Navy Yard* (New York: Institute for Urban Studies, Fordham University, May 1968).

23. Hamill, "Brooklyn," 28

24. Peter Golenbock, *Bums: An Oral History of the Brooklyn Dodgers* (New York: G. P. Putnam's Sons, 1984), 432.

25. Irving Rudd quoted in *Brooklyn, USA*, 167–68.

26. *Brooklyn Communities*, xxxviii, 162–70; Jimmy Breslin, *New York Times*, August 20, 1975.

27. *Brooklyn Communities*, xxxviii, 165–71; Ron Miller et al, "The Fourth Largest City in America," 25–27.

28. *Brooklyn Communities*, xv–xxxix, 162–70.

29. Ibid; and *Brownsville Youth Board Area Report*, 2–3; Alter Landesman, *Brownsville: The Birth, Development and Passing of a Jewish Community* (New York: Bloch Publishers, 1971), 323–28.

30. U.S. Bureau of the Census, *Seventeenth Census, 1950*, vol. 2 (Washington: Government Printing Office, 1952); *Eighteenth Census, 1960*, pt. 5c (Washington: GPO, 1961); Michael Harrington, *The Other America: Poverty in the United States* (New York: Macmillan, 1962), 171–86; *New York Times*, January 3, 1955; March 23, 1955; October 25, 1955; October 30, 1955.

31. Morton Werbel, interview with author, March 13, 1988.

32. Jonathan Rieder, *Canarsie: The Jews and Italians of Brooklyn Against Liberalism* (Cambridge: Harvard University Press, 1985), 23.

33. Jerome Krase, "Stigmatized Places, Stigmatized People: Crown Heights and Prospect Lefferts Gardens," in *Brooklyn U.S.A.*, 253–54; W. A. V. Clark and M. Cadwallader, "Residential Preferences: An Alternative View of Inter-Urban Space," *Environment and Planning* 5 (1973): 693–705; Lyn H. Lafland, *A World of Strangers: Order and Action in Urban Public Spaces* (New York: Basic Books, 1973).

34. Stanley Aronson, "Sojourners or Settlers? The Neighborhoods of Brooklyn," in *Brooklyn USA*, 279–82.

35. Ibid.

36. Harold V. Savitch, "Powerlessness in an Urban Ghetto," *Polity* (Fall 1972): 34.

37. Harold Radish, interview with author, March 12, 1987; Ben Wernikoff, interview with author, May 7, 1987.

38. Interview quoted in Rieder, *Canarsie*, 17.

39. Irving Forman, interview with author, June 27, 1988; Abe Rubenfeld, interview with author, January 12, 1987.

40. Rae Glauber, *All Neighborhoods Change: A Survey of Brownsville, Brooklyn* (New York: Rae Glauber, 1963).

41. Minutes of first general meeting, Brownsville Boys Club Alumni Association, March 31, 1948.

42. Constitution, Brownsville Boys Club Alumni Association, 1952.

43. Sid Siegel, interview with author, September 22, 1986.

44. *Brownsville Boys Club Alumni Association Newsletter*, April 1952; May 1952; assorted papers, Alumni Association Collection (in the possession of Martin Kronenberg and Joseph Feldman).

45. Constitution, Brownsville Boys Club Alumni Association, 1966.

46. Seymour Berkowitz, interview with author, June 14, 1988; Minnie Weingart, letter to author, April 6, 1988; *New York Daily News*, January 26, 1969; August 17, 1969; November 9, 1975.

47. *New York Times*, March 7, 1968.

48. Savitch, "Powerlessness in an Urban Ghetto," 30; *New York Times*, March 7, 1968; April 10, 1972.

49. *New York Times*, June 14, 1970; May 8, 1971; David Shipler, "Brownsville: The Epitome of Poverty," *New York Times*, May 6, 1971.

50. Savitch, "Powerlessness in an Urban Ghetto," 30–36; Harold X. Connolly, *A Ghetto Grows in Brooklyn* (New York: New York University Press, 1977), 189–90.

51. Savitch, "Powerlessness in an Urban Ghetto," 30–36; Connolly, *A Ghetto Grows in Brooklyn*, 192–204; *World Journal Tribune*, April 20, 1967.

52. *New York Times*, May 6, 1971

53. State Study Commission for New York City, *Urban Renewal in Brownsville, 1960–1973* (New York: Temporary State Commission, 1973), 4.

54. Ibid., 15.

55. Ibid., 3–4.

56. Ibid., 57.

57. *New York Times*, editorial, March 7, 1968.

58. Shipler, "Brownsville," *New York Times*, May 6, 1971.

59. *New York Times*, May 8, 1971.

60. Ibid., June 14, 1970.

61. Ibid., May 8, 1971.

62. *New York Sunday News*, May 16, 1971.

63. *New York Times*, June 14, 1970.

64. *New York Sunday News*, May 16, 1971.

65. Savitch, "Powerlessness in an Urban Ghetto," 55–56; for a general discussion of tenant power in this era see Joel Schwartz, "Tenant Power in the Liberal City, 1943–1971," in *The Tenant Movement in New York City, 1904–1984*, ed. Ronald Lawson (New Brunswick: Rutgers University Press, 1986), 134–208.

66. Savitch, "Powerlessness in an Urban Ghetto," 37–39.

67. Ibid., 47.

68. The discussion that follows depends heavily on Howard Savitch's persuasive essay, "Powerlessness in an Urban Ghetto." Also see Connolly, *A Ghetto Grows in Brooklyn*, 212–22.

69. Savitch, "Powerlessness in an Urban Ghetto," 46.

70. *New York Daily News*, May 6, 1971.

71. Savitch, "Powerlessness in an Urban Ghetto," 54; Connolly, *A Ghetto Grows in Brooklyn*, 176–80.

72. Diane Ravitch, *The Troubled Crusade: American Education, 1945–1980* (New York: Basic Books, 1983), 172–74; Joseph M. Cronin, *The Control of Urban Schools* (New York: Free Press, 1973), 194–97. A strike of New York City schoolteachers was precipitated by events in the Ocean Hill–Brownsville experimental school district. The issues involved were complex and not directly relevant to the points being made here. See Maurice Berube and Marilyn Gittell, eds. *Confrontation at Ocean Hill–Brownsville: The New York School Strikes*

232   6. FRIGHT, FLIGHT, AND FAILURE

of 1968 (New York: Praeger, 1969) and Melvin Urofsky, *Why Teachers Strike: Teachers' Rights and Community Control* (Garden City, N.Y.: Doubleday, 1970).
73. *New York Times*, November 10, 1968.
74. Ravitch, *The Troubled Crusade*, 174.
75. Savitch, "Powerlessness in an Urban Ghetto," 56.
76. *New York Times*, April 8, 1973.
77. *New York Daily News*, July 11, 1974; January 7, 1975.
78. Ibid.
79. *New York Daily News*, April 3, 1976.
80. Ibid., August 16, 1981.
81. Ibid., March 16, 1985; *New York Times*, August 27, 1985; April 1, 1987; September 27, 1987; October 25, 1987 (letter to the editor).
82. *New York Times*, March 27, 1987.
83. *New York Times*, July 20, 1985.
84. John Bodnar, *The Transplanted: A History of Immigrants in Urban America* (Bloomington, Indiana University Press, 1985); Ivan Light, *Ethnic Enterprise in America* (Berkeley: University of California Press, 1973); M. Mark Stolarick and Murray Friedman, eds., *Making It in America: The Role of Ethnicity in Business Enterprise, Education and Work Choices* (Lewisburg, Pa.: Bucknell University Press, 1986); David A. Bell, "The Triumph of Asian Americans," *New Republic*, July 15, 1985, 24–31.
85. Lawrence Levine, *Black Culture and Black Consciousness: Afro-American Folk Thought from Slavery to Freedom* (London: Oxford University Press, 1977); Clifford Geertz, "Religion as a Cultural System," in *Anthropological Approaches to the Study of Religion*, ed. Michael Banton (London: Tavistock Publishers, 1966), 1–46; Vincent Harding, *There is a River: The Black Struggle for Freedom in America* (New York: Harcourt Brace Jovanovich, 1981); Will Herberg, "Socialism, Zionism and Messianic Passion," *Midstream* 2 (Summer 1965): 65–74; Yehezkel Kaufman, "Israel in Canaan," in *Great Ages and Ideas of the Jewish People*, ed. L. W. Schwarz (New York: Modern Library, 1956), 30–56.
86. Gerald Sorin, *The Prophetic Minority: American Jewish Immigrant Radicals, 1880–1920* (Bloomington: Indiana University Press, 1985); Arthur Liebman, *Jews and the Left* (New York: John Wiley and Sons, 1979).
87. Eric Foner, *Reconstruction: America's Unfinished Revolution* (New York: Harper and Row, 1988).
88. Irving Howe, *World of Our Fathers* (New York: Harcourt Brace Jovanovich, 1976); Arthur Goren, *New York Jews and the Quest for Community: The Kehillah Experiment, 1908–1922* (New York: Columbia University Press, 1970); Hannah Kliger, "Traditions of Grass-Roots Organizations and Leadership: The Continuity of *Landsmanshaftn* in New York," *American Jewish History* 76, no. 1 (September 1986): 25–39; Susan Milamed, "*Proskurover Landsmanshaftn*," *American Jewish History*, 76, no. 1 (September 1986): 40–55; Shelly Tenenbaum, "Immigrants and Capital: Jewish Loan Societies in the United States," *American Jewish History*, 76, no. 1 (September 1986): 67–77.
89. Ibid.
90. Zosa Szajkowski, "The Yahudi and the Immigrant: A Reappraisal," *American Jewish Historical Quarterly* 63, no. 1 (September 1973): 13–44.
91. Herbert J. Gans, *The Urban Villagers: Group and Class in the Life of Italian Americans* (New York: Free Press, 1962), 268–73.

92. Jack Newfield, "The Bruised Apple," *New Republic*, July 3, 1985, 36–40.

93. Herbert J. Gans, *The Urban Villagers*, 268–73; Michael Harrington, "Crunched Numbers," *New Republic*, January 28, 1985, 7–9; Lisbeth B. Schorr, *Within Our Reach: Breaking the Cycle of Disadvantage* (New York: Doubleday, 1988).

94. Ivan Light, *Ethnic Enterprise in America*, 19–36; Charles H. Wesley, "The Negro in the West Indies, Slavery and Freedom," *Journal of Negro History* 32, no. 1 (January 1932): 51–66; Clifford Geertz, "The Rotating Credit Association: A 'Middle Rung' in Development," *Economic Development and Cultural Change* 10, no. 3 (April 1962): 241–63.

95. Charles Wesley, "The Negro in the West Indies," 51–66; Nancy Foner, "West Indians in New York City and London: A Comparative Analysis," *International Migration Review* 13, no. 2 (Summer 1979): 284–97.

96. *New York Times*, March 7, 1968.

97. Andrew Greeley, "Ethnics' Progress: Is Data Fact?" *Psychology Today* 15 (September 1981): 90–93; Thomas Kessner, *The Golden Door: Italian and Jewish Immigrant Mobility in New York City, 1880–1915* (New York: Oxford University Press, 1977); Stephan Thernstrom, *The Other Bostonians: Poverty and Progress in the American Metropolis, 1880–1970* (Cambridge: Harvard University Press, 1973).

98. As late as 1970 some 80 percent of Irish, Italian, and Slavic workers were in unskilled or semiskilled jobs and approximately 40 million white ethnic working-class Americans were earning less than the "modest but adequate" standard defined by the government. *New York Times*, September 28, 1970. In New York City in 1972, 250,000 Jews were living below the poverty level ($3,500) and another 150,000 had incomes under $4,500. Paul Cowan, "Jews Without Money Revisited," *Village Voice*, September 21, 1972.

99. Colin Greer, "Remembering Class: An Interpretation," in *The Divided Society: The Ethnic Experience in America*, ed. Colin Greer, (New York: Basic Books, 1974), 3–35.

100. *New York Daily News*, newsclipping, n.d.

101. William Hurley, interview with author, November 14, 1987.

102. *New York Daily News*, newsclipping, n.d.

103. William J. Wilson, *The Truly Disadvantaged: The Inner City, the Underclass, and Public Policy* (Chicago: University of Chicago Press, 1987); also see James Q. Wilson, "The Rediscovery of Character: Private Virtue and Public Policy," *The Public Interest* 81 (Fall 1985): 3–16.

104. Diane Pancoast, et al, eds., *Rediscovering Self Help: Its Role in Social Care*, Social Service Delivery Systems: An International Annual, vol. 6 (Beverly Hills: Sage Publications, 1983); Alan Gartner and Frank Reissman, *The Self-Help Revolution* (New York: Human Sciences Press, 1984).

105. E. C. Durman, "The Role of Self-Help in Service Provision," *Journal of Applied Behavioral Science* 12 (1979): 433–48; Lisbeth B. Schorr, *Within Our Reach*.

7. Livelihoods, Longings, and Legacies

1. Al Apter, "Brownsville Blues," unpublished poem.

2. Steven M. Cohen, "Vitality and Persistence in the American Jewish Family," in *The Jewish Family: Myths and Realities*, ed. Steven M. Cohen and Paula Hyman (New York: Holmes and Meiers, 1986), 221–29. "The only national comparative data we have demonstrate that the Jewish divorce rate has remained at around half the white Protestant rate, and it shows no signs of significantly surpassing that ratio. The little data we have also suggest that Jews who divorce remarry faster than others." 223.

3. Morton Werbel, interview with author, March 13, 1988.

4. *New York Times*, September 5, 6, 1986. Gerald Lenowitz, interview with author April 21, 1987.

5. Confidential interview with author.

6. Gene Ward, "Ward to the Wise," *New York Daily News*, n.d.

7. *New York Times*, July 27, 1954; July 28, 1954; Hyman Edelman, interview with author, May 21, 1989.

8. *New York Times*, February 18, 1951.

9. *New York Times*, February 21, 1951.

10. *New York Times*, February 21, 1951.

11. *New York Times*, April 22, 1951; April 23, 1951; April 25, 1951.

12. *BBC News* 6, no. 1 (February 1946).

13. *New York Times*, April 22, 1951; April 23, 1951; April 25, 1951; January 31, 1952; May 8, 1952; May 9, 1952.

14. Gilbert Sorrentino, "No Radical Chic in Brooklyn." *New York Times*, June 16, 1971.

15. William F. Whyte, *Street Corner Society: The Social Structure of an Italian Slum*, 3d ed. (Chicago: University of Chicago Press, 1981), 255–56.

16. Jack Leavitt, interview with author, February 25, 1988.

17. Arthur Granit, *The Time of the Peaches* (New York: Abelard-Schuman, 1959.

18. *Brownsville Boys Club Alumni Newsletter*, April 1952, May 1952; Minutes of BBC Alumni Association first general meeting, March 30, 1948.

19. *New York Sunday News*, March 6, 1966.

20. George Levine, interview with author, May 23, 1987; Joseph Feldman, "A Brief and Somewhat Biased History of the Brownsville Boys Club Alumni Association," typescript, February 1989.

21. *Brownsville Boys Club Alumni Newsletters* (August 1967); (October 1967); (December 1967); (February 1968); (April 1968); (January 1972); (April 1972); (March 1973); (October 1975); (January 1976); (May 1976); (October 1976); (Spring 1977); (Spring 1978); (Spring 1979); (September 1982); (Winter 1986); (July 1987); (Spring 1988); Joseph Feldman, "A Brief and Somewhat Biased History."

22. Nathan Glazer, *The Social Bases of American Communism* (New York: Harcourt Brace, 1961), 143–68.

23. N.a., "Up From Nanny Goat Park," 1953.

24. Harold Radish, interview with author, March 12, 1987; Sidney Gerchick,

interview with author, February 10, 1987; Irwin Millman, interview with author, May 5, 1988.

25. Seymour Brief, interview with author, March 10, 1987; Bernard Berman, interview with author, April 3, 1988. Neil Brief, letter to author, November 26, 1986.

26. Norman Goroff, interview with author, July 23, 1987; Irving Levine, interview with author, October 8, 1986; Jack Baroff, interview with author, July 6, 1987.

27. Abe Rubenfeld, interview with author January 12, 1987.

28. Leonard Cohen, interview with author, April 12, 1987, Al Bart, interview with author, April 14, 1988.

29. Jacob Baroff, speech, October 10, 1984.

30. Gerald Suttles, *The Social Construction of Communities* (Chicago: University of Chicago Press, 1972), 187–88; Fred Davis, *Yearning for Yesterday: A Sociology of Nostalgia* (New York: Free Press, 1979), 99.

31. Constitution, BBC Alumni Association, 1966.

32. Daniel Levinson, et al., "The Psychosocial Development of Men in Early Adulthood and the Mid-Life Transition," in *Life History Research in Psychopathology*, ed. D. Ricks, *et al*, (Minneapolis: Minnesota University Press, 1974), 243–58; Gail Sheehy, *Passages* (New York, E. P. Dutton, 1976); George Vaillant, *Adaptation to Life* (Boston: Little, Brown, 1977).

33. Karl Marx, *The Communist Manifesto* in *Karl Marx: Selected Writings* ed. David McClellan (New York: Oxford University Press, 1977), 224.

34. Fred Davis, *Yearning for Yesterday*, 115–16, 140–43.

35. Alter Landesman, *Brownsville: The Birth, Development and Passing of a Jewish Community* (New York: Bloch Publishers, 1971, 376 (emphasis mine).

Glossary

Gmiles khesed. Applied religion
Heder. Elementary Hebrew school, primarily for boys
Khevra (pl. *khevrot*). Committee or society
Kashrut. Dietary laws and rules for hygiene
Kehilla (pl. *kehillot*). Community or community council
Kishke. Stuffed derma
Landsmanshaft. Society, often mutual-aid oriented, for immigrants from
  same area or town in Eastern Europe
Mitzva (pl. *mitzvot*). Good deeds, ethical and ritual obligations
Shabos. The sabbath
Shtetl (pl. *shtetlekh*). Town in Eastern Europe with significant Jewish
  population
Shul. Synagogue
Takhles. Orientation to ultimate outcomes, accomplishment
Tikn olam. Repair or improvement of the world
Tsedaka. Justice and righteousness through performing charitable acts
  and other *mitzvot*
Yehsiva (pl. *yeshivot*). Schools for advanced Jewish learning
Yiddishkayt. Jewishness, the stuff of Jewish culture
Yikhes. Status based on family lineage or achieved by learning

Note on Sources
and Methodology

A primary source for this study has been the collective memory of the boys of Brownsville. Memory, of course, is selective, incomplete, and sometimes simply inaccurate. This is a potential pitfall of all oral history projects. However, the size of my sample—over 250 respondents—helped avoid, in large part, the more serious problems. Stories were confirmed and reconfirmed innumerable times. And on several occasions I did group interviews—once with five former BBCers.

Another great help was the fact that a significant number of these men, talking with me in 1986, 1987, and 1988, had talked four decades earlier, to radio audiences and newspaper reporters. There are substantive recorded commentaries for 1945, 1946, 1947, 1949, 1951 and 1953, including a fourteen-page transcript of an interview with four BBCers broadcast over radio station WINS in August of 1945.

In addition there are BBC newsletters and other materials related to the club for 1943 through 1948, a seven-page typescript "history" of the club written by Norman Goroff in 1947, and independent commentaries by librarians, sociologists and social workers. Particularly useful reports by direct observers of the Brownsville Boys Club were:

Florence Adamson, *A Study of the Recreational Facilities of the Brownsville Section of Brooklyn* (New York: Brownsville Neighborhood Council, 1941).

Brooklyn Council for Social Planning, "Report of Youth Activities Project," Brooklyn, April 21, 1946.

Werner J. Cahnman, "Attitudes of Minority Youth: A Methodological Introduction [investigation into the cultural interests of Jewish and Negro Youth in the Brownsville District of Brooklyn] *American Sociological Review* 14 (August 1949): 543–48.

Margaret B. Freeman, "The Brownsville Public Library: Its Origins and Development," report, Brooklyn, 1940.

New York City Youth Board, "Brownsville Youth Board Area Report," typescript, 1954.

David Suher, *The Brownsville Neighborhood Council* (New York: New York School of Social Work, 1948).

None of the documents used in the study, including the personal interviews of the late 1980s, were accepted at face value. All were examined closely and subjected to critical analyses. Indeed, during the course of the interviews, which were mainly free-flowing, I often asked pointed, but not, I hope, leading questions; and the men were as often reflective and discursive. The oral sources turned out to be a rich mine from which to draw insights and perspectives that supplemented and even redressed the bias of conventional written sources.

As I reached the end of the interviewing process, I felt reasonably sure that I had done all I could to verify and validate. I thought I had made a successful end-run around the most serious shortcomings of the participant-observer role, that I had built generalizations on a large enough sample, and that I had unearthed enough oral material and commentary from the 1940s to match against the testimony of the 1980s. And then one of those wonderfully fortuitous things happened—something which supplied a certain "icing for the cake." A former Brownsville boy, currently a very successful Madison Avenue attorney, returned a questionnaire, on which he had hastily penciled, apparently as an afterthought, "By the way I have the original books of the BBC." These "books" turned out to be the handwritten "Minute Books" for the weekly BBC meetings from May of 1940 through the end of 1946; account books; letters to and from other agencies and persons; a "Report of Activities for 1947–1948," written by Harmon Putter and Abe Stark; and the original 1940 petition to the board of education signed by the boys. These documents supplied some new material, but mainly they supplied corroboration; the historian's dream come true. The "traditionalist" in me was satisfied. I trust readers will be too.

In addition to the sources cited above, the following were very valuable for Brownsville generally, and especially for context and statistics:

Herbert Ballon, "Brooklyn Neighborhoods: A Basis for Neighborhood Studies and a District Plan for a Neighborhood Council Program in Brooklyn," manuscript, 1941, Brooklyn Collection, Brooklyn Public Library.

Brooklyn Eagle. The Main Branch of the Brooklyn Public Library has the full run on microfilm. I could find no index, but fortunately the Brooklyn Collection at the library holds the *Eagle* morgue with clippings categorized well enough to help identify particular issues of the daily paper relevant to specific researchers.

Brooklyn Communities: Population Characteristics and Neighborhood Social Resources (New York: Community Council of Greater New York, Bureau of Community Statistical Services, 1959).

Reuben Fink and Bernard Richards, eds., *Jewish Community Directory of Greater New York: A Guide to Central Organizations and Institutions* (New York: The Jewish Information Bureau, 1947).

Milton Goell, *Brownsville Must Have Public Housing* (Brooklyn: Brooklyn Community for Better Housing and the Brownsville Neighborhood Council, 1940). Goell was a lawyer, poet, and social reformer in Brownsville and neighboring East New York from the early 1930s to the early 1950s. He was a key figure in the Brownsville Neighborhood Council, and had occasional direct contact with the Brownsville Boys Club.

Milton Goell, *A Postwar Plan for Brownsville* (Brooklyn: The Brownsville Neighborhood Council, 1944).

Irving Halpern, et al., *A Statistical Study of the Distribution of Adult and Juvenile Delinquents in the Boroughs of Manhattan and Brooklyn, New York City* (New York: New York Housing Authority, 1939)

Morris Horrowitz and Lawrence Jay Kaplan, *The Jewish Population of the New York Area, 1900–1975* (New York: Federation of Philanthropies, 1959).

Alter Landesman, *Brownsville: The Birth, Development, and Passing of a Jewish Community in New York* (New York: Bloch Publishing, 1971). Landesman was a rabbi in the community and directed, for almost four decades, the Hebrew Educational Society—a settlement house on Hopkinson and Sutter avenues.

Alter Landesman, "A Neighborhood Survey of Brownsville," typescript, 1927, Jewish Division, New York Public Library.

Study of the Jewish Community of Brooklyn for the YMHA of Brooklyn. (New York: Jewish Welfare Board, 1935).

Memoirs and novels supplied additional perspectives on life in Brownsville in the 1920s, 1930s and 1940s, as well as graphic detail on the physical aspects of the neighborhood. Especially noteworthy memoirs are:

Alfred Kazin, *A Walker in the City* (New York: Harcourt Brace, 1951). The noted writer and literary critic grew up in Brownsville and returned, chronically, to visit his parents. A walk through the neighborhood in the late 1940s apparently stimulated this marvelously evocative, sensitive memoir of boyhood in Brownsville.

William Poster " 'Twas a Dark Night in Brownsville: Pitkin Avenue's Self-Made Generation," *Commentary* 9 (May 1950): 458–67; and Samuel Tenenbaum, "Brownsville's Age of Learning: When the Library Stayed Open All Week," *Commentary* 8 (August 1949): 173–78, are also well worth reading.

Noteworthy fiction depicting life in Brownsville in the 1920s, 1930s, and 1940s includes:

Arthur Granit's short stories *I Am from Brownsville* (New York: Philosophical Library, 1985) and his novel *The Time of the Peaches* (New York: Abelard-Schuman, 1959) are imaginative, resonant renditions of Brownsville life, values and "characters." Granit, was born in Brownsville to Jewish immigrants, and eventually taught English in neighborhood schools. In 1959 he said: "I think all adolescents are mad, but I like the kids and they like me."

Gerald Green, *The Last Angry Man* (New York: Charles Scribner's Sons, 1956) is largely autobiographical. Green depicts in great detail the life of his father, a Brownsville doctor in the 1930s and 1940s. He also recreates scenes of dirty, noisy streets, the interactions of shifting populations of blacks and Poles and Jews, as well as the general poverty and the gang fights.

Irving Shulman does some of the same in *The Amboy Dukes* (New York: Doubleday, 1947), a novel which makes it clear that Jews did not entirely escape the problem of juvenile delinquency.

For Brownsville in the late 1940s through the present, when the neighborhood began to become increasingly less Jewish and more populated by blacks, see: *Brooklyn Communities*, "Brownsville Youth Board Area Report," "Report of Youth Activities Project," and "Attitudes of Minority Youth," all cited above. More recent powerful and informative works dealing with Brownsville include:

Harold X. Connolly, *A Ghetto Grows in Brooklyn* (New York: New York University Press, 1977).

Harold V. Savitch, "Powerlessness in an Urban Ghetto: The Case of Political Biases and Differential Access in New York City," *Polity* (Fall 1972): 19–56.

Urban Renewal in Brownsville, 1960–1973 (New York: State Study Commission for New York City, 1973)

The *New York Times*, the *New York Daily News* and the *New York Post* often carried stories and features on Brownsville, especially in the late 1960s and early 1970s.

Valuable historical and sociological studies of ethnic neighborhoods other than Brownsville are:

Herbert J. Gans, *The Urban Villagers: Group and Class in the Life of Italian Americans* (New York: Free Press, 1962) a sensitive study of the people of the West End of Boston, where Gans lived in the late 1950s.

Jonathan Rieder, *Canarsie: The Jews and Italians of Brooklyn Against Liberalism* (Cambridge: Harvard University Press, 1985) another insightful participant-observer study, was particularly useful in that many of the Jews of Canarsie had migrated from Brownsville.

William H. Whyte, *Street Corner Society: The Social Structure of an Italian Slum* 3d. ed. (Chicago: University of Chicago Press, 1981). This classic on Boston's North End, was originally published in 1943 and became a model for many subsequent field studies.

More than 250 other works were consulted on a variety of subjects including adolescence, self-help, urban demography, housing, juvenile delinquency, nostalgia, sports, social reform, politics and crime. The items most relevant to this study are found in the notes throughout. For immigration and ethnicity, including social mobility and acculturation, see notes for the prologue and for chapters 3 and 6.

Index